Adva

Choos

M000310483

Jerry Yudelson's many years at the heart of the green building movement have led to his developing an excellent document on sustainable housing. This will be a valuable guide not only for homebuyers and consumers, but also for designers and builders. The greenest home we can build is not to build one at all; this book provides good advice on the next best thing.

— STEVEN WINTER, FAIA, Steven Winter Associates, Inc.,
Chairman, USGBC LEED for Homes Committee

Choosing Green provides the consumer with an up-to-the-minute, very thorough overview of green residential building in America. It's a guide to green construction practices, as well as a navigation system for purchasing a truly green house. Any buyer who attempts to do so without this information must beware!

— MARK BERMAN, Davis Energy Group

Jerry Yudelson, one of the foremost experts in the green building industry, has systematically gathered in-depth, hard to find information and coalesced his decades of experience into this tremendously valuable tool. *Choosing Green* provides clear guidance to navigate the complexity of the green building marketplace and its extensive resources.

— CHRISTI GRAHAM, Founder & President, West Coast Green

Today, much is being written about green housing and the myriad of related certification standards. *Choosing Green* is an excellent book by an extremely knowledgeable author, and should be a "must-read" for anyone contemplating the purchase of an "environmentally green" home. This book will help prospective green home purchasers gain a much better understanding of what constitutes a "green home" and how to make a wise purchase.

— MICHAEL GELLER, Adjunct Faculty,
Centre for Sustainable Community Development,
Simon Fraser University

Jerry Yudelson epitomizes the best of green building theory, design principles and construction practices. His work inspires and contributes to the industry's transformation and this book is no exception — it will serve any homebuyer seeking quality, efficient and healthy living very well.

— YVES KHAWAM, Pima County, Arizona, Chief Building Official

Jerry Yudelson is a rare find in the increasingly confusing world of green building scientists, policy makers, product manufacturers, and marketers. He is a jack of all trades who is able to synthesize the most salient trends, issues, and strategies down to their most compelling and useful points. *Choosing Green* is a great contribution to the consumer looking to invest wisely and make a positive impact.

— ROB BENNETT, a leading voice for green buildings in the public sector

With consumer demand for green living growing rapidly, *Choosing Green* is a very timely resource for new homebuyers who want to make smart decisions about one of their largest investments. Yudelson's book is both comprehensive and practical, acknowledging there is no "one size fits all" solution. By providing homebuyers with the right set of tools they will be better prepared to make purchase decisions that best fit their green priorities, available options and lifestyles.

— REBECCA L. FLORA, Executive Director, Green Building Alliance

As an architect with a portfolio of green homes, I can attest to the plethora of how-to books on green building, most of which are geared towards the "innovators" and "early adapters" in the design and construction industry. What makes *Choosing Green* special is that it is written for the prospective homebuyer, a milestone in the evolution of sustainable design!

— NATHAN GOOD, AIA, NathanGoodArchitect.com

Among the chief challenges to buying a green home, or greening the one you have, has been ready access to good information. *Choosing Green* is an authoritative response: it will help you ask the right questions, avoid greenwash, and create a healthier, more sustainable lifestyle for yourself and your family.

— MICHELLE MOORE, Senior Vice President, U.S. Green Building Council

Wish you had a trusted friend that could explain what is important (and not) about choosing a green home? Then Jerry Yudelson is your new best buddy! Written with the homebuyer in mind, *Choosing Green* cuts through the green fog with great anecdotes and case studies — showing what makes a truly green home, who is building them, where you can get one.

— WALKER WELLS, Green Building Program Director, Global Green USA

Finally! A comprehensive guide for anyone interested in green homes. This book is the best resource I have seen for understanding green homes, and it is presented in an easy to understand format.

— PHILIP BEERE, Green Street Development, Phoenix, Arizona

Choosing Green is a must read manual for people looking to make good environmental decisions for their homes and their families. It is clear, insightful, informative, current and timely; guiding both small steps and deep green opportunities.

— LAUREN YARMUTH, YRG Consultants, New York City

Choosing Green

THE HOMEBUYER'S GUIDE *to* GOOD GREEN HOMES

JERRY YUDELSON
Foreword by RON JONES,
Green Builder®

NEW SOCIETY PUBLISHERS

CATALOGING IN PUBLICATION DATA:
A catalog record for this publication is available from
the National Library of Canada.

Cover design by Diane McIntosh.
Leaf image: iStock   Left bottom: Courtesy of SunPower
Left middle photo: Photography by John Baker, courtesy of Homewise, Inc.
Top photo: Photography by Loren Heyns, courtesy of Green Street Properties
Right bottom: Photography by Bill Timmerman, courtesy of Modus Development

Printed in Canada. First printing April 2008.

Paperback ISBN: 978-0-86571-610-0

Inquiries regarding requests to reprint all or part of *Choosing Green*
should be addressed to New Society Publishers at the address below.

To order directly from the publishers, please call toll-free (North America)
1-800-567-6772, or order online at www.newsociety.com

Any other inquiries can be directed by mail to:

New Society Publishers
P.O. Box 189, Gabriola Island, BC V0R 1X0, Canada
(250) 247-9737

New Society Publishers' mission is to publish books that contribute
in fundamental ways to building an ecologically sustainable and just
society, and to do so with the least possible impact on the environment,
in a manner that models this vision. We are committed to doing this
not just through education, but through action. This book is one step
toward ending global deforestation and climate change. It is printed on
Forest Stewardship Council-certified acid-free paper that is **100% post-
consumer recycled** (100% old growth forest-free), processed chlorine
free, and printed with vegetable-based, low-VOC inks, with covers
produced using FSC-certified stock. Additionally, New Society purchases
carbon offsets based on an annual audit, operating with a carbon-
neutral footprint. For further information, or to browse our full list of
books and purchase securely, visit our website at: www.newsociety.com

NEW SOCIETY PUBLISHERS
www.newsociety.com

*For everyone who wants to live
a more sustainable and less impactful lifestyle,
and for all those who want to help them do so,
this book is for you.*

Contents

5. How Do I Know It's a Green Home?
Green Home Rating Programs 79

6. Where Can I Find a Green Home?
Single-family Home Developments 113

Preface

During 2006 and 2007, the new home market tanked throughout the US, with new home starts in California, for example, falling 23 percent in 2006 and an additional 9 percent through the first half of 2007. At the same time, crude oil futures in the winter of 2008 closed at record highs, above $100 per barrel, about triple the level of four years earlier. Al Gore's Academy Award-winning 2006 film, *An Inconvenient Truth*, brought home to millions of people the reality that our profligate use of energy is causing climate change on a global scale. And 2007's Live Earth concert brought the entertainment community into the global warming debate before a TV audience of hundreds of millions worldwide.

For the first time in a generation, the American public is concerned about the costs of natural gas, heating oil, propane and electricity for home operations and the price of gasoline for their cars, RVs, SUVs and pickups. Moreover, the public is becoming ever more aware of and concerned about the environmental effects of high levels of energy consumption; we're all beginning to see this concern reflected in a never-ending spate of news articles about the growing trend toward supporting green homes, installing compact fluorescent light bulbs and buying green power.

A new home is the most complex and expensive purchase of most people's lives. You want it to meet all your needs and not be a burden on the planet. In the midst of the homebuilding slowdown of 2006 and 2007 and the mortgage market debacle of 2007, the homebuilding industry began to respond to this green wave of concern. In 2006 more than 200,000 new homes, about 15 percent of all new single-family housing starts, were built to ENERGY STAR® and other green building standards. In 2007 and 2008 this wave gathered momentum as builders looked to green homes as a way to set their offerings apart from the great mass of new homes on the market.

From Seattle to Miami, from Southern California to New England, from unexpected places such as Houston, Las Vegas, Norman (Oklahoma),

Rocklin (California), New York City and northern New Jersey, green home developments are rising like wildflowers in spring. But how can you, the homebuyer, make sense of all the green home rating systems out there, including ENERGY STAR®, California Green Builder, Built Green Colorado, EarthCraft, Earth Advantage, Austin Energy, LEED® (Leadership in Energy and Environmental Design), Environments for Living, the National Association of Home Builders' *National Green Building Program*, the Green Building Initiative and some 60 additional local, regional and national rating systems for homes?

How can you decide which is more important, an energy-efficient home, a water-conserving home with dual-flush toilets, a "healthy" home with better air filtration, a solar-powered home, a walkable and bicycle-friendly community, recycled-content carpet and countertops, sustainably harvested wood cabinets, recycled-glass countertops and a hundred other variations on the green home theme? If you want all of these features, who's offering them? How much extra should you expect to pay for these features in a green home when it's getting harder to buy a home, as mortgage lenders are tightening standards right and left? What about warranties and insurance, maintenance and operational issues that might come with home features with which you're not familiar?

More importantly, where in this great land do you find a green home? If you're looking to buy a home now, where should you look to find a home builder with green homes for sale? Which rating systems should you trust, and what should be your bottom line for energy savings? How will you find a mortgage that will take these savings into account, to determine if your income qualifies for the home you want?

I wrote *Choosing Green* with you, the homebuyer, in mind and attempt to answer these questions, so that you'll feel comfortable looking for and buying a green home. I've spent my entire professional career engaged with energy and environmental issues, and for the past ten years, I've been involved daily with the design, construction and operation of residential and commercial green buildings. I've chaired the green building industry's largest conference, Greenbuild, for five years and have attended dozens of conferences, seminars, workshops, meetings and other events centered on green buildings. Last year I wrote *Green Building A to Z*, which defines 108 terms used in green building. My goal in all of these activities has been, first, to understand everything I could about green buildings, and second, to report back to various audiences how to make sense out of a field that's growing 75 percent a year.

Let *Choosing Green* be your guide to good green homes. In this book I'll show you first why choosing a green home is important for you, your family and your community, and, in some small but not insignificant measure, for the planet. Then I'll take you on a nationwide tour of green-home developments, interviewing builders, homeowners, green-technology mavens, government officials and home rating system specialists. I'll show you what's in a green home, from the most basic energy-efficiency measures, to the most elaborate solar-power systems. I'll explain green products, systems and technologies that you might encounter in your green home search, and I'll help you make sense out of them and decide which might be important for your home. I'll explain the most important green-home rating programs, tell you who sponsors them and how they can help you decide how much credence to put in a builder's claims of "greenness."

I'll show you some of the many government, utility and financial incentives for buying a green home and, if you're in the market for something other than a detached single-family home, help you locate townhouses and condominium towers in various places around the US and Canada. There are checklists and scorecards to facilitate your green-home search and give you a list of questions to ask at the model home or sales office. You might be surprised to learn that thousands of real estate salespeople, agents and brokers are learning about green homes at the same time you are. I'll show you how to decide if a homebuilder's operations are truly "green" or just make-believe green, also known as "greenwashing."

Finally, I'll show you how to do your homework, highlighting the most valuable books, magazines, online newsletters and websites to help you get your green home search off to a quick start. So, grab a cup of shade-grown, organic, fair-trade coffee, put in a dollop of organic nonfat milk and some natural sweetener, kick back and let me help you find a "good green home" that's just right for you and your family.

Acknowledgments belong in any preface. Thanks to Ron Jones, Green Builder®, for writing the foreword. Thanks to the entire staff at New Society Publishers for championing this book and getting it out in time for the 2008 homebuying season! Thanks also to everyone who allowed us to interview them for this book, including homebuilders, homeowners, public officials and rating system specialists. Thanks to everyone who contributed photos for the book. Thanks to David Ziegler-Voll for the illustrations. Thanks to James Hackler, an Atlanta freelance writer for contributing write-ups in chapter 6 of Victory Homes, New Town Builders and Leyland Alliance, along with his personal photos of those projects. Special thanks goes to my editorial associate, Gretel Hakanson, for conducting the interviews, helping with the research, sourcing all the photos and making sure that the production was accurate and timely. Thanks to the experts and friends who reviewed the draft text, including Richard Michal and Brian Maloney. Thanks to James Yudelson for taking photos of San Francisco Bay Area solar homes.

As always, any errors of omission or commission are mine alone. Thanks also to my wife, Jessica, for indulging the time spent writing yet another green-building book and for sharing my passion for green building and green homes. Finally, many, many thanks to the hundreds of passionate advocates inside homebuilding companies who have recognized the need for green homes and who have convinced their organizations to produce and market them.

— Jerry Yudelson
Tucson, Arizona
January 1, 2008

Foreword

Buying or building any home other than a green home means accepting a lower standard of living than necessary for yourself and your family. In the end, green building is simply a metaphor for quality of life, now and in the future.

At all times shelter has been a basic necessity of people. Protecting human health and safety, while providing economy and comfort, remain the primary goals of housing designers, homebuilders, product manufacturers and governments. More recently, however, we are realizing that the built environment is inextricably linked to the natural environment and that the act of building — arguably the most conspicuously consumptive activity of mankind — has a major impact on the finite resources and natural systems of our irreplaceable planet, in addition to the direct effects it has on people's lives.

For several decades the green-building movement has been gaining momentum throughout North America, and indeed, around the world. It has become undeniably evident that our traditional energy supplies, our precious fresh water and even the land resource itself are all being stressed by a rapidly expanding human population and the resulting land development. As a result, those who build and occupy houses (and other buildings) are searching for ways to reduce the ecological footprint that results from the construction and ongoing use of the homes in which they live, work and play.

Even while our understanding of building performance, resource management and the effects of the built environment on human health has grown dramatically in recent years, economic considerations, philosophical and political differences and a general resistance to change have slowed progress toward a more sustainable set of housing solutions. Sadly it has been the points of disagreement between the environmental community and the building industry that have defined an often rocky relationship

rather than the common goals of social stability, environmental stewardship and economic vitality.

While environmental organizations have demanded that all levels of
government adopt and enforce regulations requiring greater resource efficiency, accountability and stricter management practices from homebuilders, building industry trade associations often counter that affordability
must be a key factor into policy decisions. Those who supply the housing
stock resist mandates that require higher, more costly levels of performance,
arguing that freedom of choice is at the core of how we approach housing
(and most consumer decisions) in American culture. Those encouraging a
more environmentally responsive global model respond that environmental costs must be factored into the equation, because the planet cannot sus-
tain the ever-increasing levels of consumption and degradation of natural
systems that have occurred in recent years.

Climate change, or global warming, is now moving these two sides away
from their collision course and onto the path of cooperation. In the past five
years, a scientific consensus emerged, documenting the adverse effects of
all human activity, including housing, on the Earth and all of its natural systems, especially the atmosphere. While there is ongoing debate among scientific experts regarding the nature or extent of the damage, there is little
disagreement that our lifestyles are indeed having alarming and potentially
irreversible impacts on the natural world.

Fortunately, the work of course-correction has already begun. Individual pioneers have united into groups around the world to create and demonstrate housing technologies and strategies that will allow human shelter to
incorporate environmental costs along with cultural values and economic
considerations into homebuilding. In the US and Canada, green-building
groups are growing in strength and numbers. Local and regional homebuilder associations, green building councils and a variety of sustainability
advocates are working to devise and implement solutions that will provide
meaningful and achievable thresholds of performance, resulting in safer,
healthier, affordable housing options using less energy, water and materials.

Development of national standards, guidelines and rating systems from
a variety of agencies and organizations has produced a menu of options for
public policymakers. The platform of responses includes tightening building regulations to meet the demands of a better-informed public. Increased
costs for conventional energy and infrastructure, growing concerns about
water supply and purity, increasing prices for building materials, labor and
waste disposal — driven by an expanding population — all serve to make

these solutions valuable for communities everywhere, regardless of size or location.

Yet, it is you, the homebuyer, who really holds the key to the transformation of the housing stock. You, the consumer, ultimately define the market and determine what the future of housing will look like. Until now, most homebuyers have lacked the information that will allow them to demand higher standards of performance, durability and indoor environment quality, but no longer. With access to the Internet and the knowledge of authors and building experts like Jerry Yudelson, the average homebuyer now has the ability to make intelligent decisions when faced with all the choices of housing a family.

In recent years we have experienced a revolution in how intelligent consumers evaluate and select the goods and services that affect their lives. People are becoming increasingly discerning about what they put onto and into their bodies. Driven by expanding evidence that the built environment plays a huge role in the quality of our lives and our environment, those consumers are also becoming increasingly selective of buildings into which they put their bodies.

Evidence from the US Environmental Protection Agency suggests that most of us spend nearly 90 percent of our time indoors — at home, work or school — and that one in four children born today in this country will develop respiratory illnesses, diseases increasingly linked to toxins in the indoor environment. People are searching for better options, and the home-building industry is poised to deliver them.

At the very core of the problem is the way we measure the economic value of our homes. We have allowed ourselves to be steered into the trap of a *false metric* — the "dollars per square foot" calculation of home value. Homebuyers, designers, builders, mortgage lenders, appraisers, insurers and realtors have taken the easy road to valuation and created a disaster in how we evaluate the largest and most important personal financial investment most families will ever make. We have allowed ourselves to be guided into an upside-down measure of value — quantity over quality.

The critical correction that we must make is simply to change the way we look at our housing investment and ultimately alter the fundamental basis of our homebuying decision. We should determine the value of our homes not by the number of square feet of floor space, which inherently rewards inefficiencies and the spatial dilution of features and benefits, but rather by the efficiency, focus and concentration of those features and benefits — the quality — of that space.

Buying or building a home requires a leap of faith to choose quality over quantity. When making this leap, homebuyers believe that their choice will be rewarded, not only by the comfort and health of their family while they occupy that dwelling, but by the next owner of that house, someone who years from now will base his or her investment choice on the same features and benefits, the same pursuit of quality, that defined that green home in the first place.

May your goal of "choosing green" for your next home be richly rewarded!

— Ron Jones
Green Builder®
September 2007

Ron Jones is founder and editorial director of Green Builder *magazine, the leading trade journal in this field. He has been honored as Builder Advocate of the Year by the National Association of Homebuilders (NAHB). He is the only person ever to serve on the national board of directors of both the NAHB and the US Green Building Council.*

CHAPTER 1

The Green Home Revolution

It's time for you to buy a new home. Perhaps your current employer transferred you or your spouse, maybe you've decided to move to a new area for personal or family reasons, conceivably there might be a child on the way and you need more space, or possibly you're looking for a change of pace, either to upgrade your current home or (the situation many baby boomers are in right now) to downsize your living situation. You might even be looking for a bargain in markets where home prices are especially depressed (California, Arizona, Texas and Florida), owing to the overbuilding of the first half of this decade and the subprime mortgage crisis that has resulted in foreclosures on many new homes. Perhaps a local builder has too much inventory or needs to raise cash in a hurry, so that you can strike a bargain. You could have a hundred reasons for buying a new home at this time, and each one might be important to some degree to your decision.

I'd like to give you one more: buy a green home to cut your future operating costs, to get into a more comfortable and healthier home, to support your environmental values, to help force a change in our dependence on foreign oil and electricity from coal that adds carbon dioxide to the atmosphere and speeds up global warming. I'd like you to think that your next home-buying decision could have far-reaching benefits beyond the immediate gain to you and your family. I'd like you to go to the model home or sales office in the community that you want to live in and ask the builder's representative: do you have a green home I can buy, right now? Your conversation with that sales consultant can have a stimulating effect on a huge number of business decisions that will ultimately make our precious planet a more habitable place for generations to come.

But wait, you say, all I want is a home that I can afford, that's in the right part of town for me and that has the features I need or want in a home. Home buying is already complicated enough. Now you want me to ask for and demand a green home? Won't that be too much to tackle? Are there enough green homes on the market that I will really have a choice that I will like? Isn't all that soybean insulation and compost stuff for someone else? My short answer is: give it a try — you might be surprised what you wind up with! My longer answer is: read this book which will show you what to look for, help you understand what a green home is and does, arm you with the right questions to ask, help you decide among various green home offerings and, most importantly, show you where to learn about and find your "green dream home."

First, let's start with some basics: Why consider a green home? Why are green homes necessary? What's in a green home? How do you know it's a green home? Who is building green homes? How much extra should you expect to pay? Where can you get more information about green homes? These key questions form the basis for this book, and I'm glad we're making this journey of discovery together. Your choice to buy a green home will make a difference far beyond supporting your own lifestyle and economic circumstances. With your home purchase you can also help tackle broader environmental issues.

But let's focus first on your own needs: for most of us, it's a simple equation. A green home should be more comfortable, with healthier air, less-toxic finishes, more environmentally sound materials, and cheaper operating costs. About two years ago, my wife and I moved to Tucson, Arizona, from Portland, Oregon. We looked for a home that would meet as many of our "green goals" as possible. Because we wanted to be near the Sonoran desert, we looked for a development that respected the natural environment and that allowed us to be close enough to town without driving a long time to get basic services. We looked at a well-known local green development, the Civano Community, but decided against it for two reasons. It is a fairly long drive to basic services and meetings in town. My wife also objected to the nearby overhead power distribution towers, but the distance was the deciding factor against Civano, still one of the most eco-friendly developments in the country, which I'll profile later.

Eventually, we found a home in a six-year-old development that met most of our goals; because it was relatively new, we had confidence that it wouldn't be too costly to heat and cool (summer highs hit 110°F, and winter nights get down into the 20s). We also wanted good solar access, so we could plan on adding solar panels to the south-facing roof, to provide electricity and hot water. We also wanted to be able to add a rainwater harvesting system later, since we love gardens but live in a very dry area. We knew we'd have to recarpet and repaint because the family that sold it to us had two young and very active preschool children (think of fingerprints two feet above the carpet, just about everywhere!). We did find a house that met most of our criteria. (One that wasn't met was a "Guarantee Home" from the local electric utility, but more on that later.) Once we bought it, we set out to remodel with low-VOC paints and carpets, because my wife is very allergic to any chemical odors. That wasn't easy, and later you'll learn how to make sure that you don't have to experience "new home smell" after you move in. In 2008 we added solar electric panels and a rainwater harvesting system, along with a solar water heater and dual-flush toilets.

Why Choose Green? Homeowners Share Their Reasons

Other homebuyers have been able to find new green homes. Steve Rypka and his wife bought a home in 2005 in Sun City Anthem, a development by Pulte Homes, in Henderson, Nevada near Las Vegas. Steve works as a green-living consultant, so he had extra motivation to find a super-green home that would serve as a basis for his consulting practice. He says:

> We were looking for very specific features because we had a goal of green living in mind. Number one: we were looking for a smaller home. We went from about 3,000 square feet down to a home that's about 1,840 square feet with a casita that brings the total to just under 2,100 square feet, including two offices. My wife and I both work out of the house, and that's part of our green-living strategy — no commuting. We also wanted a house that was ENERGY STAR-rated and very energy-efficient. Then we looked for a floor plan that had most of windows on one face of the four sides of the home. We found a floor plan that put most of the glazing at the rear of the house. Then we picked a lot to actually put that glazing to the south. In essence, we created a passive solar

home even though the builder didn't design it that way intentionally. All of these things came together in making the decision.

Our last home was 60 percent larger; we both work from the house, but we had way more room than we needed. It was a bit of a challenge to educate my wife about the idea that she would actually be happier in a smaller home. So many people have the concept that bigger is better, and she felt like she was giving something up. But now that we've made the move, she's actually really happy we did because our new home is much more comfortable and has a better layout that makes sense for our lifestyle. We wanted the energy efficiency because our previous house was built in the mid-80s, it had an older HVAC system, and was not insulated very well. The windows weren't "low-e," they were the typical double-pane, aluminum-frame windows of that era, so they were not very efficient either.

You can see that one of the key decisions in buying a green home is size and layout, issues discussed later in the book. Steve is an exceptionally motivated person who eventually added solar panels to provide all of the electricity needed for his home, and this with a home office and in a climate that exceeds 115°F during the summer! Many green-building experts argue that size is the most important issue, because the larger the home, the more volume to be heated and cooled, and the more materials are used. I'm going to be an agnostic on this issue, but most of us interested in green homes probably feel that our homes are too large for our real needs and that we have too much stuff anyway. It's a fact that new home sizes have doubled since about 1960, while the average number of people per household has decreased!

Let's look at another situation entirely. Ideal Homes is a builder in central Oklahoma focused heavily on energy efficiency and customer service. In her mid-60s, Adri-Anne Trammell is retired from the federal government and bought her new home in the company's Royal Oaks subdivision. Here's her story:

I liked the energy-efficient features although it wasn't the primary reason for buying the house. Financially, money saving is not a huge issue for me. I miss having an open fireplace because these are sealed to save energy. On the other hand, I like flipping the switch and having a [gas] fire, so there are pros and cons. Certainly I was interested in the insulation; in fact, on my garage door, I had insulation put in and did other upgrades like that. It just wasn't really a cost-savings thing as much as it was for the energy-savings and making the home more comfortable.

For me, the three most important criteria in a home are location, physical beauty of the area, and being able to get a floor plan that I like and enjoy. The ENERGY STAR qualification was a positive factor but not the deciding factor. The floor plan and location were the deciding factors. Since I've been living in the home, I've noticed that the room temperatures tend to be really even; in other words, I don't change the thermostat much. It's not drafty. It's just nice. I don't necessarily [work at conserving] energy, but my bills do seem to be lower.

Ideal Homes gives you walk-throughs. They come back after 90 days and do more walk-throughs. They tell you how to handle everything, how to maintain the house. I just think they do a great job. I think it's a good idea to pay attention to energy efficiency, particularly for young families who might be watching their pennies, although it's important for all of us to conserve our resources. I grew up in an era where that wasn't as important to people. Now, if I sit and think about it, it is something that's really important to me but it's not something that I focus on a lot like [younger] people do.

Adri-Anne is a totally different type of green homebuyer, responding to a well-planned, energy-efficient and comfortable home, but who values energy efficiency in a more casual way than Steve.

A third homebuyer, Amy Macklin, bought a townhome in March 2005 in a close-in urban redevelopment area called Glenwood Park in Atlanta. Amy is in her early 40s and works for a non-profit in Atlanta. She and her husband now have two very young children. She says:

My husband, Eric, and I were newly married, and we were looking for a new house. We had both lived in old houses and knew about the upkeep and time required for home maintenance. When we looked at this development, we were sold on [the developer] Charles Brewer's vision for the entire community right away. We knew we would have a really nice quality of life. We like the idea of living in town and living in a [mixed-use] community that combined commercial and residential, that also would have a park, coffee shop and restaurants, and be close to where I work. [Although it was new and still much unfinished], we felt like it was going to create a really nice sense of community with the neighbors.

The EarthCraft House (energy-efficiency) certification was important to both of us, but I don't know if it was first on our list. It was just a great bonus. We were both excited about the fact that they were developing the community in a really environmentally friendly way and that they were building EarthCraft homes and townhomes.

Our house is 50 percent larger than the house we were living in before we bought this one, yet our utility bills are 25 to 30 percent lower. I think it's a tightly wrapped house, and I like that it protects the environment. I like living in a home that's less draining [on resources] than other homes. I don't think it's that much different to operate, and it's not drafty. The carpet on the second floor is low-VOC, and that's a good thing especially with children in the house. Our daughter was diagnosed with reactive airway disease (a precursor to asthma) when we first moved, and we were glad to be living in a home that wasn't contributing to it or making it worse.

[For anyone buying a new home], I would recommend that buyers stay intimately involved in the building process. We walked through our house frequently and stayed in close contact with the developer. If we saw things that we had questions about or that concerned us, we brought it up right away and got everything addressed on the front end. For example, on the third story of our townhouse, there's a balcony on the rear that didn't have an appropriate slope for water drainage. We brought that up, and they addressed it.

I visited Glenwood Park in the summer of 2007 and walked through townhomes that were still being built. There's an elevated, noisy interstate highway right at the north edge of the development less than 100 feet from the townhomes, but when we closed the doors on the units, they were so quiet that it was easy to see that the insulation, weatherstripping and general building approach were doing their job of keeping noise out as well as reducing energy use. For many consumers like Amy Macklin and her husband, the EarthCraft Home label has become a certification of choice for homebuilders in the Atlanta area, because of the rigorous criteria and onsite inspections included in the program.

The Global Warming Challenge

Imagine a world in which the Arctic Ocean is ice-free most of the year, in which the permafrost of Alaska and Canada is melting, so that people, animals and vehicles can't get around most of the year. Imagine a permanent drought in the US and Canada west of the 100th meridian, so that our fastest growing cities, with millions of people, face chronic water shortages. Imagine a world that's warm enough so that most of the pest species that now are held in check by winter cold can grow and spread far beyond their historical ranges. Imagine a world in which hurricanes are more frequent, more severe and more damaging than anything we've known in our lifetimes. That is the stark future facing North America, as envisioned by climate scientists.

Anyone who follows current affairs knows that the United Nation's Intergovernmental Panel on Climate Change (IPCC) issued its *Fourth Report* in the spring of 2007, pegging the probability of human-induced (vs. naturally occurring) climate change at 90 percent, owing to the large increase in greenhouse gas emissions since 1950 and the consequent increase in carbon dioxide (CO_2) concentrations in the atmosphere. Recent analyses put the level of CO_2 at 380 parts per million (ppm), about 40 percent greater than the level of 150 years ago, before the start of the Industrial Revolution in developed countries. Informed projections to the year 2050 indicate that it will be hard to stop the growth of CO_2 emissions and concentrations at 450 ppm, the level at which many climate scientists expect irreversible effects on the global environment. If we want to hold back irreversible climate changes, acting now is far better than acting later. In fact some respected climate scientists put the "year of no return" as early as 2016! It's obvious that pulling back from the brink of irreversible effects is better now than waiting to see what happens later and "hoping for the best." This is not science fiction, or some far-fetched Hollywood thriller like *The Day After Tomorrow*, this is the best guess of the world's leading scientists.

In 2007 the Nobel Foundation awarded former Vice-President Al Gore and the IPCC scientists the 2007 Nobel Peace Prize for their role in highlighting and documenting the threat of global warming and irreversible climate change. This award shows that the entire world is waking up to that danger. Among the advanced industrial nations, Canada and the US lead the way in per capita emissions of CO_2, primarily because of widespread use of fossil fuels for buildings, homes, industry and transportation. If the peoples of the world are going to have a chance to avoid the dangers of unpredictable climate change, it will be largely due to the actions of more than 330 million consumers in the US and Canada, in making their choices for cars, consumer products, food, travel and homes. This is an awesome burden as well as an unprecedented opportunity for all of us.

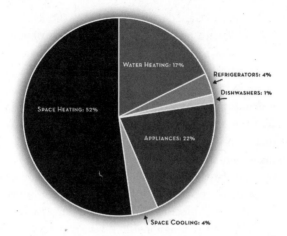

Figure 1.1. While air conditioning is a small percentage of overall energy use, it does contribute 16 percent of total electricity use, a figure that is dwarfed by the consumption of appliances, which constitutes 65 percent of total electricity use in a 2001 national residential energy consumption survey (Figure 1.2). Of the total appliance use, nearly 14 percent was for the refrigerator. *End Use Consumption of Energy 2001 [online], www.eia.doe.gov/emeu/recs/ recs2001/enduse2001.html, accessed January 2008*

Energy Use in the Home and Climate Change

Let's "drill down" a little farther and see how much our housing and transportation choices influence CO_2 production. Most estimates put housing at 20 percent of total US greenhouse gas emissions, stemming from such mundane activities as heating and cooling the home, heating water for bathing, dishwashing and clothes washing, and providing electrical power for our appliances and lights. Figure 1.1 shows the distribution of energy consumption in the average US home, based on end uses. (Cutting home energy use by 50 percent is like getting rid of one of your cars!)

Interestingly, more than half of all US energy consumption goes for space heating (think Michigan, New York, New England, Minnesota and Iowa in the winter), while only 4 percent goes for air conditioning. Lighting and appliances account for 22 percent of the total (less than half the level of space heating), while water heating makes up 17 percent of total housing energy consumption, with refrigeration taking about 4 percent of total energy use.

However, in Texas, which has both cold and hot extreme temperatures and dramatic differences in climate from the northern plains to the southern Gulf Coast, the percentages are a bit different, with far more energy used for air conditioning:[1]

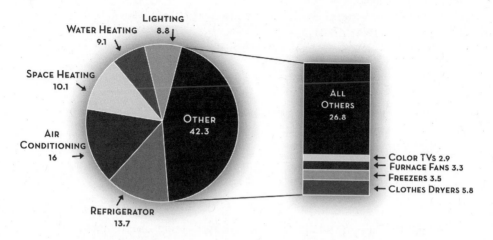

Figure 1.2. Distribution of electricity use in American households, showing the importance of controlling not only air conditioning but all connected "plug" loads. *Redrawn from* The Carbon Buster's Home Energy Handbook *by Godo Stoyke, New Society Publishers, 2006*

Space heating	29%
Lighting and appliances	29%
Water heating	18%
Air conditioning	17%
Refrigeration	8%

In terms of total annual energy use, location is obviously a big factor. In New York, with its cold winters and hot, humid summers, average energy use is 101 million BTU (British Thermal Units) — or 1,010 therms — per household, about $1,250 per year, while in Florida it's only 58 million BTU and in California, 58 million BTU, only two-thirds of New York's total cost. Part of the reason for these discrepancies may be that both California and Florida are faster growing than New York, with milder climates and a far younger average housing stock. The US average home-energy consumption in 2001 was 95 million BTU, so you can see that New York is far closer to average than either California or Florida. When you assess your green home's prospective total energy use, it helps to compare it not only to national averages but also to the average use for homes in your region of the country, as shown in Figure 1.3.

Consider the value of energy savings for each region of the country. If you're in New England, for example, reducing energy use by 50 percent

Figure 1.3. Average energy use per household, million (MM) BTU, most populous states, in 2001

	New York	California	Texas	Florida
Electricity (MM BTU)	20	20	51	52
Natural Gas (MM BTU)	71	46	57	26
Total (all fuels) Million BTU	99	62	89	58

Note: 1 million BTU = 10 therms = 293 kwh. *US Energy Information Administration [online], eia.doe.gov/ emeu/recs/recs2001/ce_pdf/enduse/ce1-7c_4popstates2001.pdf, accessed January 4, 2008*

Figure 1.4. Average retail price of electricity, by region, September 2007

Region	Average Retail Price, cents per kwh	Energy Savings (Equivalent kwh)	
		5,000	10,000
New England	16.5	$825	$1,650
Middle Atlantic (NY, NJ, PA)	14.6	$730	$1,460
East North Central (IL, IN, MI, OH, WI)	10.0	$500	$1,000
West North Central (IA, KS, MN, MO, NE, ND, SD)	8.5	$425	$850
South Atlantic (DE, DC, FL, GA, MD, NC, SC, VA, WV)	10.4	$520	$1,040
East South Central (AL, KY, MS, TN)	8.2	$420	$820
West South Central (AR, LA, OK, TX)	11.4	$570	$1,140
Mountain (AZ, CO, ID, MT, NV, NM, UT, WY)	9.8	$490	$980
Pacific Contiguous (CA, OR, WA)	13.1	$655	$1,310
Alaska	15.4	$770	$1,540
Hawaii	23.5	$1,175	$2,350
US Total	10.9	$545	$1,090

US Energy Information Administration [online], eia.doe.gov/cneaf/electricity/epm/table5_6_a.html, accessed January 4, 2008

(approximately the equivalent of 5,000 kilowatt-hours) could be worth $825 per year, just like earning a 4.1 percent tax-free yield on a $20,000 bond.

Considering that the total annual value of new residential construction and renovations in the US and Canada, at more than $300 billion,[2] exceeds the total value of all commercial building construction, it's not hard to understand the importance of controlling total home energy use in the broader picture of reducing national and global carbon dioxide emissions.

Looking Ahead

In the next chapter, I'll show you what the emerging field of building science has to say about how far we can go to reduce home energy use. There are a lot of potential energy savings in new homes, if they're built right. Also, it's important to realize that whatever homes we build today will likely be in use 50 years from now. (I grew up in Los Angeles in a home built in 1948, and it's still in use today.) So, whatever structural measures we put in a new home to conserve energy, particularly for space heating and cooling, will still have a major influence on home energy consumption in the year 2050 and possibly even 2075! Considering both residential and commercial construction, one estimate is that 75 percent of the built environment in the US will be new or renovated during the next 30 years. This shows how much potential there is to affect national energy use (and climate effects) with seemingly small individual choices. That's where you, the homebuyer, come in.

Figure 1.5 shows the growth in CO_2 emissions from buildings, homes, transportation and industry in the US since 1950. The only sector that is not increasing emissions rapidly is industry, partly because of energy conservation measures taken since the 1970s, partly because of the continued growth of the service economy, and certainly in large part because of the off-shoring of much industrial production (think of Chinese toys imported by most major retailers). Looking ahead to 2020, we can see that, without stringent conservation measures, US energy production and CO_2 emissions are likely to grow another 37 percent from the 2000 base. Given this projected growth, you can see that scaling back emissions in 2020 to 1990 levels will be a gargantuan task for all of us. You have an opportunity (and an obligation) to help in this task, with your individual and family housing choices. Saving energy is a core feature of green homes, one that actually pays you back over time, in terms of a return on investment, by reducing future utility bills. As one wag put it, "Not only do you get a free lunch, but you get paid to eat it too!"

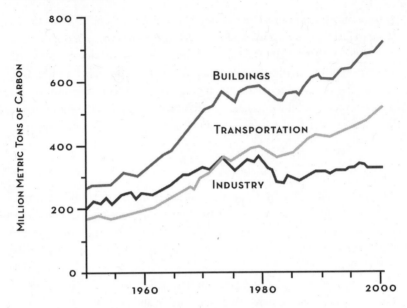

Figure 1.5. CO_2 emissions from major sectors. *Architecture 2030, architecture2030.org, redrawn with permission*

In Canada the situation is not as dire. According to a 2006 report, only 6 percent of Canadian greenhouse gas emissions came from residences, versus 20 percent in the US. The report says that, thanks to improved home-heating equipment and cleaner fuel sources, residential emissions remained fairly constant between 1990 and 2002, even while Canadians formed almost 22 percent more households.[3] However, because Canada is colder than most of the US, Canadians care more about energy-conserving homes for their fuel savings, better indoor air quality and greater comfort.

Figure 1.6 shows that, with a concerted Climate Action Plan involving all sectors of US buildings, transportation and industry, we have a chance to take a different path, one that leads us away from the brink of unprecedented climate change and toward a more livable future. There are two divergent paths to the future, in terms of energy use and global warming. In this context, I'm reminded of Robert Frost's famous poem, something you might have read in school, that concludes:

> Two roads diverged in a yellow wood, and I —
> I took the one less traveled by
> And that has made all the difference.

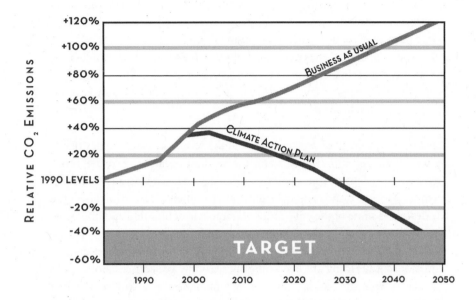

Figure 1.6. The two paths of US building sector carbon dioxide emissions to 2050.
Architecture 2030, architecture2030.org, redrawn with permission

These two pathways to the future are starkly different: one creates some breathing room for building energy efficiency and other approaches to reducing CO_2 emissions to become effective; and one continues business as usual, a path that probably results in a lot more suffering, economic disruption and foreclosing of any easy options for dealing with climate change. You have the power, with your next housing choice, to make a difference in this great debate. Your choice of an energy-efficient home, one with solar power systems, will help create a more livable future for yourself, your family and everyone else.

Environmental Impacts of Homes

Besides energy use, what are the other consequences of housing choices? From 1992 through 2002, more than 20 million acres of land (1 percent of the country's total area) were developed for urban and industrial uses, much of it for new housing. One US federal government study found that homes are a major contributor to the overall environmental impacts of building development, construction and operations. Take a look at these facts. Buildings contribute:

- 39 percent of total national energy use (55 percent of the total comes from homes)
- 12 percent of total water consumption (74 percent from homes)
- 68 percent of total electricity consumption (51 percent from homes)
- 38 percent of total carbon dioxide emissions (54 percent from homes)
- 136 million tons of construction and demolition debris each year (43 percent from homes)[4]

Clearly we should all be concerned about the resource-use efficiency of our homes, their pollution impacts and the amount of land use for new subdivisions. Here again, your choice of green housing can help alleviate some of these symptoms and create a brighter environmental future for all. Figure 1.7 describes some of the environmental impacts of building and operating our homes.

Beyond the environmental impacts of energy use and carbon dioxide emissions, Americans are becoming increasingly concerned about water shortages. According to the federal government, homes use more than half of publicly supplied water. A family of four uses about 400 gallons of water every day. In the West, much of it arid, landscape irrigation leads to much higher per capita residential water use. Los Angeles gets an average of only 16 inches per year of rainfall, compared with 42 inches in New York City and 48 inches in Orlando. In Los Angeles, there is almost no rainfall from May through October, the prime growing seasons for plants, so irrigation is a must for lawns, gardens and landscape plants. According to the US Environmental Protection Agency, in the last five years, nearly every region of the country has experienced water shortages. At least 36 states are anticipating local, regional or statewide water shortages by 2013, even under non-drought conditions.[5]

Homes are also getting bigger, increasing their resource consumption. From 1970 to 2005, the average size of a new single-family (detached) home increased 62 percent, from 1,500 square feet to 2,434 square feet. Since 1990, I have lived in both a 1970s average-size single-family home and a current average-size home, and I know that both are quite livable. In 1970 only one-third of all new homes had central air conditioning, but in 2005 nearly 90 percent did. We have more volume of space to heat and more use of cooling in that space. It stands to reason that energy consumption will increase.[6] Everything has its limits, and in 2006 the average home size stopped increasing, for the first time since the end of World War II.

Figure 1.7. Homebuilding and operations environmental impact

Number of trees required to build an average American home, as estimated by the US Forest Service	88 (3.2 acres of forest).[7]
Amount of water an average household can save per year by using conservation practices and water-efficient products	30,000 gallons.[8]
Amount of CO_2 emissions that can be averted each year when an incandescent light bulb is replaced with a compact fluorescent	104 pounds.[9]
Of all the power consumed by electronic devices in US homes, percent of that power consumed when the devices are supposedly turned off	5 percent.[10]
Percent of energy that is wasted by unplanned air infiltration and exfiltration in most homes	30 percent or more (equivalent to the energy supplied by the entire Alaska pipeline).[11]
Weight of a 1,500 square foot home: 37 tons. Amount of space that home would occupy in a landfill if entirely discarded	120 cubic yards.[12]
Amount of mercury emitted by a coal power plant to produce the electricity to light one incandescent bulb for five years	10 milligrams. Amount of mercury produced to light a compact fluorescent for five years: 2.4 milligrams.[13]
Amount of formaldehyde given off by hardwood plywood imported from China	up to 100 times more than is legal in Japan and 30 times that allowed in Europe and China.[14]
In 2005 the average floor area of a newly built home	2,434 square feet, up 48 percent from 1,645 square feet in 1975.[15]
Change in average household size since 1967	10 percent reduction.[16] This means the average person's use of living area has grown more than 50 percent in a little more than one generation. (This might be a sign of progress, but it consumes more resources.)

Craig Tanner, courtesy of Monte Hewett Home

Figure 1.8. This EarthCraft certified home, built by Monte Hewett Homes, is one of 20 homes in the Greenwood community near Atlanta.

Green Home Builders and Buyers Respond to Climate Change

In my research for this book, I found homebuilders and homebuyers alike passionate about doing a better job on these issues with their new homes. For example, Dina Gundersen of Monte Hewett Homes in Atlanta (model home shown in Figure 1.8) says:

> We are one of the few builders in Atlanta that builds every one of our homes to EarthCraft Home standards. It's a company policy, and Monte, the company owner, believes in it wholeheartedly. Monte was attracted to the EarthCraft program in its infancy because there weren't then any other building standards that prove to a homeowner that their home had been certified by an [independent] third-party, that specific energy-efficient and sustainable features had been included, and that it had been inspected. The third-party inspection is the biggest piece. That rings true and is important to homebuyers, they want to know that you're not just saying [that you're a green builder], but that it's really true.

Buying a green home, in our world, is not just about the benefits to the buyers. It's also about the benefits to the environment. You can get points through the EarthCraft program based on how you dispose of materials and how the site is laid out in terms of stormwater drainage and tree-saving properties, for example. Environmentally healthy comes down to little things such as how you frame a house. A builder can drastically change the amount of material used and reduce waste simply based on how the boards are cut. We think the benefits to the environment are a big part of what we do.[17]

Another homebuilder, Nat Hodgson, Vice-President of Construction for Pulte Homes/Del Webb, Las Vegas Division, says:

To be honest with you, "going green" has been a lot of extra work. Sometimes I ask myself why the heck am I doing this? My answer: Because it's the right thing to do. My vision is to build a community that has just about every green thing that I can get my hands on.[18]

Rich Coyle, of DR Horton Homes, Sacramento Division, shares similar feelings:

Green building has been an evolution for our division and DR Horton as a company. At DR Horton, Sacramento was a start-up division almost nine years ago. We started offering homes that included guarantees on heating and cooling...and incrementally tried to do what we could to build a better house. As a result, each home helps mitigate over 4,200 pounds of greenhouse gas emissions per year. Multiply that by the 5,000 homes under this program and it equates to over 21 million pounds fewer carbon emissions. When you start looking at those things and educating the buyer, light bulbs go off — and hopefully they're compact fluorescent light bulbs![19]

Steve Tapio of New Tradition Homes, in Vancouver, Washington, concurs:

We want to build the best possible product at the most affordable price. The best product could be defined as a house that has healthy indoor air, higher energy savings, durable construction and one that gives the homeowner enhanced comfort and peace of mind. One of the owners of the company likes to say, "We want to do the right thing." That means doing the right thing for the homeowner, the environment and for the company, for our employees as well as our trade contractors.[20]

Homebuyers are equally passionate about their green homes. Interestingly, in most interviews with buyers of green homes, among both men and women, we found a high level of awareness about environmental issues, coupled with considerable knowledge about the benefits of their green homes' energy savings. For example, one Northern California homeowner, Larry Brittain, who bought into the Carsten Crossings development offered by the Grupe Company, a regional builder, says:

> The money that I'm saving is just incredible. I have to tell you that after living here for one complete year, my Pacific Gas and Electric bill was about $430 for the whole year — and that's both gas and electricity. I'm not aware of how much electricity that I've sold back to the utility; I just know what I paid in usage.
>
> [To a friend looking to buy a green house] I'd say, "Go for it." We didn't know how much we were going to save until we started living here. Then I starting getting the bills and I said, "I can't believe this." Our old house was four years old when we moved into it; we lived there for four years, and now we're saving over $200 a month in this house. It helped us in offsetting our increased mortgage payment [for a more expensive new home].[21]

Kenny Trapp, another homebuyer at Ideal Homes in Oklahoma, says:

> I'm a meteorologist for the University of Oklahoma. I'm very well aware of energy costs and energy demand and how those will increase with climate change, not necessarily long-term, but also short-term as far as the seasons go. My goal was to find a highly energy-efficient home. I could've bought a very cheap home in an older neighborhood, but it would not have been nearly as energy-efficient. I found out that Ideal Homes has invested a lot in research and development — in trying and testing new things — all for the betterment of making sure their homes were as energy-efficient as they could be, which ultimately saves on the bottom line for their customers. They went through the process of testing the entire home as far as exactly how energy-efficient it is so they could get the ENERGY STAR rating. That was all in an effort to keep my energy costs down.[22]

Jeff Baxter, a homeowner at the Oak Terrace Preserve development in North Charleston, South Carolina, says:

> I chose this development because I'm a big proponent of the strategies and philosophies that are going to be implemented there. I felt like, number one, it was a way to put my money where my mouth is, and also it's an up and coming area, so there's a lot of new investment coming into the area. It's an older part of town that had declined a little bit, but there's still some great older housing stock where a lot of people have been fixing up houses. It has a great feel to it.
>
> The green features were very important to me. Not many homebuilders are completely focused on this sort of thing. That was a big encouragement to push me over the edge on purchasing the home in this area. I also like the fact that all of the other homes in the area have to meet the same standard. I think it's going to have a lot of impact on the way homes are built and neighborhoods are designed. It just seems to me, it would be irresponsible to not have ENERGY STAR appliances and the basic things that really don't add much cost to the house.[23]

CHAPTER 2

What Is a Green Home?

We've explored why people are building and buying green homes. But what exactly do we mean by the term "green home?" Reading the first chapter, you might surmise that there are many possible definitions, depending on what features a builder includes in a home and what rating or certification system a builder uses. There are no "Consumer Reports" or "J. D. Power" ratings for green homes, as there are for cars, home appliances and so many other consumer products, so to some degree you're on your own in looking for a green home.

Sam Rashkin, head of the ENERGY STAR for Homes program of the US Environmental Protection Agency, says his simple rule for homebuyers is: "First blue, then green."[1] Blue is the ENERGY STAR logo's color, so what he means is that your home should first of all be at least 15 percent more energy-efficient than a standard home. Then you should add the other green features described in this chapter, such as water conservation, better ventilation and healthy finishes. So, as a homebuyer, your first question for the builder should be: "How energy-efficient is this home and who vouches for that?"

I wholeheartedly agree. Not only does Rashkin's rule save you money in the long run, but it also helps reduce your carbon footprint by reducing the amount of coal, oil or gas that needs to be burned to provide your home's energy needs. (Remember the electricity production and distribution

Figure 2.1. Six elements of a green home.

system is less than 30 percent efficient from start to finish, so for every unit of electricity you don't use at the home, you're saving three-plus units at the source.) Moreover, once the home is built, it's very hard, and often expensive, to change its basic energy demand for heating, cooling and hot water, since most of these features are built into the home's structure and core energy-conversion systems. Your new home will probably last 50 years or more and its "embedded" energy use will remain for most of that period, with all the impacts on the environment that come with energy production.

Key Features of a Green Home

Figure 2.1 shows the elements that most people consider when they talk about buying a green home.

Sustainable Site Development/Location and Linkages
- Avoiding development on inappropriate sites such as prime farmland, flood plains and near wetlands
- Orienting the lots so that you can get warm sunlight in the home in the winter and keep it out during the summer (good lot orientation can save you 10 percent or more of your home's energy use)
- Locating sites near transit and neighborhood amenities, so that you don't have to get in a car to get a quart of milk or travel to work
- Treating stormwater on or near the development, so that less contaminated runoff goes in local streams or, eventually, the ocean or nearby lakes
- Designing roads and other hard surfaces to absorb less sunlight, reducing the temperature of the local microclimate, so there's less need for air conditioning.

Water Conservation

- Using native and locally adapted plants that require less water to thrive
- Using efficient drip irrigation or high-efficiency irrigation for public spaces (remember more than half the water used by a single-family home is typically for irrigation)
- Installing more efficient water-using features in the home, such as dual-flush toilets, low-flow faucet aerators and "home runs" or recirculation loops for hot water distribution (this means you won't run the water so long before you get hot water at the faucet)
- Installing water-efficient appliances such as dishwashers and clothes washers with an EPA WaterSense™ certification.

Energy Conservation

- Passive design measures, including overhangs over south and west-facing windows and deciduous vegetation on the south and west sides, that will shade the home in summer while still allowing light — and heat — in during the winter
- An ENERGY STAR home rating, assuring you that your home will use at least 15 percent less energy than a typical home in the area, operated in a similar fashion
- To achieve the ENERGY STAR home rating, expect increased insulation and better insulated windows, along with a host of smaller measures grounded in "building science" (more about this later in this chapter)
- ENERGY STAR home appliances (as you saw in chapter 1, a minority of your energy use comes from heating and cooling)
- A well-insulated, efficient water heater or tankless water heater (water heating can account for 25 percent of your total home energy use)
- Easily programmable thermostat, so that you can set back temperatures at night and let the home cool off or heat up (depending on the season) when you're away at work
- Efficient lighting fixtures, including compact fluorescent bulbs (CFLs) throughout the home, especially in those areas you're likely to be using a lot, such as living room, kitchen, study and bedrooms. Outdoor lighting should also rely on CFLs (there are special types that can take the cold)
- In colder climates, look for a "heat (or energy) recovery ventilation" system that will use the heat in the exhaust air to preheat the colder incoming air, saving you energy

- Solar power systems to provide 10 percent to 20 percent (or more) of your annual electricity needs
- Solar water heaters to provide 50 percent or more of annual hot water needs.

Materials and Resource Conservation

- Your homebuilder should be recycling 50 percent or more of construction waste
- Your home should contain recycled content materials wherever possi-

Energy Conservation at DR Horton, Sacramento (CA) Division

We interviewed Rich Coyle of DR Horton in Sacramento about the company's program. He says:

Green building has been an evolution. Here in Sacramento, we have embraced energy-efficient homes since 2001. We looked at energy-efficient, sustainable houses as our niche in our marketplace. We started offering homes that offer guarantees on heating and cooling [costs]. At that same time we started a Building America project designed to reach Environments for Living (EFL) Platinum levels. Now for every new project, we offer the guarantee. We do at least the Gold Plus level for Environments for Living which is about 15 percent better than [California's Title 24 Energy] code. All of our projects are ENERGY STAR rated.

A few years ago we started to offer solar as an option, and now we're starting a project where solar is standard — we're working to rate that project as LEED for Homes Silver.

We've tried to do things that make sense for a production builder. That's been our progression. We've probably built over 5,000 homes that have energy [usage] guaranteed with them. Last year [2006] we built 1,100 alone. This year [2007] it will also be about 1,100 homes. All of our homes are guaranteed by Environments for Living (EFL). There are different levels of energy efficiency in the EFL program, with the minimum being "Gold Plus" level. We guarantee the maximum amount of heating therms and cooling kilowatt-hours that will be used by the homes for a three-year period. We also have a guarantee that the center of the room will not vary by more than three degrees from the thermostat temperature.

ble, but these must have the same quality, durability and aesthetic appeal as the rest of the home
- You might consider upgrading to cabinets using wood from sustainably harvested forests
- Similarly, you might want to look at flooring made from rapidly renewable materials such as cork, bamboo and linoleum, again with full consideration of aesthetics, durability and quality (materials from the local region may be more sustainable because of reduced transportation energy use).

We were finding it's hard to get the word out to buyers about our green offerings. It's important to educate the buyers because they are comparing builder A and builder C to DR Horton. Even though a green home may cost a little more, we need to let them know that in the long run, buyers are going to come out ahead because they are going to save money on their energy bills.[2]

Keith Sutter, courtesy of DR Horton, Sacramento Division

Figure 2.2. Equipped with solar electric systems and other energy-efficient features, each home in DR Horton's Provence community in Sacramento will reduce CO_2 emissions by 4,700 pounds a year, the equivalent of not consuming 244 gallons of gasoline.

Indoor Environmental Quality

- Look for a home with the ENERGY STAR indoor-air-quality package that will assure you of a healthier home with superior ventilation (the trick of course is to have good ventilation without increasing energy use for heating and cooling incoming air)
- Your home should be made with low-toxicity finishes, especially paints and carpets, so that there is no "new home" smell when you move in, which consists of the off-gassing of potentially harmful contaminants
- Look for cabinets and other finishing touches made without urea-formaldehyde resins (go into any furniture store and smell the furniture: you can tell if it is off-gassing formaldehyde)
- Look for a quiet, efficient bathroom fan, to keep mold out of the bathroom; this will ventilate adjacent spaces as well

Indoor Air Quality in North Texas Homes

We interviewed Steve Hayes, division president for McGuyer Homebuilders, Inc., Dallas. He says:

> We have a fresh-air intake on all of our air conditioners. It's mechanically controlled and computer-operated to make sure that a certain amount of fresh air comes in throughout the entire year. It's not a hand-controlled damper system [that might not allow enough fresh air into the home]. Indoor air quality, according to the [federal] EPA, is one of the top five health concerns in the nation right now. The air inside of the home a lot of the time is worse than the air outside the home, because of the furnace, cooking oils burning and different things that go on when someone lives in a home. That air becomes very stale, and there's a lot of moisture in the air. The fresh-air intake at the air conditioning unit allows for the circulation of new fresh air into that home and circulates the old, stale air back out of the home. Having fresh air for the family living inside the home is very important. We also do a four-inch media filter on all our air conditioning units. Our air conditioning company gave us an interesting analogy: the normal one-inch air filter, which you see at the return air grill [in most homes], is designed to catch the softballs, baseballs and golf balls. The four-inch media filters are designed to catch grains of sand. It's made to filter fine particles out of the air coming into the house, compared to the one-inch typical filter which is simply designed to keep large dust particles out of the A/C unit.[3]

- Good daylighting without glare is the hallmark of a green home; this can come from large windows (with overhangs), clerestory windows in a cathedral ceiling, north-facing skylights, light tubes and other means. Good daylighting allows you to do many of your daily tasks without turning on the lights.

Most good green-home rating systems incorporate each of these five features, even though they might give them different emphasis. Some green-home rating and certification systems, such as the US Green Building Council's (USGBC) Leadership in Energy and Environmental Design (LEED), have prerequisites in each category, while others, such as the National Association of Homebuilders (NAHB) Model Green Home Guidelines, require builders to achieve a minimum score in each category. Most good green-home rating systems require onsite inspection and testing of at least leaks in the home (this is done by pressurizing the home with a "blower door" and seeing how much air leaks out) and in the ventilation ductwork (in this case, the home rater pressurizes the ducts and measures leakage). We'll talk more about the requirements and merits of various rating and certification systems in chapter 5.

Sometimes homebuilders and homebuyers have different views about what's important in a green home beyond energy conservation measures. For example, Richard Barna of Pepper Viner Homes, a builder at the Civano green community in Tucson, Arizona, says:

Civano is a unique community. A lot of people that are looking here are looking for something that's green and energy-efficient. ENERGY STAR is a good starting point. If the home isn't meeting that level then you should ask, why not? It can be done.

When we started this project we asked "What is quality?" We wanted to build a higher-quality house than the average builder. Everybody uses the same subcontractors; they all use the same sheetrock, etc. So we thought that if we could design a house that works better than the average house and you can document it and prove it by third-party testing, then there's no more debate about quality.

We're also working with Building America, which is the US Department of Energy's program to make production housing more energy-efficient. They help us and suggest things that we can be doing to improve our methods. There are labels now for greenbuilding programs, and if somebody is just saying "ours is green" but they don't have anything to back it up, it probably isn't green.

We thought that if we built a house that was super-energy-efficient, it should have just a tiny increase in cost. You wouldn't even notice the price difference from what we sold before to now. It really didn't cost us that much to do it. It took a lot of effort and a lot of time, but some things that you do [to meet that standard] actually save you money. Plus there are government tax credits for the builder. Our goal is to build an energy-efficient house so people don't have that decision to make: Would I pay a whole bunch more? The goal would be to get it for the exact same price that they were paying anyway and get a house that's worth a lot more. Some of our houses are saving 50 to 54 percent on heating and cooling costs — that's pretty major savings. That meets the federal EPACT 2005 standard, and it doesn't cost all that much to get there.

We've been a design-oriented company, but now we're positioning ourselves both as a high-performance and a high-design company. This has taken a change in the mindset of our company. We decided that our whole company culture had to reflect a green approach. We decided that it wasn't mandatory to build simple little boxes. There's a stereotype about that with super-energy-efficient homes, because people think that you probably don't have a lot of design features in it.[4]

Jeff Baxter bought a home at the Noisette Company's Oak Terrace Preserve subdivision in North Charleston, South Carolina. He says:

There are about 20 houses built or being built in this neighborhood [this year]. Ultimately there will be 300 single-family homes and about 60 or 70 townhomes. The community itself has a New Urbanism premise, so there are alley-fed houses [garages at the back of the property]. From a community standpoint, they are encouraging activity on the street-front as opposed to having a garage for your front door. It's also very dense housing. The average lot is 4,000 to 5,000 square feet which is small — it equates to eight to 10 homes per net acre.

Community-wide, you have to use native plants or plants that don't require special irrigation needs for landscaping. So sod and turf grass are discouraged; you can only have a certain percentage of turf grass. The stormwater system is a low-impact design. Ideally 95 percent of the rainfall is dealt with onsite through a system of bioswales and rain gardens, as opposed to having it run off the site as quickly as possible into pipes and channeling it out to the river.

Figure 2.3. Each home in the Oak Terrace Preserve community is built and certified according to stringent green building standards in healthy, efficient, durable and comfortable residential design. The entire community was developed according to traditional neighborhood design; homes have front porches and are within easy walking or bicycling distance to schools, retail establishments and recreational areas.

This builder specializes in "back-to-the-basics," proven methods to build a good house that's more energy-efficient. They don't push things like photovoltaics and real unusual features or things that add cost. It's great to have an efficient air conditioning system, but if the envelope of your house isn't up to par, then it's still inefficient. They look at it as a whole-house concept. They're using a smaller air conditioning system because they have a really tight envelope with high R-value insulation. Their goal is to compete at the same price point as a normal house but deliver one that is more durable and saves you money on your energy bill.

I would have been willing to pay more for the house because of the green features. I would associate a premium to it, and I'm willing to pay a premium for something that is well designed, is going to hold up and that I have confidence in. The price point was competitive with a regular house that does not include those features.[5]

Building Science Basics

"Building science," a term that's coming into vogue as home energy efficiency becomes more important, means using sound scientific and engineering principles in home design to achieve lower energy use, more comfort, healthier indoor air quality and fewer moisture-related problems such as mold. Building science has also developed "advanced framing techniques" that reduce the use of building materials, especially wood, while still achieving a strong, energy-efficient home. Over the past 20 years, through the federal government's Building America program, scientists and engineers have built up an impressive array of tools and techniques that many progressive builders have begun to adopt. This collection of homebuilding "best practices," known as "building science," is all about the control of temperature, air movement, moisture and radiation (in areas with radon gas in the ground).

A house is an interactive system of many different parts. Change any part, and you impact the whole — favorably or unfavorably. That's a key premise behind building science. A growing number of residential builders are looking to the answers of building science to assist them in constructing better homes.

Building science is based on seven key phenomena, easily recognizable to anyone who's taken high-school science:

1. Heat flows from hot to cold. (A warm house wants to lose heat in winter and a cool house wants to gain heat in summer.)
2. It takes energy to maintain a constant temperature in the home and to move air around, because heat is always being lost or gained. (Even a "net-zero-energy" home requires input from solar power or other renewable sources.)
3. Warmer air rises and cooler air falls. (This leads to convection currents — drafts — caused by cold windows and warm rooms.)
4. Air moves from higher to lower pressure. (Air ducts not well sealed will leak conditioned air into unconditioned spaces; if the leak is large, air may not get to all the rooms of the house. Also, if the wind is blowing, the outside air can be higher or lower pressure than the home, depending on wind direction, so both infiltration and exfiltration may occur — unwanted air coming in on the high-pressure side and conditioned air leaking out on the low-pressure side.)
5. Moisture flows from higher to lower concentrations. (If it's moist outside and dry inside, moisture wants to enter the house.)
6. Moisture condenses on a cool or cold surface, when there's enough humidity in the air. (If outside humid air gets through a vapor barrier to an air conditioned wall, it will condense and stay there, potentially causing mold.)

7. Gravity pulls everything down, so water that gets through the cladding of the home has to be taken out at the bottom of the wall. (Anyone over 50 will see this principle at work daily in the bathroom mirror!)

One of North America's leading experts in building science, Dr. Joe Lstiburek of Building Science Corporation, says:

> Controlling rain intrusion is the single most important factor in the design and construction of durable buildings and in the control of mold. Drainage planes (water-resistant barriers such as DuPont's Tyvek®) located inside the exterior cladding of a home (stucco, brick, etc.) are used in the design and construction of building enclosures to control rain and direct it down and away from the house.[6]

Building science calls for home designs that are regionally specific. The US Department of Energy has identified eight main climatic regions in the US and Canada.[7] Each one calls for different approaches to heating, cooling, moisture control and human comfort:

1. **Hot-humid** (East Texas through the lower Southeast) — more than 20 inches of rain and more than 3,000 hours with a wet-bulb temperature above 67°F. (This means that the air is warmer than that temperature.)
2. **Mixed-humid** (the upper Southeast, plus Oklahoma, Kansas, Missouri, the Ohio Valley, parts of Illinois and Indiana, plus southern New Jersey and southeastern Pennsylvania) — more than 20 inches of rain, less than 5,400 heating degree-days and average monthly winter temperature below 45°F. (See Glossary, after chapter 11, for definition of degree-day.)
3. **Hot-dry** (West Texas, southern Arizona and the California Central Valley) — less than 20 inches of rain and average monthly outdoor temperatures (even in winter) above 45°F.
4. **Mixed-dry** (Las Vegas, southern New Mexico and the Texas Panhandle) — less than 20 inches of rain, less than 5,400 heating degree-days and average winter monthly outdoor temperature below 45°F for one or more months.
5. **Marine** (West coast from San Diego to Vancouver and Victoria, BC) — a summer dry season, at least four months with average temperatures above 50°F, plus a warmest month average below 72°F, and with an average temperature of the coldest month between 27°F and 65°F.

6. **Cold** (as you might guess, everything else in the US up through western BC and southeastern Alaska, including southern Ontario and the Canadian Maritimes) — 5,400 to 9,000 heating degree-days.

7. **Very cold** (Most of the rest of populated Canada and Alaska, plus pieces of northern Minnesota, Wisconsin and North Dakota) — 9,000 to 12,600 heating degree-days

8. **Subarctic/Arctic** (interior and northern Alaska, Nunavut and caribou country) — more than 12,600 heating degree-days.

Heating degree-days are measured from a 65°F base and determine the amount of heating energy you'll need for the home. For example, a day with an average temperature of 45°F will represent a 20 heating degree-day. Add that up for a 30-day month and you get 600 heating degree-days. If the monthly average were 30 degrees Fahrenheit instead, there would 1,050 heating degree days. The key point here is that sizing of heating and cooling equipment and approaches to moisture management are going to vary greatly depending on where you live, so that there are no "one size fits all" design approaches. This means that if you're moving from one region to another, don't be surprised if some of the building practices are markedly different; there's usually a good reason.

The essence of building science can be summed up in ten core principles. Some of these elements are shown in Figure 2.4, for a home in the hot-humid region.

1. Design a comfortable home that uses as little energy as possible. (Sounds easy, but it's not!)

2. Build a tight building envelope (something we heard about from Richard Barna), so that all ventilation air goes through the air filtration system (except when you purposefully open the windows or doors).

3. Ventilate adequately and purposefully, so that the home is always getting fresh air and is not losing conditioned air inadvertently.

4. Use more insulation than standard practice to make sure that the home is more like a thermos bottle than a glass carafe, as shown in Figure 2.5.

5. Control moisture, so that it doesn't hide in the walls, foundations and other places of the home, where it will eventually wear away the building materials. In this way, the home is more sustainable because it's more durable.

6. Make sure that all homes are oriented so that there is a south-facing roof slope that can accommodate solar panels, without being shaded, either now or in the future. (This could also be a garage roof.)

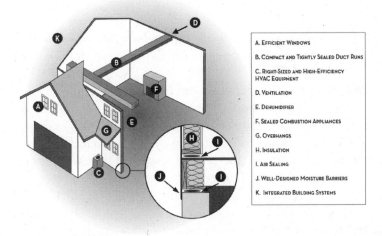

A. Efficient Windows

B. Compact and Tightly Sealed Duct Runs

C. Right-Sized and High-Efficiency HVAC Equipment

D. Ventilation

E. Dehumidifier

F. Sealed Combustion Appliances

G. Overhangs

H. Insulation

I. Air Sealing

J. Well-Designed Moisture Barriers

K. Integrated Building Systems

Figure 2.4. Elements of building science. *Adapted from US Department of Energy's Building America Best Practice Series, Volume 1*

7. Use the most efficient heating, cooling and hot water systems properly sized for the job. In most cases, the HVAC system is 20 percent to 40 percent oversized, which adds cost and results in less efficient operation. (See Figure 2.6)

8. Use efficient lighting and appliances matched to actual needs. Since such equipment can use more than 25 percent of a home's total energy, this is very important. For example, more task lighting and less ambient (overhead) lighting would be a better match to actual needs in most homes and would reduce energy use.

9. Reduce home energy use 40 percent to 70 percent (compared with conventional homes) before adding solar power systems for electricity and hot water.

10. Make sure all systems are working properly according to design intent (a process called "building commissioning" using a

Figure 2.5. The well-insulated thermos bottle will keep liquids hot for a long time, while the uninsulated carafe always needs supplemental heat to stay warm.

third-party — independent — inspector) before the eventual owners move into the home.[8]

Figure 2.6 shows how these principles might be applied by a builder to get a home that could save almost 10,000 kilowatt-hours yearly in North Carolina.

From this example, you can see that following simple building science principles allows a homeowner to save almost $900 per year on energy costs (assuming electricity costs $0.09 per kWh) AND a homebuilder to save considerable money by installing an electric heat pump that's just half the conventional size! Since the only extra costs are for higher-efficiency insulation and windows, the builder's *net* extra costs are about zero, but the

Figure 2.6. Reducing HVAC size with energy-efficiency upgrades (2,000 square foot home in Raleigh, North Carolina)

	Conventional Construction	With Energy-efficiency Upgrades
Wall insulation level	R-11	R-19
Ceiling insulation level	R-19	R-38
Window glass	Single-pane	Double-pane with low-e coating
Window overhangs	One foot	Two feet
Duct leakage	Average, with ducts in unconditioned space	None, with ducts inside conditioned space
House air leakage[1]	8 air changes per day	6 air changes per day
Manual J design heating load	46,100 BTU/hour	21,300 BTU/hour
Manual J design cooling load	52,100 BTU/hour	23,300 BTU/hour
Electric heat pump size	4.0 to 5.0 ton	2.0 ton
Annual heating energy usage	12,641 kWh	4,677 kWh
Heating savings[2]	—	$717
Annual cooling energy usage	3,808 kWh	1,790 kWh
Cooling savings	—	$182
Total annual energy savings	—	$899

1. Measured by blower door test, at 50 Pascal pressure.
2. At $0.09 per kWh.
US Department of Energy, "Right Sizing Heating and Cooling Equipment," eere.energy.gov/buildings/info/documents/pdfs/31318.pdf, accessed January 5, 2008

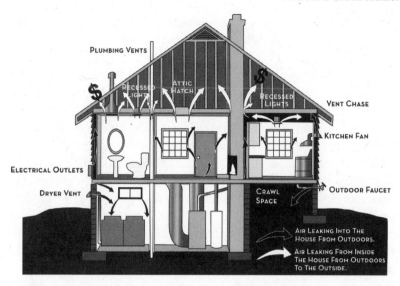

Figure 2.7. In typical homes, energy loss can occur because of holes and penetrations for plumbing, wiring, lighting and ductwork. *Adapted from ENERGY STAR*

sales benefit should be considerable. You can estimate the value of your potential savings from similar measures by consulting Figure 2.8.

What's Wrong with Typical New Homes?

The first five building science principles are the most important, according to building science experts we interviewed for this book. The first problem in single-family housing design is locating the mechanical (heating, cooling and ventilation) equipment in a vented space that is unconditioned. It's just a bad idea to put equipment and ducts in a vented crawlspace — things like furnaces and boilers and air handlers.

The same is true with attics; there are many houses built today — the majority of production homes — that have their air handlers and ductwork in vented attics. Even in a cold climate, in a larger house with a basement, you might find two systems — one in the basement and one in the attic, where the basement isn't vented but the attic is.

According to the experts, all crawl spaces and attics should be conditioned spaces, meaning they should be properly insulated. Why is this one issue so important? A building could lose up to 30 percent of its energy due to air leakage associated with having vented attics and vented crawl spaces. That includes energy loss from duct leakage, air-handler leakage and openings between the ceiling and the attic, as well as those between the floor and the crawl space. Because of plumbing, wiring and vents, we have openings in floors and ceilings to connect everything and those make the entire house leaky.

The second big problem results from the fact that a house is a six-sided cube, and there are often big holes somewhere because of the way that it was built or designed. For example, there can be bathtubs on outside walls where the bathtub was put in place before the sheetrock was put in, and as a result, the connection of the tub lip to the interior drywall isn't tight. Air will leak out of the house because the closure wasn't finished behind the wall of the tub or shower enclosure. In another situation, there might be kitchen cabinets on an outside wall, and the builder installed the soffit above the cabinets before the drywall, creating a place that's open to the outside forever. In another case, there might be a porch roof where, for whatever reason, the sheathing didn't go continuously. There could be a lot of big holes that result in air leakage that you can't see when you're ready to buy your house.

How can you know if you have any of those problems? Make sure you buy a home that's had a blower door test, so you can determine the air tightness of the home. There are hundreds of RESNET (home energy raters) around the country who do these tests. The homebuyer should ask the builder for the blower door test results and look at the numbers to see that they meet a standard of air tightness, such as no more than 0.35 air changes per hour.

Another common situation results from ineffective (read "cheap") exhaust fans in the bathrooms. There are good, quiet fans today that are energy efficient and pull out air very well. When you're looking at buying a home, go in and switch on the fan in the bathroom. If it makes a lot of noise, it's probably not working very well. You can also do a simple "tissue test": Take a piece of tissue and see if it will actually stick to the fan grill; if it doesn't, there is a problem, because the purpose of the fan is to take the moisture out of the bathroom. If it can't hold up a tissue, it's not going to get rid of moisture very well.

Believe it or not, some bathroom fans may not exhaust directly outdoors. Buyers should see if they can follow the duct from the fan up through the roof. Otherwise, the fan will be depositing moist air into the attic where it could lead to mold or mildew problems. To avoid building up moisture, you have to have air changes in the house. Without getting moisture out of the attic, especially if it is a sealed (conditioned) attic, you could be creating indoor air quality problems. What's the point of having an energy-efficient house with poor indoor air quality?

Make sure that you or your home inspector gets up into the attic and see where the ducts go. You or the inspector should be able to figure out where the space above each bathroom would be. You can always look on the outside to see if there are any exhaust vents anywhere. If there aren't or you can't figure out where things vent, you need to ask the builder where the bathroom vent exhaust goes until you're satisfied there is a clear path for moisture out of the home.

If a home is leak-free, it won't cause excessive air changes by mistake. Your goal should be to have only purposeful air changes. Obviously, you'll be opening your windows and screen doors during mild weather, which you can think of as intentional holes, which is fine. What you don't want are unintentional holes, and most homes have lots of them!

Having intentional air changes (or leakage) improves indoor air quality, but it does affect the energy efficiency. If you had a home that was hermetically sealed and well insulated, you wouldn't have to add any heat to maintain a certain temperature for a long time. The minute you exchange indoor air with outside air at a different temperature, you have to use energy to keep indoor temperatures stable.

But we need fresh air to live. We need oxygen, and we need to change the air in our homes. We can't live in a hermetically sealed house. So it's how you cause that air change that really matters. If you don't cause air changes in a controlled way, you'll be using more energy than necessary for comfort and health. Your objective should be: when you're using energy to heat, cool, humidify, dehumidify or filter the air, you do it in a way that results in as few air changes as possible and only what you really need for your health. This is where you have to rely first on the builder to provide a high-quality design and secondly on the HERS raters to test the design as built.

There's a lot more you can learn about building science, if you're interested. From my own reading, I can tell you that the details of the actual science are fairly complex (it's easier if you have an undergraduate degree in science or engineering), but the basic principles are pretty straightforward. In the end, however, as a homebuyer, you have to rely on the builder to be familiar with these principles and to incorporate these best practices into the construction of each home. Make sure to get a home that has had a certified "HERS rater" (see chapter 5) do at least a blower door test and duct pressurization test, so that the actual construction has been tested. Make that part of your home inspection requirements. Then, make sure that the builder participates in a formal home-rating and evaluation system, such as those I profile in chapter 5, preferably with independent third-party certification.

Make sure the home has an ENERGY STAR rating as well. One other thing: try to talk with other homeowners who've bought from the same builder, if you can, to see what their experience has been. All of these tools will give you more assurance that your new home will be healthy, comfortable and less expensive to operate.

Finally, you might like to look "under the hood" at the economics of energy efficiency upgrades from both your perspective and that of the home-builder. In my research for this book, I found one builder willing to share his costs and your estimated benefits.

Tom Hoyt of McStain Neighborhoods (Denver, Colorado) prepared an analysis of the economics of green homes, from a homebuilder's perspective. His independent surveys showed that McStain's homes' resale value is 4 percent to 11 percent higher than homes of comparable age and size in the same market. His surveys also show that McStain's new homes command a $10 per square foot premium ($20,000 on a 2,000 square foot home) against direct competitors in the seven-county Denver Metro area. Such premiums are one way to convince a builder to offer the high-performing green home you are looking for. Customer referrals in 2006 ran at 33 percent; in other words, one buyer out of three bought from a personal referral.[9] Think of what this does to reduce the builder's advertising and marketing expenses!

Figure 2.8 shows what McStain pays for energy-efficiency upgrades and the expected savings they deliver to occupants, from a homebuilder's perspective, for a 1,733 square foot townhome in the Denver area. You can see from Figure 2.8 that a builder could invest less than $5,000 to save you $555 on your annual heating, cooling and hot water bills, a tax-free return on investment (for you) of 11 percent or more.

Would you be willing to pay $5,000 extra for a home that was certified to have all of these features? From the builder's perspective, that's where the rubber meets the road. If builders can't command a cost premium for these measures, they'll do just the minimum possible to get an ENERGY STAR certification or some other (less difficult) local certification, but you'll be the one paying the bills as long as you live in the home.

Figure 2.8. Economics of energy-efficiency upgrades, Denver townhome

Features	Estimated Annual Savings ($)	Extra Cost ($)
Advanced framing 2" × 6"	36	545
Low-e, argon-filled windows	55	210
92.1% efficient direct vent furnace	88	900
Water heater — sealed combustion	22	400
Advanced insulation system	89	975
Infiltration/advanced air sealing	81	410
Sealed conditioned crawl space	19	110
Engineering duct distribution system • all ducted system inside conditioned space • set-back digital thermostat	60	920
Fireplace with added electronic ignition	72	0
Downsize furnace/air conditioning (reduces builder's cost)	43	−750
Mechanical (forced) ventilation	−10	300
Third-party verification/energy commissioning	0	580
Total	$555	$4,600
Payback period (Years)	—	8.3
Annual return on Investment (%)	—	12.0

CHAPTER 3

The Experience of Living in a Green Home

N ow that your head is stuffed with building science knowledge and green homebuilding logic, you may wonder what it's like living in a green home. What's the difference with a regular home? Are you just going to notice a lower monthly utility bill, a quieter home, or are there additional benefits?

I can share with you my own experience living in a LEED Gold-certified apartment in Portland, Oregon. After selling our home in Portland in late 2005 and prior to moving to Arizona six months later, my wife and I decided to move from a suburban wooded area to an emerging upscale district in downtown Portland. We signed a short-term lease on an upper-floor apartment in a 16-story building, with a great view of the snow-capped Mount St. Helens volcano in southwestern Washington, and moved in on a rainy day in early November. We were the first tenants in this particular apartment, but among the last to move into a unit; the building had opened six months earlier. Since my wife has severe chemical sensitivities, we were especially interested in the indoor air quality. We were not disappointed: there were no odors, no "new building" smell, because to secure the LEED rating, the developer used low-VOC paints, adhesives and sealants, as well as low-VOC carpet and formaldehyde-free cabinets. The second thing we noticed: we

Figure 3.1. Located in Chicago's Lake Shore East community, 340 on the Park expects to become the first LEED-certified residential building in the Midwest.

were on the 14th floor and had a view to the Interstate 405 freeway less than 100 yards away. With the balcony door open, the noise was incredibly loud; when I closed it, there were no traffic sounds. The double-glazing and other energy-efficiency features made the apartment incredibly quiet (except for the twenty-something neighbor across the hall, whose parties seemed to start at 2 am Friday and Saturday nights — but that's urban living!).

We also had low-flow faucets and showerheads and dual-flush toilets, so water use was lower than normal. Add the bamboo floors and energy-efficient lighting systems, along with the recycling room down the hall, and we felt we were living in a truly green home. Oh yes, the entire apartment building was non-smoking, so the quality of the indoor air was maintained throughout the entire building. The building even supplied non-toxic household cleaning products to prevent toxic fumes from conventional products entering the building's vent system. While I lived there, we only had one car, and I walked to work. In fact, we walked across the street to the grocery store, the first Whole Foods Market in Portland, and walked everywhere (including to the dog's favorite pet store). Even on a cold, rainy day (of which Portland has an abundance), I could walk one block and pick up a public streetcar that would take me close to work. Except for the fact we were paying the highest apartment rents in town, we hated to move!

This personal vignette illustrates some of the characteristics of living in a green home: energy-efficient, water-efficient, high indoor air quality, quiet and comfortable indoors and walkable neighborhoods located close to public transit. Unfortunately, not every new development is in such an idyllic location.

Homeowners in green homes (defined as "containing a specific green building element in at least three of the five categories" described in chapter 2 — energy efficiency, water conservation, improved indoor air quality, resource conservation and improved site management) express considerable satisfaction with the homes. For example, in a 2007 survey, 85 percent of people in green homes said they were "likely" or "highly likely" to recommend these homes to others. The top four reasons for buying green homes were operating cost savings (90 percent), environmental concerns (84 percent), healthier indoor environment (82 percent) and potentially higher resale value (73 percent).[1]

Reported at the 2007 National Green Building conference by McGraw-Hill Analytics, a 2007 survey of 341 green home purchasers showed that green homebuyers tended to be wealthier and better educated and to reside more in the South and West of the country. Women constituted 71 percent of the total, married couples made up 65 percent of the group and the average age was 45. The most intriguing part of the survey was that the highest percentage of buyers who bought a green home did so (28 percent) because they learned about it from a friend, again indicating a high level of homeowner satisfaction with their green home purchase. Some 20 percent learned about green buildings from TV and 14 percent from the Internet.

What motivated the green homebuyers? Some 69 percent were worried about rising energy costs, while 52 percent cited third-party certification as a reason for buying. The survey had a margin of error of eight percent. The green homebuyer rated the top three influencers — cost savings, environmental concerns and healthy indoor environment — as basically equal in importance. Your feelings may be very similar: you want to save money, help the environment and have a healthy, comfortable home to live in.

Pulte Homes, Las Vegas division

Figure 3.2. The Las Vegas division of Pulte Homes participates in the Southern Nevada Green Building Partnership program. Buyers of homes certified under the program benefit in several ways: lower operating costs because of the reduced use of water, electricity and gas, and a higher level of indoor air quality because of the partnership's requirements for environmentally sensitive building materials and superior ventilation systems.

So, let's hear the stories of some homeowners about their experiences living in green homes. Some homeowners feel that living in a green home allows them to share their environmental passions with others. Steve Rypka, a homeowner in Pulte's Sun City Anthem development in Henderson, Nevada, says: "I like the fact that my home provides me with an opportunity to share the benefits of green living with others and to show how easy it is to make a difference. That's absolutely the best part for me. It's not just about the energy savings and environmental benefits. They're huge, of course, but for me, my house has become a leverage tool that has allowed me to educate thousands of other people about the benefits of green living. When they see our $8 per month electric bill, that really gets their attention!"[2] Steve owns a business called GreenDream Enterprises and consults with area homeowners and businesses about green buildings and renewable energy, so he's made his passion into his livelihood.

Other homeowners are surprised by what they get in a green home. Consider the experience of Paul Kriescher, living in an ENERGY STAR and Colorado Built Green-certified home in the Garden Courts area of Denver's Stapleton redevelopment, in a home built by Wonderland Homes:

We were looking to find a new and larger home because we were living in a very small home in Denver's Washington Park neighborhood. We decided where we wanted to live first, and Stapleton was the only place we wanted to live as far as a new home would go. It is a friendly neighborhood type of development, in that there are sidewalks, front porches, bike paths that lead to stores, walking access that allows you to bump into and meet people easily and there are good schools.

The key thing for my wife and I was that we wanted a home that had very good passive solar gain and also had roof lines that allowed us to put on solar energy technologies if we wanted. We chose to have solar water heating put on the house, and in the future, we may do solar electric. Another thing we really liked about Wonderland is that they build many of their homes in courtyard configurations in Stapleton. There are five houses on the corner of a block, and it is arranged in a half-circle. In front of us we have a nice little common area of trees, grass and xeriscape plants that makes for a great place when you have a two-year-old to just go out the front door and play. We also wanted the lot that allowed us to have very good southern exposure because I know enough from my training and my work that I can cut my energy costs more than $200 a year just by having a lot that lets me bring in all of this free sun that we get in Colorado. While we get cold weather, there are still lots of sunny days, and we get lots of free heating from the sun because we have a lot of good windows on the south side that let the heat in.

Prior to this one, I lived in a home that was built in 1929, and I did a lot to try to make it more comfortable and more efficient. The biggest difference in our new home, compared to that one, or even compared to homes that are brand new and built to code, is truly just how much more comfortable the house is. It's not always going to be the case, and I don't want to misrepresent anything. ENERGY STAR and green building programs are getting ever closer to tying in comfort with the energy savings and reduced environmental impact. In my case, having a modulating furnace and variable-speed fan makes a huge difference in comfort, especially when the weather is pretty cold.[3]

Amy Macklin, a buyer in Glenwood Park, Atlanta, shares her experiences of buying and living in an EarthCraft-certified home in an urban infill development. She and her husband had decided beforehand that they wanted to be in a walkable community close to downtown Atlanta to avoid having to drive so much.

Loren Heyns, courtesy of Green Street Properties

Figure 3.3. Through the use of shade trees, sidewalks and narrow streets, the Glenwood Park community in Atlanta emphasizes pedestrian comfort and safety. The neighborhood offers a variety of housing types, open space, restaurants and retail stores that serve the everyday needs of the residents. All homes are EarthCraft Home certified.

We like the way the housing here is structured to promote building community, friendships, relationships and interactions with your neighbors. We walk to the restaurants and coffee shops. My husband, Eric, and I want our lifestyle to be minimized in terms of using the car. I live two miles from my office, and he works from home. It's a big deal if we drive to a restaurant instead of going to one in our neighborhood.

It's been a great experience, and we couldn't be happier living in this community and moving into this townhouse. We really have no complaints. We were a little skeptical about a townhouse as a product, but we've really enjoyed it.[4]

Kenny Trapp of Norman, Oklahoma, bought into a development built by Ideal Homes, an ENERGY STAR homebuilder that completed about 500 homes in 2006. Here's his story:

If I don't have to use as much energy to heat and cool my home, then I'm not emitting as much carbon dioxide from my power demand. To give you an idea, my energy bills for an 1,800 square foot, four-bedroom home have been consistently lower (by significant dollars) than a lot of my colleagues' who are in two-bedroom apartments.

One of the things that I was impressed with by Ideal Homes is that they don't use duct tape on the ductwork for the air conditioning in the house. Over time — and that time can be very short — especially in an attic where temperatures are really hot, the duct tape will wear away, causing air leaks. The key thing to energy efficiency in a home is controlling leaks. If you can control leaks, your home is much more energy-efficient than a standard home. Also in my home, there are vents above the doors in every room, which allow air to flow through rooms even if the doors are shut. The motion of the air moving around the home helps to evenly distribute the air so the system is not constantly trying to cool down one room and balance things out if the door opens.

I did about six months of research before I bought this house, and that included looking at many other homebuilders. Nobody had the kind of detail and explanation that Ideal Homes had on how their homes are energy efficient.

There's not much of a difference living in a green home compared to a non-green home. I've had family and friends from across the country visit, and I don't think they really noticed a big difference. And that's the beauty of it; *you don't have to sacrifice your lifestyle in any way to live in a green home.* The great thing is the *lower utility bills* so you have more disposable income to go out to dinner or buy things to improve your home.

One more thing: The home is really quiet, because of the extra insulation and the care with which the home was built. The backyard of my house is a major street that has a lot of traffic. Because of the insulation in the house, the only vehicles that I hear are emergency vehicles or very heavy industrial trucks. I don't notice the traffic. I grew up in the country so I'm used to quiet, and traffic noise is something that I usually notice immediately when I'm in a new home.[5]

J. R. Kramer, a homebuyer at the Oak Terrace Preserve project in North Charleston, South Carolina, says:

Our house is made from structurally insulated panels so it really holds in the heat in the winter and the coolness from the air conditioning. It's very tight and energy efficient. Our windows are all low-e. As far as our

Ideal Homes

Figure 3.4. Named America's Best Builder in 2007 by the National Association of Home Builders, Ideal Homes offers heating and cooling cost guarantees for its Signature line of homes.

roof goes, we chose a metal roof because of the longevity factor plus the recyclability of steel. For us a 40-year life on the roof is a sustainable factor. All of our appliances, ceiling fans and the mechanical system are ENERGY STAR rated. All of our lights are compact fluorescents. We have bamboo floor throughout the majority of the house, there's cork in the kitchen, and two upstairs bedrooms have carpet that was recycled from plastic Coke bottles. When it's complete, our landscaping will have 100 percent native plants so there won't be a need for irrigation. We also have low-flow toilets, with the two buttons: one for low flush and one for super-low flush.

We felt like we had a calling to be in that neighborhood. But also as far as the sustainability factor, we really wanted to walk the talk by buying a house in a neighborhood that was conscious of the environment. It is also an infill neighborhood, and my wife and I felt that was an essential component to raising our son in a diverse environment.

Our three most important criteria were the sustainability factor as far as energy efficiency; the quality of the home and the design aesthetic of the home.

Figure 3.5. The Carsten Crossings neighborhood was the first US subdivision made up entirely of LEED-certified homes. The 144 homes in this neighborhood save about 65 percent on the monthly utility bills compared to a standard home. In addition to solar-integrated roof tiles, the homes include tankless water heaters; low-e, dual-pane windows; enhanced attic insulation (R-49) and foam-wrapped (R-5) building exterior.

I think, overall, as far as price point, we paid more for our home. But as far as what we thought we were getting for quality, we would do it over again. There are other builders that are doing the EarthCraft program, but they're not going to the lengths that Noisette [the developer] went to here. We could have had a bigger house, but we would rather have a smaller house that is much more energy-efficient and well-built. It's going to last a lot longer and meet our needs.

The certification was very important because you had someone other than the builder that was making sure everything was done correctly. In reality, living in a green home is just like living in a regular house except our energy bills are lower.[6]

One more example may convince you that you may want to live in a green home. Larry Brittain is a salesman and homeowner in Carsten Crossings, a subdivision in the Whitney Ranch development, built by the regional homebuilder, the Grupe Company, in the foothill country near Sacramento, California. He bought a new LEED-certified home in that subdivision, almost by chance. Here's his story.

It caught us by surprise that the builder was offering solar and the other energy-saving features. The way it happened was this: we had friends visiting from out-of-town that wanted to see what the builders were doing at Whitney Ranch. So my wife and I and our friends hopped into our Yukon and went from builder to builder late on a Saturday afternoon. After looking around, on our way out of the development, my friend noticed another builder, so I put on the brakes and turned in. And this is exactly how it happened verbatim: We walked in; they were very, very pleasant; no high-pressure; and to me that was great. We walked into the first model, I was the first one in the house, and I made a comment: "Wow, I could really live here." And my wife grabbed me by the shoulder and said: "What did you just say?" I got this sense of, I don't know what came over me, it was like a peaceful feeling. The reason I felt that way is when you close the door and you have that soy-based insulation, you don't hear anything outside. We walked through the single-story model and really liked the features such as the size of the rooms, the granite counter-tops, the kitchen-island, the shower and this and that.

Then we walked through the next model and liked some things there. Then we walked into the third model; in the garage there was an energy showroom. It showed what the other builders offer, what Grupe offers, and a sample of the PV panels, the tankless water heater, and a sample of the TechShield® roofing sheathing. They also had an interesting demonstration of the soy-based insulation versus conventional insulation, which appealed to me. It consisted of a little hairdryer, temperature gauges and samples of the two types of insulation covered with Plexiglas. You could see that both were at the same temperature. When you turned the hairdryer on, all of a sudden you could see the pink side [of the insulation] heating up all the way past 90 degrees, and the soy-based insulation was still at the starting temperature. I said, "Oh my God, that's better than sliced bread."

Back at the sales office, they said that we could save up to 60 percent of our energy costs. And my wife, the sales agent and I started talking further. I ended up writing a $5,000 check that night. Now I talk about this stuff to my friends and customers. I have close to 300 customers, and they talk about how hot it is, and I tell them that I can't wait to get back to my house because it will be 76 degrees and I don't even have the air conditioning on. Last year in July, we had 17 days over 110 degrees.

I did not find out that my home was LEED-certified until about six months after we moved in — we got a certificate in the mail. When all this green stuff comes to light all over the country and more people become educated, the LEED certification will be a great opportunity for me if I ever decide to sell my home.

I don't think I could find a home as good as this one. There's another builder in the area that's offering solar, but it's a smaller system in terms of what it'll produce. They're not offering the soy-based insulation, and they're not doing the tankless water heater. Personally, I think the tankless water heater alone is probably saving me $20 to $30 per month in natural gas costs.[7]

Let's look once again at the benefits of choosing green and living in a green home. By making a good choice, you're going to live in a home that will save you several hundred dollars a year in energy and water costs. If it's built right, according to the principles of building science outlined in chapter 2, it's likely to have better indoor air quality and fewer drafts or cold windows. Your home will likely be more comfortable and quiet to live in. If you're locating in an urban infill project, you might be close to transit stops or even be able to walk to work, as I was able to do in Portland. Leaving the car at home might save you an additional couple of hundred dollars a year, especially if your employer subsidizes public transit costs. If you have allergies, asthma or other physical problems, you may notice you're breathing easier because of better filtration systems and low-VOC carpet and paint. You might even enjoy showing off your solar power system to friends and other family members, and giving your kids some "bragging rights" at school (or even material for their science projects). Finally, you may take some personal satisfaction in knowing that you're living a little more lightly on the planet or reducing your carbon footprint.

CHAPTER 4

What Goes into a Green Home?

Green Products, Systems and Technologies

N ow that we've learned how building science experts look at green homes and how homebuyers think about the purchase and experience the benefits of a green home, it's time to look at how homebuilders think about building them. Figure 4.1 shows how the various features of a green home can translate into benefits for the homeowner, according to one builder. For example, a tighter building envelope lowers utility bills, results (along with other measures) in higher indoor air quality, affords greater comfort, produces a quieter home, has less air infiltration, may use recycled materials (such as cellulose fiber insulation) and is friendlier to the environment because it uses less energy to operate. You get the idea. Take a moment and consider which of the features and benefits might appeal most to you.

Let's hear from some builders as to what they see as the essential features of green homes, by taking a brief tour around the US and Canada, starting with Canada. John Gilvesy is the owner of Gentrac Building Corporation, which built the first solar-powered, ENERGY STAR home in Ontario, as part of the Wood Haven Subdivision development in Tillsonburg.

Figure 4.1. Features and benefits of a green home

Features \ Benefits	Lower Utility Bills	Higher Indoor Air Quality	Greater Comfort	Higher Energy Efficiency	Quieter Home	Less Air Infiltration	Better Moisture Control	Insect Repellent	Fire Retardant	Recycled Materials	Environment Friendly
Tighter Building Envelope	✓	✓	✓	✓	✓	✓	✓	✓	✓	✓	✓
Improved Construction Methods	✓	✓	✓	✓	✓	✓	✓	✓	✓	✓	✓
Blown Cellulose Insulation	✓	✓	✓	✓	✓	✓	✓	✓	✓	✓	✓
Air-Sealing Measures	✓	✓	✓	✓	✓	✓	✓				
Tight Ductwork	✓	✓	✓	✓		✓	✓				✓
Low-e Windows	✓	✓	✓	✓							✓
House Wrap	✓	✓	✓	✓		✓	✓				
Engineered Wood Products										✓	✓
Solar Power (PV) System	✓										✓
Water-conserving Fixtures	✓										✓
ENERGY STAR Appliances	✓				✓						✓

Adapted from "Features and Benefits of an EarthCraft Home built by Monte Hewett Homes," Monte Hewett Homes, Atlanta, Georgia, montehewetthomes.com

Solar photovoltaics (PV) have always intrigued me…the fact that solar energy can be converted to electricity. You can envision the heat from the sun warming up water, but creating electricity from a resource that is renewable is exciting. We felt that in order to promote the growth of solar PV, it would be important for a working system to be on display. We were unaware of a working display, so we decided to not just make our homes *solar-ready* but to actually put a system in place. Realizing

Gentrac Building Corporation

Figure 4.2. The 1,530 square foot Merlot model green home, built by Gentrac Building Corporation, consists of a 785-watt Sanyo solar array. The system also has a backup power system, which can, during power interruption, supply designated essential circuits about three days worth of electricity.

the potential benefits, Carmanah Technologies and RE Source Store agreed to install the system at cost and extended the time to pay for it. The local utility also shared our excitement and agreed to contribute to the project.

When we had our official opening, conditions were ideal and the four-panel system was actually feeding electricity back into the grid. We turned off a few things, and we were able to get the meter to run backwards. Our community is not set up yet for selling electricity back into the grid but according the manufacturers, the system should serve approximately one-third of the expected electric requirements.

Gentrac designs and builds what we believe are distinctive homes. In the past, solar panels have been considered a bit of an eyesore...somewhat like TV antennas in what would otherwise be a quality, planned development. The first comments that often come from people who heard about our planned solar installation... 'How can you get away with this in a subdivision? It's going to be unsightly and the impact will be negative.' Panel and mounting bracket color, size, details, location and efficiency were all considered. When you look at the installed system, it blends in well with the roof and other materials...making it aesthetically viable. That was one of the comments at our official opening. The solar panel installation must not be unsightly so that it will be more acceptable in larger developments.[1]

Another builder with a major commitment to energy-efficient and green homes is Pulte Homes, Las Vegas, Nevada, Division. We spoke with Nat Hodgson, its Vice-President of Construction. Pulte Homes' Las Vegas Division built more than 4,500 homes in 2006, and the majority were more than 50 percent energy efficient, compared with the national standard. That's really impressive for such a large builder!

Our interest in energy efficiency started back in the late '90s when Pulte Homes' current COO, Steve Petruska, was the Las Vegas division president. We always wanted to be the innovators and the leaders, and we started with energy efficiency. We did a lot of research and wanted to be the first to do new things. We got started on a pilot program that focused on installing less A/C (tonnage), built homes with conditioned attic spaces and looked at the whole house as a system.

The biggest energy-saving step that we do involves tonnage. We can reduce the tonnage from the old rule of thumb (the amount of A/C tons per square foot) because of the efficiency and the tightness of our homes. Believe it or not, that's probably the biggest trade-off there is — extra tonnage costs money, and it's not necessary because of the way that Pulte Homes builds homes here in Las Vegas. The $2,000 federal tax credit[2] helped us to launch our energy efficiency program. Between the federal tax credit and Nevada Power's rebate (for installing A/C units rated better than SEER-13), we were able to do it cost-effectively and make it desirable to the consumer.

There's a lot of engineering that goes into our homes that the consumer doesn't see. At the end of the day, I have to make sure that the house is going to perform, because we guarantee it. We have a three-year comfort and energy usage guarantee. We guarantee plus or minus two degrees in each room, and in our (Environments for Living) Platinum, Diamond and above houses — which are the majority of them — we guarantee plus or minus five degrees from the livable house to the conditioned attic. For example, on a hot day, your attic is probably 130 to 140 degrees. In one of Pulte Homes' Las Vegas area houses, if you're cooling your house to 76 degrees, the attic is about 80 degrees.

Our energy usage guarantee is in BTUs and therms, but we try to put it into dollar figures at the current daily price of utilities, with a monthly guarantee of the maximum a consumer might pay. Out of the 10,000 or so homes sold in Las Vegas with this guarantee, we've only had a few dozen that went over. Those exceptions are usually houses with four or five refrigerators or a pool and spa. Historically, we still cut them a check. Even those homeowners will tell you that operating their Pulte home in Las Vegas is still a lot cheaper than their last house.

As a company, we built about 4,650 homes last year, and over 4,500 were at least 50 percent more efficient in heating and cooling usage than code. Most of Pulte Homes' Las Vegas area houses, like Timber Creek which is our Southern Nevada green project, are 50 percent or more in energy-efficient than code. To me, saving energy through reduced heating and cooling usage, especially in our extreme desert climate, is a key part of green building. That's where you're really conserving natural resources and reducing air pollution.

Another important part of our green program is recycling the building materials. Our framing and clean-up company both help with this effort. The Pulte Homes' Las Vegas cleanup contractor has realized that there's some value in recycling lumber and plastics. They separate it back at their yard and turn it in for recycling credits.

The comfort guarantee is a huge customer benefit. There's a lot of engineering that goes into it and a lot of items that affect it, especially the tightness. Pulte Homes' Las Vegas area houses are sealed like you wouldn't believe, and most of it is done at the framing stage. It took us nearly six years to train framers how to properly make air barriers (that's how we condition the attic). From the livable — the conditioned — to the unconditioned space, we actually seal it air-tight. Every nook and cranny that is unconditioned space has to be air-tight sealed. Once the buyers are in the home, they really see and feel the benefits.

In terms of utilities savings, it's hard to define "save." We say that our houses in Las Vegas are 50 percent more efficient but that's compared to current energy code. Compared to a house that's 15 years older, a Pulte Home in Las Vegas could save upwards of 90 percent in heating and cooling costs. So it's hard to give a percentage savings that means something to a new buyer.

We always ask the buyers what brought them in. Energy efficiency and green are still new and we don't have a lot of data on it yet, but over 90 percent of the people say it was a major factor in considering buying at our communities. Energy efficiency and customer satisfaction are what we're known best for in Las Vegas. I know why other Las Vegas area builders haven't embraced energy efficiency and green building in the way we have — it's a lot of work. Many builders look only at what price they can sell their homes per square foot to get their volume up

Figure 4.3. In the Legacy Homes Brookside Woods subdivision, just outside Grand Rapids, every home is certified according Michigan Green Built program standards.

and while meeting the minimum code, then they're happy. I guess the Pulte Homes Las Vegas team and I are just crazy the other way.[3]

What drives a lot of homebuilders is a passion for getting the home "right" as well as a passion to protect the environment, not the first things you might associate with homebuilders, but it's there! With so many of the homebuilders interviewed for this book, ranging from the CEO to the division president, the construction chief and the superintendent on the job site, we found people who were eager students of building science and were willing to put up their own money to test out new ideas.

Here's another homebuilder's take on green homes, this time from Jeff Wassenaar, president of Legacy Homes, Grand Rapids, Michigan, and developer of the Brookside Woods neighborhood.

The project started four years ago. The original plans included a ten-acre nature conservancy area and green building practices. One thing led to another, and we decided to make each home in the whole neighborhood certified by Michigan GreenBuilt.[4] We committed to doing each one of the homes as a GreenBuilt certified home, which requires ENERGY STAR certification. There are 15 lots in total with nine or ten of the homes already built. It's located in Ada Township, a small borough near Grand Rapids.

Building green is absolutely a market differentiator for us. When you're in a slower market like we're in now, everything that you can add to that is going to help. We're always looking at how we can help someone who is not in the home building business understand how significant building green is. As we walk the project and talk with the prospective homeowners, building green is just who we are and what we're doing. When we walk through homes with our clients, it's a natural thing to talk about — the things that we do versus what the builder down the street does.

What we've found is that the aspects of green building, for us, are like a tripod. First, it is a healthier environment because of indoor air quality. The second leg is energy-efficiency. Efficiency just makes sense from a pocketbook standpoint. It's not hard to convince somebody from that perspective, especially with how natural gas prices in our area have gone up substantially over the last few years. The third leg on the tripod is that green building is environmentally friendly, and a lot of people care about that now.

From a company standpoint, we want to be good stewards of the environment. From that end it makes sense, and I have my own convictions about that from a religious/spiritual standpoint. We're supposed to be good stewards of the Earth, so it's just natural for me to want to do that with our homebuilding business. I think that this approach has really paid dividends for us.[5]

Finally, consider Tom Hoyt, founder and now "mission adviser" of McStain Neighborhoods, Denver, Colorado. I've heard Tom Hoyt speak at two conferences and I have been moved and surprised by his passion for "getting homes right" and for his vision about where green homes should be going. McStain is a regional builder active just in the Denver metropolitan area, but their vision and achievements have inspired mid-size builders across the nation.

The way we approach building at McStain, the very first decision, and maybe the biggest one of all, is where should we build? You could build the greenest home in the world, and if it's 30 miles out on a school bus run and its footprint, in terms of infrastructure service (water, sewer, roads, drainage), is really expensive from a sustainability standpoint, then that's not a good decision for the world. If you really want to be green, where you build is one of the first pieces. We ask: Is the development a place you really can live without running all over town to support yourself? Is the school within walking distance, if you have children? Are services easy to get to, if you're a senior? All of those things are what we call neighborhood aspects. Then when you get into the house, it's a combination of energy-efficiency, indoor air quality and sustainability of the materials that you're actually using.

We tend to brand ourselves more by the fact that we're constantly working to be at the leading edge. So if you buy from us, you're buying the best package that we've been able to assemble while making a good value investment at the same time. There is no magic answer at any one time. This business is changing so fast, and there are new materials and new research on durability and other aspects showing up all of the time. I think finding professionals that you really trust is one of the most important things for a homebuyer. [A homebuyer can do that by] talking to the builder, asking for their credentials, their referrals and finding out what they really believe in. So it shouldn't be a pure "price and pretty picture" decision. It really needs to be your relationship with the builder and trust in the information the company provides to you.

Homeowners should ask builders why they think what they're doing is going to be a better long-term value compared to the competitor. *What we try to do in our production homes is focus on the elements that cannot be easily retrofitted* . The building envelope is a really important piece of how a home is put together. It's a real pain in the neck and very expensive to go back and rip the walls off and change the way they're put together sometime in the future. But you can buy an energy-efficient refrigerator when yours wears out; that's a pretty easy fix. You can even change out a furnace and other things later on. Things like windows and wall structures, in essence, how well the house is built, are really important in terms of how the house is going to perform over the long haul [and can't be changed easily or cheaply].[6]

Products Used in Green Homes

We've heard a lot from builders and buyers about results. What creates the final result, however, are the dozens, even hundreds, of decisions that builders make about products and services that go into a green home, and of course a few that buyers make, in terms of options and upgrades. Here are the things you should be looking for, ranked in rough order of importance. To understand the order of importance, consider Figure 4.4, from a study by Building Science Corporation for the Building America program. This study was done for the Chenier House, built in Cameron Parish (county), Louisiana, in cooperation with the Louisiana State University AgCenter. If a builder is willing to add less than $6,000 to the cost of a home and does it in

Figure 4.4. Energy-efficiency measures in order of importance[7]

Feature	Annual Energy Costs	Total Energy Savings	Incremental Investment	Cumulative Cost of Change	Payback (time to recover investment)
Conventional home	$1,346	n.a.	0	0	n.a.
First, upgrade building envelope (insulation, windows)	$1,031	23.0%	$400	$400	15 months
Then, upgrade mechanical system efficiency	$910	31.8%	$1,000	$1,400	3 years
Then, install CFLs and ENERGY STAR appliances, etc.	$779	42.6%	$350	$1,750	3 years
Then, install 40 sq. ft. of solar water heating panels	$663	51.1%	$3,700	$5,450	8 years
Then, install 2.0 kW of PV panels	$473	64.9%	$10,000 (net of buyer incentives)	$15,450	18 years

the right way (assuming nothing important is taken away), in general, you should expect about a 50 percent annual energy savings over a conventional home, even before adding a solar electric system. (These figures may vary dramatically by region and/or climate zone.)

The Building Envelope

From Figure 4.4, you can see that an energy-efficient home should, first and foremost, have an energy-efficient building envelope. That means high levels of insulation or high R-value walls, with efficient windows, a well-designed vapor retardant layer and almost no unintended air or ventilation leaks, along with attention to details such as putting ductwork in conditioned and unvented space. There are many approaches to doing this. Some of the newer systems include insulated concrete forms and structural insulated panels, along with products such as Tyvek® or Fortifiber® vapor retarders and TechShield® radiant barrier roof panels. Additionally, the home should have, as a minimum, double-pane low-e coated windows with thermal breaks throughout.[8]

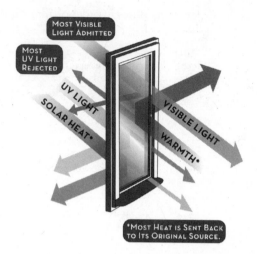

Figure 4.5. Low-e windows have a metal-oxide coating that reflects infrared heat and ul-
traviolet rays, while admitting visible light; in the summer, the heat of outdoors is reflected
away from the home, cutting cooling demand. In the winter, the heat of indoors is reflected
into the house instead of being lost out the windows, reducing heating demand. Low-e
coatings can be designed to let in varying amounts of sunlight, depending on the climate.
Adapted from ENERGY STAR

There are almost as many approaches to constructing an efficient envelope as there are builders and building styles. Some of the older-style buildings (so-called indigenous architecture) are making a comeback, but the
modern style of wood-framing and stucco or brick exteriors is likely to persist. In the Southeast, this could mean homes with screened front porches
(for sitting outside at night), lots of cross-ventilation and similar measures.
In the Pacific Northwest, it may mean homes with lots of wood construction, including exterior shakes and shingles, large overhangs to keep the
rain away from the entrance and even a mud room off the kitchen for taking
off wet clothing and shoes.

In Tucson, Arizona, where I live, it would make all the sense in the
world to build homes with thick masonry walls, flat roofs and lots of "thermal mass" inside the home to moderate temperature swings, especially in
summer, as long as you pay attention to other design issues. In 2007, for
example, Tucson had 65 days over 100°F and of course many days with
highs in the 90s.[9] Yet there are fairly cool nights that allow for night ventilation of heat that comes in during the day. However, most of our homes
use California building techniques of "slab on grade" construction and a
wood-frame structure with stucco exteriors and sloped roofs. I've been in

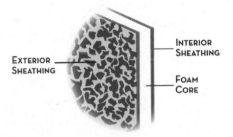

EXTERIOR
SHEATHING

INTERIOR
SHEATHING

FOAM
CORE

Figure 4.6. Structural insulated panels (SIPs) consist of a core of rigid foam sandwiched between two sheets of OSB. Building with SIPs costs about the same as wood-frame construction because the panels reduce construction time and job-site waste. *Courtesy of SIP Home Systems, Inc., redrawn with permission*

older Tucson homes, particularly those built before air conditioning became widespread, and they are quite comfortable, even on very hot summer days, without the use of air conditioning.

Structural Insulated Panels

A green home can be built with structural insulated panels (SIPs), a composite building material, made of engineered wood products and foam insulation. They consist of a sandwich of two layers of structural board with an insulating layer of foam in between. The board is usually oriented strand board (OSB), and the foam is either expanded polystyrene foam (EPS), extruded polystyrene foam (XPS) or polyurethane foam. SIPs share the same structural properties as a steel I-beam or I-column, providing structural framing, insulation and exterior sheathing in a one-piece solid component.[10] SIPs replace several components of conventional building, such as studs and joists, insulation, vapor barrier and air barrier. As such they can be used for many different homebuilding applications including exterior wall, roof, floor and foundation systems. In May of 2007, SIPs were formally accepted into the International Residential Code by the International Code Council.[11]

The OSB used in SIP skins is made from small plantation-grown trees that can be sustainably harvested. Because engineered wood products use wood more efficiently than sawn lumber, it requires less forest acreage to build a SIP home than a conventional wood-frame house. Expanded polystyrene (EPS), polyurethane and other foam cores used in SIPs are made of mostly air and very little petroleum. In the first year after installation, the average SIP home saves 19 times the energy it took to make the EPS insulation.

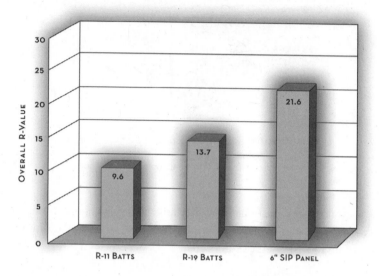

Figure 4.7. SIP panels have more insulating value than fiberglass batts and offer fewer pathways for heat to leak out of the home in winter or into the home in summer. *Building Green with SIPs by SIP Home Systems*

SIPs have a high R-value foam core without any thermal-bridging studs (i.e., in a conventional home, studs are not insulated) or areas of potential compression or voids in the insulation, which might compromise the insulating value. Buildings made with SIPs have higher R-values than conventional frame buildings, as shown in Figure 4.7. SIP homes also have extremely low levels of air infiltration because there are fewer gaps to seal. When combined with other high-efficiency systems, SIP homes commonly demonstrate 50 to 70 percent savings over the Model Energy Code (MEC). SIPs have been a key component in the creation of many zero-energy buildings, which produce more energy than they consume.[12] Finally, SIPs can help a home meet the ENERGY STAR requirements quite easily, a rating system discussed in the next chapter.

Insulating Concrete Forms

Another innovative technology appearing in new homes is the use of insulating concrete forms (ICFs). These hollow, lightweight forms are manufactured using two expanded polystyrene or extruded polystyrene panels that are connected by high-impact polypropylene webs or other means. Instead of an SIP, which is a sandwich with the insulation in the middle, ICFs are a

Figure 4.8. ICFs are stacked and then filled with concrete. The installation of ICF walls incorporates framing, insulation, vapor barrier and shear resistance all into one step.

sandwich with concrete in the middle and insulation on the outside. Neat idea! The forms are interlocking modular units that lock together somewhat like Lego® bricks and serve to create a form for the structural walls of a home.[13]

During construction, the forms are stacked, then filled with concrete, making stable, durable and sustainable walls. Concrete is pumped into the cavity to form the structural element of the walls. Usually, reinforcing steel (rebar) is added before concrete placement to give the resulting walls flexural strength, similar to bridges and high-rise buildings. After the concrete has cured, or firmed up, the forms are left in place. ICFs may be a little more costly than conventional construction, but the payback in energy savings and comfort is rather quick. Also, the concrete needs to dry out, so drywall and other interior treatments need to wait. Finally, they are not easy to change once installed, so later additions such as extra windows, doors and electrical outlets are harder to accomplish.[14]

ICFs combine the insulating effectiveness of EPS or XPS with the thermal mass (which reduces temperature fluctuations in the home) and structural strength of a reinforced concrete wall. They also offer a "5 in 1" solution: structural strength, high levels of insulation, vapor barrier, sound barrier and attachments for interior drywall and exterior siding in one easy step. ICF walls 6-inches thick can provide a fire rating of 3+ hours, a sound transmission class (STC) of 50 (meaning they are very quiet, two-thirds less noise than a conventional home) and an insulation value of R-22 or more. By combining the performance R-value of EPS, the stabilizing effects of concrete, thermal mass and the lower air infiltration rates, ICF walls can perform up to an equivalent insulation value of R-22, compared with R-11 or R-19 values for conventional "stick-built" construction.[15]

Mechanical Systems

There is a simple message here: if your climate requires a lot of cooling and dehumidification of incoming air, ask for a higher SEER-rated air conditioner! The Seasonal Energy-Efficiency Ratio (SEER) measures how much cooling you get for each unit of electricity you buy. Since 2005 residential air conditioners or heat pumps have had to have a SEER ratio of 13.[16] If you opt for a SEER 17 air conditioner, you get a savings of about 23.5 percent on your cooling bills.

So much for efficiency. The builder also needs to know how big to make the air conditioner (this is called tons, each ton representing 12,000 BTU per hour of cooling capacity). A necessary first step in designing a quality residential HVAC system is conducting a proper Manual J° load calculation. Manual J, the national standard for calculating heat gain and heat loss, is produced by the Air Conditioning Contractors of America (ACCA), a nationwide non-profit contractors' association.[17] Most air conditioning units are oversized, because most contractors use "rules of thumb" to size them, based on the energy-inefficient homes that they see every day, rather than analysis of the actual components of the home. However, an air conditioner that's too big is working inefficiently and is costing you money for no real benefit, so make sure that the HVAC system in your green home was sized using Manual J. That's required for LEED and other rating systems anyway.

As for heating, when you have a really tight home, with good insulation and efficient windows, you should be able to stay warm with a high-efficiency boiler or gas heating system, even in the coldest of winters, without paying a fortune for energy. You should be able to get 90 percent or better efficient gas furnaces and home water heating systems from most responsible builders. You're going to be paying the bills every year, so demand

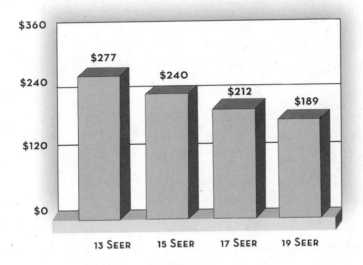

Figure 4.9. Annual energy savings on air conditioning in Nebraska at $0.10 per kwh. *Nebraska Public Power District [online], nppd.com/my_home/services/additional_files/airconditioning_calculator.asp, accessed December 2007.*

the best quality systems. The rating is typically expressed as Annual Fuel Utilization Efficiency, or AFUE. Indicated as a percentage, your furnace's AFUE tells you how much input energy is being converted to heat. With a 90 percent AFUE furnace, you'll save about $100 to $140 per year, at $0.80 per therm, not a lot, but you won't be wasting energy so much as with an 80 percent AFUE system that just meets current codes.[18]

With a whole-house heat-recovery ventilation system in winter, you'll pay even less because the stale air leaving your home will give up a good portion of its heat (and humidity) to the colder, drier incoming air. Most heat-recovery ventilation systems can recover about 70 to 80 percent of the energy in the exiting air and deliver that energy to the incoming air. However, they are most cost-effective in climates with extreme winters, where fuel costs are high. In mild climates, the cost of the additional electricity consumed by the system's fans may exceed the energy savings from not having to fully warm the supply air.[19]

Vapor Barriers

Most people have seen yellow Tyvek® housewraps in new home construction. They're hard to miss. I was surprised to learn, however, how many dif-

Figure 4.10. By keeping the interior walls dry, a weather-resistive barrier cuts utility costs, increases comfort, improves durability, decreases maintenance costs and reduces the risk of moisture-related problems such as insects, mold, mildew and dry rot.

ferent types of vapor barriers or, more correctly, vapor retarders there are. As the earlier discussion of building science principles pointed out, rain will always get through the first layer of protection, either stucco, brick, fiber cement or shingles, so it's very important that another layer of protection stop the water from getting into the wall cavity. That's where vapor retarders come in.

A weather-resistive barrier plays a key function in a residential wall system because of its capacity to control moisture. The weather-resistive barrier:

- forms the vertical surface behind the exterior wall cladding (stucco, brick, siding, etc.) that allows water to safely drain out of the wall system
- lets wet wall components dry safely, because of its ability to allow moisture to pass through the barrier material
- protects the wall from water that makes its way through the exterior cladding, thereby acting as a barricade. This helps prevent water from damaging the interior wall system components such as insulation and framing.
- when properly installed and integrated with flashing systems, a weather-resistive barrier can make a major difference in the long-term durability of walls.[20]

Plumbing Systems

The current plumbing code requires toilets that use no more than 1.6 gallons (6.0 liters) per flush. This standard was adopted in 1992 (replacing the old limit of 3.5 gallons per flush) and has not changed in 15 years, even as water supply problems in the US are escalating. Responding to the growing concern over excessive water use in buildings, many manufacturers have begun to offer even lower-flush toilets and urinals. A good example is a dual-flush toilet with a 1.6 gallon flush for solid matter and a 0.8-gallon flush for liquid. I have two in my home, and I save an average of 37 percent on water use for toilet flushing. Remember the 70s water conservation mantra? "If it's yellow, let it mellow; if it's brown, flush it down." Now you have a technologically superior alternative.

In January 2007 the US Environmental Protection Agency (EPA) introduced a voluntary higher standard, with a 20 percent reduction in the 1992 levels, down to 1.28 gallons per flush. Manufacturers who meet this new standard can display the WaterSense logo on their products. One manufacturer estimated that a family of four could save 7,000 more gallons of water per year using a dual-flush toilet.[21]

A good green home should use water-conserving fixtures in the kitchen and bathroom and have a low-impact landscaping system, with native and adapted plants and the least amount of turf possible. Ask your builder if they are using appliances with an EPA WaterSense logo. For example, there are currently 12 different manufacturers of toilets with EPA recognition; that means there are plenty of competitively priced options out there for builders.[22]

In the late summer and early fall of 2007, water storage in reservoirs serving Atlanta, Georgia, fell to less than 30 percent of capacity. An unprecedented drought in the summer of 2007 stretching across the southeastern United States forced some of the region's largest cities to declare water emergencies. In October the situation became so serious that officials in Atlanta, where rainfall was more than 16 inches below normal, said they could have run out of drinking water in a matter of weeks.[23] That year Atlanta recorded the lowest rainfall since 1954.

Australia is suffering through its worst drought in 150 years. Because of this condition, dual-flush toilets have been mandatory in all Australian new homes since 2003. American homes would be well served with similar requirements, as we get used to more permanent drought conditions and water shortages in the West and Southwest, brought about by population growth and global warming.

Figure 4.11. Most residential tankless water heaters are about the size of a suitcase and are more efficient than water heaters with storage tanks because water is only heated when needed, thereby reducing standby losses.

Rinnai.

Tankless Water Heaters

In recent years, more homes have begun to use gas-fired tankless water heaters to replace the standard 50-gallon storage-type water heater. Tankless water heaters cost about twice as much to buy and install as conventional water heaters, but can last twice as long and never run out of hot water. Think of never running out of hot water if you are buying a new home that you'll have to share with teenagers! With flow rates up to 10 gallons per minute (a showerhead might use 2.5 gallons per minute (so you can see why you'll never run out of water!), tankless water heaters also provide instantaneous hot water. (There are other ways to reduce water waste, as you wait for hot water, including a "home run" or recirculation-type plumbing system and insulating hot water pipes, even in the slab, but most builders don't use these approaches.) If you're going to use a solar water heater, you could combine it with a tankless unit and have only one solar storage tank (with electric backup) that feeds into the tankless water heater.

Lighting Systems

The key issue in lighting design in new homes is to replace all the incandescent lamps, inside and outside, with screw-in compact fluorescent bulbs (CFLs) that use about 70 percent less electricity for the same amount of illumination and last ten times longer.[24] There are CFL flood lamps as well as standard lamps and other fixtures. Dozens of attractive lighting fixtures are ENERGY STAR qualified, so make sure the builder is using these also. The priority for a new home should be to install CFLs in all high-use areas, such as kitchen, bathroom, living room and bedrooms. In closets or places such as storage areas, where you're only going to turn the light on for a minute or two each day, incandescents are just fine (for now). Also, CFLs don't like the cold, so putting them outdoors reduces their energy savings. If they are to be used outdoors, they need to be specially marked for that use.

CFLs are getting really popular. In the first nine months of 2007, Wal-Mart sold more than 100 million CFL lamps, so prices are really coming down.[25] There's no excuse for builders promoting incandescent bulbs in any high-use area when there's a CFL fixture available on the market. The Energy Independence and Security Act of 2007 (EISA) provides for a phase-out of 100-watt incandescent light bulbs by 2012 to 2014, by raising the minimum efficiency requirements by 30 percent.[26]

Just one note of caution. As with all fluorescent bulbs, CFLs require small amounts of mercury, a hazardous substance, to function. There's no problem when they're in use, but if you break one, you need to clean it up carefully and thoroughly, and then double-bag it for disposal. CFLs that wear out (and this might take many years) should be taken to recycling centers for fluorescents.

ENERGY STAR Appliances

Clothes washers, refrigerators, dishwashers and freezers are all available with ENERGY STAR labels. Make sure that your homebuilder is offering these appliances in every new home. Most buyers know to look for the ENERGY STAR label on these standard home appliances.

Solar Water Heating Systems

I've long been a fan of solar water heating systems. After the first Arab oil embargo of 1973 and 1974, for about the next ten years, solar water heating technologies were thoroughly explored in the US. In California I was in charge of the state's efforts to commercialize solar technology in the late 1970s. At that time, I estimated that more than 250,000 solar water heating systems were installed for homes, apartments and factories, along with tens of thousands of pool heating systems and thousands of solar home heating systems. In almost all cases, conventional heating systems were used as backups during winter and periods of low sunshine and cloudiness. In fact, solar thermal technology has been used in some form for more than 100 years in the US and elsewhere.[27]

The US Energy Policy Act of 2005 gave renewed impetus to the solar thermal industry, providing (currently through the end of 2008) federal

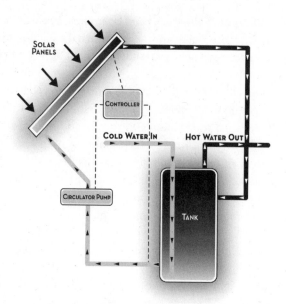

Figure 4.12. Solar water heaters can be a cost-effective way to generate hot water for your home and can be used in any climate. *Adapted from Building America Best Practices Series*

tax credits of 30 percent for residential solar water heating (up to $2,000 tax credit). Many states and some utility companies also offer tax credits or incentive payments for solar water heaters. In most parts of the US, solar water heating systems can easily supply 50 percent or more of annual requirements for a family home.

From the standpoint of basic physics, using a very low-intensity energy source such as solar for heating water is intuitively appealing. With a single-glazed, metal-finned collector, the sun can easily heat water to 160°F, more than enough for a typical water heater (usually set about 125°F to 135°F), and protecting the collector against freezing is not difficult. Many of you may have used an elevated black plastic water bag as a way to have a hot shower while camping. The technology is that simple. There are a few variations that you may see from Figure 4.12. For example, there are high-tech "evacuated tube" systems that use vacuum-tube technology. Another type (thermosiphon) puts the electric water heater on the roof along with the collector panels (these systems have been used in Australia and Israel, for example, for decades and in large numbers). What you'll see most commonly is a one- or two-panel (about 40 to 64 square foot) system with the storage tank in the garage, connected to the home hot water pipes.

Many parts of the world that have to rely on diesel or heating oil (or even wood) for water heating have used solar water heating for decades, including a good part of the Mediterranean and Australia. On a trip through Greece a couple of years ago, I saw many solar water heaters atop apartment buildings in Athens, a testament to the basic utility of this technology.

Solar Electric Systems (Photovoltaics)

I really love photovoltaic (PV) systems, especially in the southerly reaches of the US. Interestingly, the largest users of solar electric systems in the world are the Japanese and Germans, people in two countries with less sunshine than most of the US. On an annual basis in the US, a 5 kW PV system will supply about 6,000 to 9,000 kilowatt-hours (kWh) of electricity, about 50 to 75 percent of a typical home's annual use of 12,000 kWh. Because they are made from silicon, the most abundant element on Earth, they're pretty close to a renewable technology. In 2008 estimates are that more silicon will be used worldwide for PV systems than for microprocessors! They share the same basic technology; as a result, PV prices have been dropping consistently since widespread use began globally in the early 2000s.

Photovoltaic solar electric systems ("photo-voltaics" means electricity from light, especially sunlight) have been around since the 1950s, and have been used extensively in the world's space programs to power satellites, the International Space Station and other spacecraft needing solar power for operations. Using semiconductor-grade silicon, solar cells convert the energy in sunlight to electricity, typically at efficiencies of 5 to 12 percent, or with power output of about 5 to 12 watts per square foot. Sunlight is a very diffuse energy, falling on the Earth's equator at the rate of about one kilowatt (the input for ten 100-watt bulbs) per square meter. Electricity is a very concentrated form of energy, so it's not surprising that it takes considerable collection area (80 to 200 square feet per kilowatt) to make any sizable amount of electricity from the sun.

Nevertheless, solar electricity is rapidly gaining popularity around the world. For many years, solar power in the US has made thousands of homes "grid-independent" and enabled larger projects to make a quite visible statement about their use of solar energy. Despite our abundant solar resources, especially in the Sunbelt states and the West, the US government has never put much of a priority on commercializing photovoltaics.

In addition to promoting solar thermal systems, the 2005 Energy Policy Act (EPACT) created a 30 percent federal tax credit (residential credit limit is $2,000; commercial is unlimited) for solar electric installations, currently

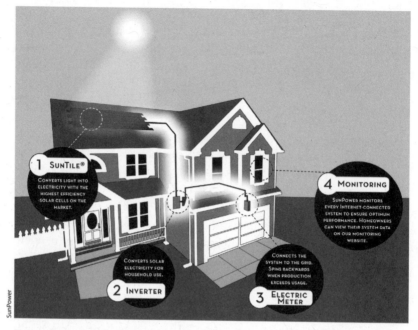

Figure 4.13. SunPower offers a turnkey solar electric solution for production homebuilders. The low-profile SunTile® solar shingles integrate into any concrete tile roof. The system is connected to the local utility for net metering.

set to expire at the end of 2008. Many utilities also have solar electric promotional programs, and some state governments such as Oregon, New York and Arizona have additional tax credits. In 2007 the California Public Utilities Commission enacted a $2.2 billion "million solar roofs" program that requires the state's investor-owned electric utilities (serving a majority of California residents) to offer incentives in the range of $2,400 per kilowatt for photovoltaics.[28] Tucson Electric Power, my hometown utility, offers a $3,000 per kilowatt rebate for residential PV systems.

The largest drawback to increased use of photovoltaics has been cost. Today's consumer systems can cost $7,500 to $9,000 per installed kilowatt. You may find in various parts of the US and Canada that government and utility incentives lower the cost of PV systems by 50 percent. This gets you awfully close to making a real return on the investment. Beyond a financial return, are there still reasons to do this? Yes, there may be several. For example, what is it worth to have a supply of electricity that is fixed in price today, no matter what future utility prices may be? Or that allows you to make a statement that you are producing domestic renewable energy, with-

Kyocera Solar

Figure 4.14. The solar system on this home, manufactured by Kyocera Solar, is built directly into the roof. After the solar panel frames are installed with the roofing tile, the modules are placed into the frames using a cassette-like system, allowing easy installation by any roofing crew.

out any environmental impacts? What if your roof could be made from PV-powered shingles or tiles, so that when you had to replace your roof, you could combine it with a PV system at a lower total cost? The real benefit of a PV system for me is the statement it makes that we don't have to be dependent on imported fossil fuels as individuals and as a country.

For my own seven-year-old home, in late 2007 I got a bid on a 1.5 kW system that will produce about 2,400 kWh per year, at a cost of about $8,000 per kW. After state and federal tax credits and a local utility incentive, my net payment is $4,500, and my annual benefit is about $240, so the return on my net investment (by having the local utility buy all my output at retail rates) is about 4.5 percent. That's not terrific, but remember that saving on utility bills is after-tax money, and I'll have more than what tax-free municipal bonds are paying now. As long as the system works, the return is guaranteed. Also, it's an inflation-protected return, unlike a muni, so that as electric power rates go up, so does my benefit. As part of one's investment portfolio, that's not a bad proposition. And if I sell the home, I may be able to take the system with me.

Many homebuilders began to offer 1.5 kW or 2.5 kW systems as standard on a lot of California and Nevada homes in 2007. I predict that this trend will spread throughout the Sunbelt and will accelerate if Congress decides in 2008 to extend the residential solar tax credit of 30 percent (up to $2,000) and as more utilities offer investments as part of their development of Renewable Portfolio Standards for solar and wind power. The builder may pass on the value of the system to you as a homebuyer, so that you can claim the $2,000 federal tax credit and any local utility incentive payments.

Interior Finishes

We've talked a lot about energy savings, water savings, moisture control and comfort. There's one more area where you need to pay attention, and that's the interior finishes. To my mind, a green home should not contain any materials made with volatile organic compounds (VOCs) that might cause allergic reactions to some family members. The off-gassing of these compounds is what gives a new home a particular smell. My concern applies to paints, carpets, adhesives, sealants, coatings and especially cabinets. You should ask the builder questions about low- or zero-VOC finishes before you buy the home, particularly if the home is not already constructed. Why go to all the effort to get a healthy home and then have it contaminated before you move in with substances that might cause you harm and take many months to leave the home? These days, with so many people having environmental allergies, it just makes good sense to reduce the level of VOCs to which you expose yourself.

What's a VOC (pronounced "vee-oh-cee")? The acronym stands for volatile organic compound, an entire class of carbon-based chemicals that gives off vapors at normal room temperatures. VOCs are emitted by thousands of products. Examples include: paints and lacquers, paint strippers, adhesives and sealants, carpets and carpet backing, cleaning supplies, building materials and furnishings, office equipment (copiers and printers), graphics and craft materials including glues and adhesives, and permanent markers.[29]

When I was growing up, our five-child family got a new car only every three to five years. And it was a real treat to sit in a new car and inhale the new-car smell, an odor that disappeared after a few months. Of course, as kids we didn't realize that we were breathing several toxic chemicals, even suspected carcinogens! Once they finished off-gassing, of course, the smell disappeared.

Paints and coatings in green buildings must meet VOC limits established in the Green Seal GS-11 standard, while clear wood finishes, floor coatings and similar substances have their own special standards. Many VOC concentrations are regulated by local air pollution control agencies, since they eventually escape a building through the ventilation system and become an ingredient in creating urban smog.

Adhesives with high VOC levels are often found in general construction adhesives (think of anything that comes in a tube), flooring and fire-stopping adhesives, caulking, duct sealants and plumbing adhesives. There are also aerosol adhesives, carpet pad adhesives and ceramic tile adhesives. A builder has to be especially vigilant in monitoring all the things a subcontractor might bring onto a site in a tube.

Carpets and carpet cushions are also sources for VOCs in buildings. In green buildings, they must be certified under the Carpet and Rug Institute's Green Label Plus and Green Label programs, respectively. Since builders buy lots of carpet, they can certainly specify low-VOC carpets and carpet backing from their installers and suppliers.

Composite wood and agrifiber products in green buildings must be free of any added urea-formaldehyde resins. This category includes particleboard, medium-density fiberboard, plywood, wheatboard and strawboard, and door cores. This especially applies to the cabinets a builder will put in, and you should diligently inquire about this subject when specifying cabinets. It won't be easy, but you should try. There are alternative non-toxic resins that some manufacturers are using, including phenol formaldehyde, so you can find substitute resins for typical cabinetry.

New furniture and furnishings are also sources of VOCs. Try to buy a piece of furniture that doesn't have pressed wood fibers soaked with smelly urea-formaldehyde, and you'll understand. Now think about all the people in your new home who will be subjected to the off-gassing of urea-formaldehyde from new furniture! For your own health, please take care in your purchases. You might have to buy slightly more expensive solid wood furniture and furnishings to avoid the smell, but it will be well worth it. Many new products with low or no VOCs are coming on the market as consumer preferences for them get better articulated.

FUSIONPARTNERS

BUSBY PERKINS & WILL

PRYDE & JOHNSON

Top: High Point was Seattle's first Built Green neighborhood. All homes meet a minimum of Built Green 3-Star standards, with many achieving 4-Star level and ENERGY STAR certification.

Bottom left: The Acqua+Vento in Calgary, Alberta was the first multi-family residence to receive LEED Platinum certification in North America. Each unit is 50 percent more energy efficient than the Model National Energy Code of Canada and consumes up to 60 percent less water than a typical condo. Each unit features a heat recovery ventilator, radiant floor heating, R-22 insulation, double-glazed low-e argon-filled windows, ENERGY STAR appliances, dual-flush toilets, low-flow fixtures and recycled kitchen countertops.

Bottom right: The Ashworth Cottages, a community of 20 homes in Seattle, are certified Built Green, ENERGY STAR and LEED Platinum. Each home is estimated to reduce water use by 40 percent and energy use by 50 percent. Over 90 percent of the construction waste was recycled and most of the paints, windows, countertops, brick masonry and framing materials were locally sourced.

ED ROSENBERGER, KENNECOTT LAND

© 2007 DOVERWOOD COMMUNICATIONS, INC., COURTESY OF HARMONY

Top: Front porches are a common feature on the homes in the Daybreak neighborhood in South Jordan, Utah. The landscape plan for the community includes the planting of 100,000 trees and lots of open space for parks, wetlands and natural green space. Every home is ENERGY STAR-certified which can save homeowners $200 to $400 per year on their utility bills.

Bottom: Located in Central Florida, a 40-minute drive from Orlando, Harmony was recognized by the Council for Sustainable Florida for its dedication to environmental stewardship. A 7,700-acre network of protected habitat is near enough to the community to make nature a part of every day living.

DODSON HOMES

KB HOME

Top: This ENERGY STAR certified home in the Oden Ridge community in Front Royal was built by Dodson Homes, a local builder that has built over 350 ENERGY STAR Homes in Virginia (as of the end of 2007).

Bottom: This home at the Belmont development in the Discovery Trails community in Palmdale, California is one of KB Home's 42,000+ ENERGY STAR-qualified homes. One of the nation's largest homebuilders, the company announced at the beginning of 2008 that all new homes will include ENERGY STAR-qualified appliances.

FIRESIDE HOMES

MCSTAIN NEIGHBORHOODS

Top: Hidden Springs is a 1,844-acre master planned community developed around a 130-year-old working farm just north of Boise. The community is home to the first LEED Gold-certified residence in the state. Built by Fireside Homes, the home features local, recycled materials; an air-filtration system that includes a fan in the garage to exhaust carbon monoxide; and multiple thermostats that allow residents to reduce heat or A/C in little-used rooms.

Bottom: The experimental Discovery House in High Plains Village received the highest energy rating ever given by Built Green Colorado and was the first non-custom home in the state to qualify for the American Lung Association's Health House certification. The builder, McStain Neighborhoods, constantly tests new, environmentally friendly building products and practices in an effort to continually increase the energy efficiency of their homes.

PARDEE HOMES

OVERLAND PARTNERS

Top: Solar electric systems are integrated into the roof on select homes in this Santa Rosa neighborhood located in coastal San Diego. The builder, Pardee Homes, offers their LivingSmart program, which combines environmentally sensitive, energy conscious and healthy features and options with high-quality functional design.

Bottom: The 3,000-square foot Stone House at the Skywater community in Horseshoe Bay, Texas will function first as a sales office, then as a community center and is aiming for LEED Gold certification. The 1,600-acre master-planned community will include 1,000 homes, all expected to be LEED certified.

FOREST CITY STAPLETON

LEIGH WACHTER, PRAIRIE HOLDINGS CORPORATION

Top: When complete, the Stapleton community will increase the area of Denver City Parks by nearly 30 percent. The master-planned community of 1,100 acres of parks and open space, 12,000 homes, and 13-million square feet of retail and commercial development is located on the site of Denver's former airport.

Bottom: Now a nationally recognized conservation community, the land that makes up the Prairie Crossing community in Illinois was purchased in 1987 by a group of neighbors who wanted to preserve open space and agricultural land. They formed a company with the goal of responsible development of the 677 acres, building a total of 359 single-family homes and 36 condominiums (as opposed to the 2,400 homes that were planned by another developer).

EDAW

NEW TRADITION HOMES

W.H. HULL COMPANY

Top: Terramor Village, a green community located in Ladera Ranch, California, consists of 1,260 single-family and multi-family units. Based on homeowner surveys, owners save as much as $239 a month on electricity bills, $26 on water and $8 on gas, equaling $3,276 per year. All homes are ENERGY STAR qualified, include ENERGY STAR appliances, exceed California's energy code (Title 24) by 20 percent, have low flow water fixtures and incorporate national ventilation. Photovoltaic systems were offered as an option.

Center: These homes in the Sixth Street Station community in Battle Ground, Washington are Earth Advantage and ENERGY STAR certified. In their efforts to build energy-efficient homes, New Tradition Homes installs ENERGY STAR appliances; vinyl-framed, low-E windows and Tyvek housewrap.

Bottom: Built by W.H. Hull Company, this home in NorthWest Crossing was one of the winners in the NAHB's 2007 National Green Building Competition. Each home in the 486-acre community in Bend, Oregon is built to Earth Advantage standards.

Top: Aiming for LEED Core and Shell certification, the Terrazzo is a 14-story building in Nashville, Tennessee, that has 109 high-end condominiums.

Center right: The Ponderosa Colony at Alamo Creek community participates in the California Solar Initiative program. Along with other energy efficiency measures, the roof-integrated photovoltaic system on this home can save up to 60 percent on utility costs.

Bottom left: Elleven is the first newly-built residential structure in downtown Los Angeles in 20 years. The LEED Gold-certified, 13-story building has 176 units and saves 817,000 pounds of CO_2 emissions and 500,000 gallons of water a year.

Bottom right: Developed by Extell Development Company and designed by Cook + Fox Architects, the Lucida is an 18-story building that includes both retail and high-end residential condominiums located in New York City's Upper East Side. The 110 LEED-certified residential units range in size from 1,445 to 3,500 square feet and feature double-height ceilings and large outdoor spaces with cityscape views.

CHAPTER 5

How Do I Know It's a Green Home?

Green Home Rating Programs

S o you're convinced that a green home is the way to go, and you're now ready to buy. How will you know a good green home from one that's just pretending? How will you set your sights on the greenest home for your budget? This chapter will help you learn about green home rating programs and decide which are worthy of attention. Unlike the commercial building sector, where the US Green Building Council's LEED (Leadership in Energy and Environmental Design) is the only widely accepted green building rating system, in the new home arena there are more than 60 local, regional and national home rating systems, sponsored by governments, utilities, nonprofits and even for-profit entities. As the saying goes, "You can't tell the players without a program," so here's the program.

HERS Story

The backbone of all rating systems is a way to evaluate prospective home energy use, considering the home size, insulation and window characteristics, climate and a host of other factors. Over the past 20 years in the US, we've developed a group of Home Energy Rating System evaluators, known as HERS raters. There are about 300 rating firms in the country serving the building industry. They're independent and well trained.

Based on the home's plans, the Home Energy Rater uses energy-modeling software to estimate future energy use. This analysis yields a projected HERS Index. The software models the impact of heating, cooling, water heating, lighting, appliances and, where applicable, onsite power systems, typically solar. After calculating the HERS Index, the rater works with the builder to identify energy-efficiency upgrades needed to ensure the house will meet ENERGY STAR performance guidelines. The rater then conducts onsite inspections, typically including a blower door test (to test the leakiness of the house) and a duct blast (to test the leakiness of the ducts), and then completes a thermal bypass checklist (a visual inspection of common construction areas where air can flow through or around insulation).[1] Results of these tests, along with inputs derived from the plan review, are used to generate the HERS Index score for the home. Be sure to ask for the results of these tests, plus the bypass checklist.

The HERS Index is a scoring system established by the Residential Energy Services Network (RESNET).[2] A home built to the specifications of the HERS Reference Home (currently based on the 2006 International Energy Conservation Code — IECC) scores a HERS Index of 100, while a net-zero-energy home would score a HERS Index of 0. The lower a home's HERS Index, the more energy-efficient it is, in comparison to a standard home just meeting the requirements of the 2006 IECC. Each one-point decrease in the HERS Index corresponds to a one percent reduction in energy consumption compared to the HERS Reference Home. Thus a home with a HERS Index of 85 is 15 percent more energy-efficient than the HERS Reference Home, and a home with a HERS Index of 80 is 20 percent more energy efficient.[3]

ENERGY STAR

ENERGY STAR, a home rating system developed and administered by the US Environmental Protection Agency (EPA), is a voluntary partnership between the government and more than 9,000 organizations, including more than 3,500 of the nation's home builders.[4] An ENERGY STAR home expects to reduce energy use at least 15 percent versus a conventional home. Each ENERGY STAR-rated home is estimated to save about 2,000 kilowatt hours of electricity annually, worth about $200 to $300 in utility bill reductions.[5] In addition

Figure 5.1. "First blue, then green." *Courtesy of ENERGY STAR*

to site-built, single-family homes, there are ENERGY STAR-qualified multi-family homes as well as ENERGY STAR-qualified manufactured homes.[6]

A HERS rating of 85 (15 percent savings) is required in most of the southern tier of the US (technically climate zones 1 to 5) to qualify for an ENERGY STAR label; 80 (20 percent savings) is the minimum in the northern tier (climate zones 6 to 8), stretching from northern New England to Montana, including parts of Idaho and western Colorado. Due to the unique nature of some state codes and/or climates, EPA has agreed to allow locally developed energy codes and definitions of ENERGY STAR in California, Hawaii and the Pacific Northwest to continue to meet program requirements.[7]

In addition to certifying the energy efficiency of a home, EPA has developed guidance for indoor air quality measures. Homebuyers can also look for the ENERGY STAR Indoor Air Package label. Homes that achieve this level of excellence are first qualified as ENERGY STAR, and then also incorporate more than 60 additional home design and construction features to control moisture, chemical exposure, radon, pests, ventilation and filtration. Together, these features help protect qualified homes and their residents from mold, chemicals, combustion gases and other airborne pollutants.

ENERGY STAR is by far the most popular home energy rating system in the US. In 2006 ENERGY STAR certified more than 180,000 homes, representing 12 percent of all new single-family housing starts. Because of the pronounced housing slowdown of 2007, EPA only certified 121,000 homes in 2007. Taken together, more than 700,000 homes were ENERGY STAR certified from 2003 through 2007, compared with less than 50,000 by all other homebuilder-run voluntary certification programs.[8]

As an example of homebuilder participation in the ENERGY STAR program, KB Home, one of the country's top ten builders, certified more than 11,000 homes in California, Nevada, Arizona, Colorado and Texas in the 12-month period ending June 2007. The Austin and Houston, Texas, divisions both committed to certifying 100 percent of their homes to ENERGY STAR standards. Overall, the company has certified more than 42,000 homes to ENERGY STAR.[9] Lisa Kalmbach, senior vice-president of the Studios division for KB Home, describes their commitment to ENERGY STAR:

As our CEO said, "It's the right thing to do." We need to be leaders although we're just starting off in the process of how green building can impact the company as well as the communities and the people that we

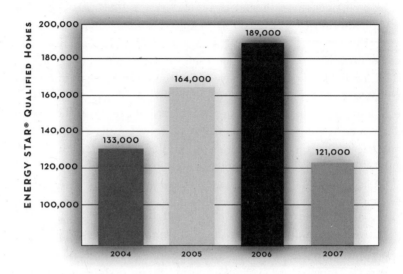

Figure 5.2. ENERGY STAR home certifications, 2004–2007. *Data courtesy of ENERGY STAR*

serve and of course the environment. ENERGY STAR resonated with us because a lot of our homebuyers are first-time buyers or first-time move-up buyers, and we're educating them about how to live in their homes and reduce energy usage and energy costs. Costs are something that they are concerned about when they move into a home. It's top of mind for them. They're interested in keeping their operating costs low. If it helps the environment also, it's two good deeds for the price of one. It works out well for everybody.[10]

Some states may also offer versions of ENERGY STAR. For example, in cooperation with many of the state's electric utilities, New York State has offered its own version of ENERGY STAR since 2001 and has already certified more than 10,800 homes.[11] The state estimates that their certification process helps homes reduce energy use by 30 percent. The program says:

While many builders claim to build energy efficient homes, only New York ENERGY STAR Labeled Homes pass a stringent evaluation that involves a computer-based energy analysis, inspections of systems and the way they work together as a whole, and certification testing. This advanced whole-house performance testing helps ensure that the home is properly insulated, doors and windows are installed correctly, cracks and gaps in a home are sealed, and carbon monoxide gases from appliances and heating and cooling systems are vented properly.[12]

National Association of Home Builders (NAHB) National Green Building Program

The largest and most established organization in the homebuilding field is the NAHB, claiming 235,000 members, 80 percent of the nation's homebuilders. NAHB introduced its Model Green Home Guidelines as a voluntary standard in 2005[13] and has created a National Green Building Program, accredited by the American National Standards Institute, using similar guidelines and an online scoring tool as part of the updated rating system, that debuted in the spring of 2008. At the same time, NAHB unveiled a new Certified Green Professional educational designation for homebuilders, remodelers and other industry professionals.[14]

From 2004 to 2007, approximately 36,000 homes were certified under green guidelines by local builders' associations.[15] The NAHB National Green Building Program provides three levels of certification — Bronze, Silver and Gold — requiring minimum scores (varying by certification level) in seven guiding principles of builder and environmental concern, to ensure a balanced whole-systems approach:

- Lot Design, Preparation and Development
- Resource (Materials) Efficiency
- Energy Efficiency
- Water Efficiency
- Indoor Environmental Quality
- Operation, Maintenance and Homeowner Education
- Global Impact[16]

Let's take a closer look at the National Green Building Program. For each certification level, there are a minimum number of points required for each of the seven guiding principles. After reaching the thresholds, an additional 100 points must be achieved by implementing a number of items from a list of possible measures.

Unlike LEED, which requires that every home be inspected and tested for energy efficiency, the older NAHB Guidelines only required that if multiple homes of the same model were built by the same builder then a representative sample (15 percent) of homes would be reviewed according to a sampling protocol. While this approach saved the builder a little cost, it did

Figure 5.3. NAHB National Green Building Program Rating System

Category	Bronze (minimum)	Silver (minimum)	Gold (minimum)
Lot Design and Development	8	10	12
Resource/Materials Efficiency	44	60	77
Energy Efficiency	37	62	100
Water Efficiency	6	13	19
Indoor Environmental Quality	32	54	72
Homeowner Education	7	7	9
Global Impact	3	5	6
Additional Points Required	100	100	100
Minimum Points for Certification	237	311	395

not address one of the key findings of building scientists, which is that every house needs to be tested, since quality control of site-built homes is not strong enough, and mistakes of omission and commission are often made by the dozens of subcontractors working on every home. NAHB's new National Green Building Program will provide for 100 percent testing.

At the Gold level, the homebuilder must provide you with a manual detailing the operation and maintenance of the home, including all of the following items. Even if the home isn't Gold certified, you should ask for a manual from any builder with an NAHB or local home builder association (HBA) green home certification, that includes these items:

- Narrative detailing the importance of maintenance and operation to keep a green-built home green
- Local green building program certificate (this could be valuable for resale)
- Warranty, operation and maintenance instructions for all equipment and appliances
- Household recycling opportunities
- Information on how to enroll in a local green power purchase program
- Explanation of the benefits of using compact fluorescent light bulbs in high-usage areas (and telling you where they have installed them)
- A list of habits or actions to optimize water and energy use
- Local public transportation options (if applicable)
- Clearly labeled diagram showing safety valves and controls for all major home systems.[17]

If you've been following the suggestions in this book so far, you'll recognize that these are really *de minimus* requirements for any responsible homebuilder and don't represent a real step forward in helping you to understand how to live in a green home. At the very least, you want to know exactly which of the myriad of guideline items are actually included in the home; so if it's certified by the local HBA or by NAHB, demand to see a copy of the checklist for certification. Then see what the builder has actually done to make it a green home.

The Certification Process

What does it take for a home to be certified under the NAHB Program? First of all, the certification comes from a recognized third-party verifier, using checklist information provided by the builder, installer or manufacturer. At this time, there are also more than 30 local certification programs based on the Model Guidelines.[18] Through the Green Building Initiative™, there are rating and certification programs operated by home builders associations in the following areas. This list will undoubtedly expand during 2008, as more HBAs seize the chance to create their own programs, to forestall other independent programs from gaining a foothold in their marketplace. Detailed contact information for these programs is provided in the Resources section.

Interior Alaska	Western Nevada
Southern Nevada	Central Washington
Central Oregon	Missoula, MT
Utah	New Mexico
Houston	North Texas
Little Rock, AR	St. Louis
Kansas City	Northeast Ohio
Indianapolis	Kentucky
Central Ohio	Michigan
Columbia, SC	Rochester, NY
Long Island, NY	Keystone, PA
Boston, MA	Maryland
Columbia, SC	Hawaii
Durham, Orange and Chatham Counties, NC	

In addition, there are Built Green certification programs run by local HBAs, in the following six regions:

1. Colorado (Built Green Colorado), operated by the Home Builders Association of Metro Denver, with a rating of one to five stars. This program has certified about 30,000 homes in the past ten years.[19] In this program, only five percent of homes are inspected in a typical development.[20] ENERGY STAR certification is not required, but the program requires a HERS rating of 85 or less, equivalent to ENERGY STAR requirements for Colorado's Front Range (but not for the mountain regions). To receive a rating, homes must accumulate 75 points from a 186-point checklist.

2. Washington State (Built Green Washington),[21] with a rating of one to five stars. Many local HBAs offer this program all around the state, and a total of 15,000 homes had been certified through the summer of 2007. Figure 5.4 shows how a Built Green Washington home actually goes through the certification process.

3. BuiltGreen Society of Canada (Alberta and British Columbia), had more than 7,000 homes enrolled as of late 2007.[22] Ratings are based on the federal Natural Resources Canada's "EnerGuide for New Houses" initiative. Ratings range from Bronze to Silver, Gold and Platinum, with minimum EnerGuide scores ranging from 72 to 82. The highest-rated house to date is an 88 on the EnerGuide scale, which goes up to 100 for a zero-net-energy home.

4. Hawaii Built Green, with a one to three-star rating program.[23]

5. Build Green New Mexico (dba Green Builder Program), HBA of Central New Mexico.

6. Green Built Certified, HBA of Greater Grand Rapids, MI.[24]

In the nation's largest state, the California Building Industry Association runs California Green Builder, a ratings program available in 35 developments as of December 2007.[25]

From a consumer perspective, you should be vigilant when buying homes that are, in essence, self-certified by the homebuilder, or by a trade organization to which the builder belongs. You should insist on some form of independent third-party testing of every home, especially for the vital issues of energy efficiency and indoor air quality (as demonstrated by a blower door test and a duct blast test). Without that, you have only to rely on the builder's assurances that every home was built to the referenced standard, without the backup of independent third-party testing. In this case, I suggest you ask for ENERGY STAR certification with Indoor Air Package. That will give you the best assurance that the home will be less expensive to

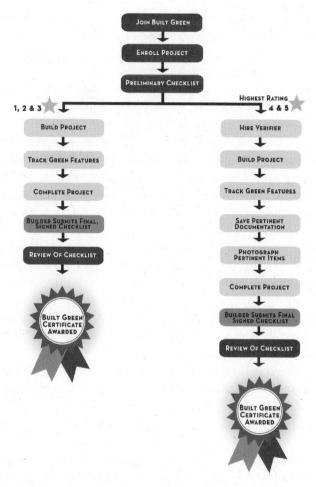

Figure 5.4. The Built Green certification process. *Courtesy of Built Green® of King and Snohomish Counties*

operate, reasonably comfortable, with healthy indoor air quality, and that the required tests have been done. Be sure to ask for the test results, plus the thermal bypass checklist.

US Green Building Council's LEED for Homes (LEED-H)

At this time, it's safe to say that LEED-H is the gold standard of home rating systems. A LEED-H Gold or Platinum certified home would score at the top of any other rating system in the country, but the reverse is not always true. LEED-H was first developed in 2005 as a pilot program by an independent non-profit, the US Green Building Council (USGBC), an organization of more than 14,000 companies, environmental groups, public agencies, universities and colleges, schools, non-profits, architects, engineers and contractors. It is the largest such independent organization serving the building industry and is recognized as an authoritative source on green buildings. The LEED-H pilot program consisted of more than 10,000 homes and the final LEED-H version was released at the end of 2007. For high-rise residential buildings, the system in use is the LEED-NC rating system (LEED for New Construction), introduced in March of 2000. LEED-NC commanded more than 15 percent of the commercial new construction market in 2007.[26] Like all national home rating systems, LEED does not specifically account for the importance of regional environmental issues such as water conservation.

Michelle Moore, Senior Vice-President of Policy and Public Affairs heads up the LEED-H program at the USGBC. She describes some of the rationale for this program:

> We've found that there is interest in LEED from three big sectors: production builders, custom builders and multi-family developers. Throughout the pilot phase [which ended in October 2007], we learned about the specific needs and issues related to each sector. We're learning how to accommodate those needs both in the rating system and delivery system.
>
> There are two aspects that we're working on now. One is a neighborhood-scale solution. We've been developing guidelines for our LEED for Homes providers on how to use a customized or single set of requirements for a whole subdivision. It's not applicable for all credits, but certain credits can be used across the subdivision.
>
> We're also working on sampling protocol to reward strong in-house quality control processes of a production builder. The protocol will allow the provider [home rater] to work with the production builder as they gain more familiarity with the program and begin to start verifying homes using a sampling protocol [instead of testing every home].
>
> Builders have played a central role in the LEED for Homes program as committee members, reviewers and active pilot participants. During the pilot, they generated multiple questions that have led to several hundred refinements to the rating system. It's equally important to ensure that the LEED measures are integrated into the design process as early as possible.

Visko Hatfield, courtesy of Pringle Creek

Figure 5.5. At the time of certification, Pringle Creek's first model home was named the greenest single-family home in America by the US Green Building Council and received 103 points (out of a possible 129), earning a LEED Platinum certification.

The key piece is that LEED is a national program that provides independent third-party validation and certification. The important component of the program is that USGBC stands behind the third-party verification; this enables buyers to understand that they are getting a home that makes sense for the environment and their budgets.[27]

Single-family Homes

In many ways, LEED-H has a similar rating system to NAHB, but the current requirement for testing and certifying every home is more stringent. Both programs require ENERGY STAR certification as a prerequisite for their certification.[28] As of January 2008, LEED-H had 12,900 participating residential units, about evenly divided between single-family detached and multi-family (low-rise) attached homes. At that time, 540 homes had achieved formal certification, with hundreds more expected to follow in short order in the first quarter of 2008.[30] While LEED-H is the newest of the national residential certification programs, it is likely to be one of the two or three major national programs by 2010.

LEED-H can also be used to certify existing homes, as demonstrated in December 2007, when former vice-president and Nobel Prize laureate Al Gore certified his 10,000 square foot Tennessee home at the Gold level, by adding solar power, ground-source heat pumps and a rainwater collection system, and re-lamping with CFLs. He was able to reduce his total energy consumption by 11 percent during the summer months of 2007, when Nashville was sweltering under a record heat wave.[31]

The Details of LEED for Homes

What does it take to get a LEED-H certification for a home? In a new home, LEED-H version 2.0, in force since November 2007, requires each home to get a minimum number of points from four of the eight credit categories, with 18 prerequisites that have to be met by every home. Here you can see the eight categories of concern, containing 67 specific credits (with associated maximum number of LEED points in each credit category):

- Location & Linkages (10 points)
- Sustainable Sites (22 points)
- Water Efficiency (15 points)
- Energy and Atmosphere (38 points)
- Materials and Resources (16 points)
- Indoor Environmental Quality (21 points)
- Awareness and Education (3 points)
- Innovation and Design Process (11 points)

What Does It Take to Get Certified?

LEED-H is a point-based rating system with a total of 136 points available. Figure 5.6 shows the number of points required for each level of certification. There is no minimum required in any of the eight categories; however, all 18 prerequisites must be met, a requirement not found in the NAHB system.

Location and Linkages

Home-building projects have substantial site-related environmental effects, in terms of both the impact to the site and the impacts from choosing the location. The Location and Linkages section addresses how builders can choose site locations that promote environmentally responsible land use patterns and neighborhoods. Well-chosen development sites need fewer

Figure 5.6. LEED certification levels/points

Certification Level	Number of Points
Certified	45–59
Silver	60–74
Gold	75–89
Platinum	90–136

infrastructure elements, especially roads, and water and sewer lines. Such developments promote many transportation options, including walking, bicycling and public transit, reducing auto use and dependence. Site choices can also include compact and walkable neighborhoods, with services close by; New Urbanist developments which foster interaction between neighbors, and access to protected open space.

Sustainable Sites

Green homes should consider more than just the home, because site use can have a significant environmental impact. This category rewards projects that minimize site impacts. Good home design aims to create attractive, easy-to-maintain landscaping that protects and promotes use of native plants and contributes to the health of local habitat. Good landscape design

John Baker, courtesy of Homewise, Inc

Figure 5.7. Open space borders the Evergreen community in Santa Fe, New Mexico, on three sides, allowing for easy access to the local network of trails. The community's location takes advantage of existing roads and trails, which connect residents to shopping areas, work places, a library, a youth center, parks and schools.

provides shade, aesthetic value, habitat for native species and a mechanism for absorbing carbon and enriching the soil. This credit category also promotes the use of bioswales, retention ponds and other means for absorbing stormwater runoff and recharging local groundwater basins.

Water Efficiency

Water-efficiency measures in new homes can easily reduce water usage by 30 percent or more. Exterior water conservation strategies may involve irrigating with collected rainwater harvesting and graywater systems, but these cost money and are not used by most builders. They also require homeowner maintenance, and let's face it, most of us want our new homes to be maintenance-free, at least for the first few years. LEED also rewards use of water-efficient fixtures and appliances, something addressed in chapter 4.

Energy and Atmosphere

Because home sizes have doubled since 1960, the average energy use per home has increased also. The goal of the energy and atmosphere credits is to reduce home energy use and carbon dioxide generation, both through efficiency measures in the home and the use of solar power. Because homes last so long, it makes all the sense in the world to build them so that their inherent structural energy use is as low as possible. That means an efficient building envelope above all, since most of the systems in the home will become more energy-efficient over time (think of all the people right now relamping with CFLs).

According to the USGBC, the average LEED-certified home will use 30 to 40 percent less electricity and save more than 100 metric tons of carbon dioxide emissions over its lifetime.[31] LEED awards up to 34 points in the "Optimize Energy Performance" category, based on the HERS rating (and

Figure 5.8. LEED energy points and HERS ratings

HERS Rating	Percent Energy Savings vs. Standard Home	LEED Energy Points Climate Zones 1–5 (southern)	LEED Energy Points Climate Zones 6–8 (northern)
80	20	6	0
70	30	13	9.5
60	40	18.5	15.5
50	50	22.5	20
40	60	26	24

climate zone), as shown in Figure 5.8. It takes a zero-net-energy home to get all 34 points!

Materials and Resources

The choice of building materials is important for sustainable homes because of the energy and environmental costs of harvesting or extracting, processing, transporting and disposing of them. One key statistic: construction and demolition debris represents about 40 percent of the total solid waste generated in the US. Good decisions about framing can significantly reduce demand for lumber and other framing materials, as well as the associated waste and loss of embodied energy.

In this category, LEED also awards points for environmentally preferable purchasing and use of building materials, including reclaimed timber, recycled-content materials, locally sourced materials, third-party-certified wood products and low-VOC materials.

Indoor Environmental Quality

This is the credit category that directly affects your health. Many of the pollutants found indoors can cause health reactions in the estimated 17 million Americans who suffer from asthma and 40 million who have allergies, contributing to millions of days absent from school and work.[32]

There are three major ways to improve indoor environmental quality.

- Source removal is the most practical way to ensure that harmful chemicals don't enter the home. Evaluating the properties of adhesives, paints, carpets, composite-wood products and furniture, and then selecting materials with low levels of potentially irritating VOCs, can reduce residents' exposure. Good construction practices that reduce or eliminate the potential for VOCs to be absorbed into finish materials are also important.
- Source control strategies focus on capturing pollutants that are known to exist in a home. For example, good air filters are important to control particulate matter that gets into the home. Keeping the ductwork clean and wrapped during construction and flushing out the home prior to occupancy can also reduce the potential for problems.
- Dilution involves the use of fresh outside air to ventilate a home and exhaust pollutants to the outdoors, a strategy that may also control moisture (see the earlier discussion on building science). It's important to have mechanical fresh-air ventilation systems, something that most new homes do not have, to get fresh air in and take stale, polluted air out.

Most homes accomplish this task through unintended leaks, as I point out in chapter 3.

Your comfort is also important, so LEED promotes the proper installation and use of automatic sensors and controls to maintain temperature, humidity and ventilation in rooms that you use. All new homes should have carbon monoxide sensors, but not all building codes require this. If your builder uses the ENERGY STAR with Indoor Air Package approach, LEED will automatically award the home an additional 13 points for indoor air quality.

Awareness and Education

The environmental impact of a home continues throughout its life cycle, and most new homes are expected to last 50 to 100 years, during which the residents consume energy, water and other resources. Since most homebuyers are going to know little about the details of green home construction, this credit category promotes broad awareness among homebuyers and tenants that LEED homes are built differently and need to be operated and maintained accordingly. You should ask for and get a fairly thorough Homeowner's Guide and a complete walk-through of all the key building systems when you get ready to move in. Keep the guide in an easily accessible place and use it to help you throughout the first year of residence.

Innovation and Design Process

The Innovation and Design Process credit category encourages project planning and design to improve the coordination and integration of the various elements in a green home. Credits can be earned for innovative designs, exemplary performance against LEED standards or regional best-practices that produce quantifiable environmental and human health benefits. These practices include integrated project planning and durability management.

Summary

Well, now you probably know far more than you ever thought you wanted to about the LEED for Homes rating system. I think it's the best one around, and I hope you will find a builder who's willing to engage in the learning required (and the extra costs) to bring this superior green home evaluation system to you. Failing that, there are still excellent regional green home rating systems (described later in the chapter), as well as the NAHB National Green Building Program, that will still get you a better home than a

Maxwell MacKenzie, courtesy of PN Hoffman

Figure 5.9. The Alta at Thomas Circle was the first new residential building to achieve LEED certification in Washington, D.C. The building features a green roof, ENERGY STAR appliances, low-VOC paints and finishes, recycled content materials and Green-Seal certified carpet.

standard homebuilder product. Remember, it's your money and your health (it's a lot of your money, actually); don't hesitate to ask for the best!

Multi-family Homes

The LEED market for multi-family homes is quite strong, reflecting the interest of city people in environmental issues. LEED for Homes can be used for townhouse and condo projects of three stories or less, so expect to see a lot more of those projects. Condos above four stories tall use the standard LEED for New Construction (LEED-NC) rating system. Many high-rise condos have begun to achieve the LEED rating, in places as diverse as New York, Chicago, Seattle, Boston, Los Angeles and Portland, Oregon. At the beginning of 2008, there were more than 100 large LEED-NC certified apartment and condo projects, as well as 112 multifamily projects certified under LEED for Homes. The LEED rating system for high-rise condos is very different from what's described above, since these are far more like commercial office buildings. You'll find out more about such projects in chapter 7.

Local Utility Programs

There are a few local electric utility programs in the US that have very strong testing and certification programs. If you're fortunate enough to live in one of those areas, you can rely on these programs for at least the energy-efficiency and indoor air quality components of a green building. Because utility programs focus primarily on energy conservation, they are not as fully rounded as the NAHB and USGBC programs described above. However, there is no reason why a builder cannot certify to both a local utility program and a national non-profit program, and some do. The three most notable utility programs are Austin Electric (City of Austin, Texas), Earth Advantage (developed by Portland General Electric and serving primarily its service territory in northwest Oregon and southwest Washington) and Tucson Electric Power's Guarantee Homes program. Memphis Light, Gas and Water city utility in Tennessee is another more recent program. Most of these programs now enroll one-third or more of all new homes in their service territory, so the odds of finding a home built to these standards in those areas are good; in fact, I would recommend NOT buying from a builder that isn't using one of these programs or something even more stringent such as LEED.

Austin Energy's S.M.A.R.T., the oldest program in the country, rates homes from one to five stars. By the end of 2007, it had rated about 7,500 single-family homes and 13,000 multi-family units.[33] Builders or developers who choose to participate in the S.M.A.R.T. housing program are required to meet a minimum one-star Green Building Rating. There are entire subdivisions where the builder complies with a minimum Green Building Rating. This ensures that moderate-income buyers get the benefit of a green home. Usually about 15 to 20 percent of the new homes built in the Austin Energy service area are rated by this program. Through 2006, Austin Energy reduced peak electric demand by 78,000 kW, avoided consumption of 135,000 megawatt-hours of energy and avoided over 40,000 tons of carbon dioxide emissions. Water conservation is also a component of the rating system, because the largest use of electricity among city departments is for the processing, delivery and reclamation of water and wastewater.

By the start of 2008, Earth Advantage had certified 8,600 homes in northern and central Oregon and southwest Washington. Randy Hansell has been with the Earth Advantage program since 1995 and works closely with homebuilders. He talked about what it costs a builder.

The additional cost to build a house to our program standards varies depending on when the builder came on board [in the building process] and what measures they choose. If they are building strictly to code, the additional cost will be close to 2 percent, but if they're already using some of the green features that we require, the additional cost is closer to 0.5 percent (of construction cost of home). In addition, some of the builders are adding more green features that aren't a requirement of the program, so that adds an additional cost as well.

Homebuyers tell us that they are willing to pay more for a green home. Some of our builders say they've been able to incorporate the energy and environmental measures into their construction systems, and therefore they don't have to charge more for an Earth Advantage-certified home. On the other hand, a couple of other builders are charging a little more, and people are still buying from them. We also have a few builders that have been able to communicate the value proposition in their sales process to homebuyers, and they are able to sell the houses at higher prices.

We feel third-party certification is important. We have always verified, inspected and performance tested (blower door and duct blast) our program houses. We feel that this process helps us ensure that the houses that go through our program meet our standards. Our required and optional features are inspected during construction and after the home is completed. We find a strong value in that because the builder is able to say that an outside organization has proven that the standards are being met. Even though it costs them more, the builders continually tell us that it is a feature that they really like. We work with the builders, helping educate their staff and subcontractors to help them get their homes certified. Our program is voluntary, so builders know what they're getting into when they come on board: they're hiring us to consult with them to build these homes to our program standards and get them certified.[34]

Duane Woik, also a consultant with the Earth Advantage program in Oregon, describes how his program benefits the homebuyer.

The main thing that we bring to the table is that we're out there testing the homes. Performance testing proves that the builder is building to the performance requirements of the program. It also ensures that cost-effective strategies are happening during construction. If the builder doesn't do things right during the construction phase, it's a lost opportunity for the life of the home. With an Earth Advantage certification, we say that the home is meeting certain standards such as improved indoor air quality requirements and energy efficiency. Consumers think that a code house is a good house, but one thing to remember is that a code house is the minimum standard that a home can be built to. For most people, a home is the largest purchase of their life, so why buy a home that's built only to the lowest minimum standard?[35]

Linda Douglas-Worthy is manager of Tucson Electric Power's Guarantee Homes program in Arizona, one of the best in the country. She describes what her program does and how it benefits the utility to offer this program:

We give the homeowner a written guarantee that the home is going to be comfortable, and if it's not, then we work with them. In the event that we can't make it comfortable, we install a different piece of equipment; we're that confident in the program. We guarantee that the annual heating and cooling costs will not exceed a certain amount. If it does exceed that, then we give the homeowner a credit on their electric bill for the difference. The other benefit that the homeowner gets is a special electric rate that is lower than the standard rate. We can do that because the load curve is different on the Guarantee homes compared to a home that is not built to these standards. We provide them a different rate, which comes out to be a lower cost per kilowatt-hour. That reduced rate is for the lifetime of the home. It transfers from one homeowner to the next. As long as someone doesn't remodel and remove insulation, install new windows or tear out duct systems, that home will perform the same way for its entire life.

There are a lot of similarities between the Guarantee Home program and ENERGY STAR. The new 2006 ENERGY STAR requirements added a lot of things that we've done all along. ENERGY STAR does not require fresh air ventilation in every home, and it still does not manage air pressures, which are two big items [we require]. They do a blower door test on homes for infiltration. We do that also but it's a less important piece than the pressures.[36]

Local Government Programs

There are a number of local governments now offering home certification programs, including the cities of Austin (mentioned above), Scottsdale (AZ), Irvine and San Jose (CA), Portland (OR), San Antonio and Frisco (TX), Boulder (CO) and the state of North Carolina HealthyBuilt Homes.

Figure 5.10. Photovoltaic and solar thermal systems with on-demand water heater backup systems are standard features in the Armory Park del Sol neighborhood in Tucson, Arizona. Each home comes with a five-year energy cost guarantee from the local utility. This high-density community won the NAHB 2007 Livable Communities Award, Governor Janet Napolitano's 2007 Arizona Innovation Award and the 2005 NAHB Energy Value Housing Award.

Each has different requirements. As before, you should insist on at least an ENERGY STAR home with onsite inspection of each home by an independent third-party home rater.

Scottsdale Green Building Program

The Scottsdale program has 28 mandatory measures and 14 rating categories. The rating categories consist of the following elements:
- Site
- Roofing
- Structural Elements
- Exterior Finishes
- Energy Rating/Performance
- Interior Finishes
- Thermal Envelope
- Interior Doors, Cabinets and Woodwork
- Heating, Ventilation and Air Conditioning
- Flooring
- Electrical Power, Lighting and Appliances
- Solid Waste
- Plumbing System
- Innovative Design

The Scottsdale Green Building Program also uses a size-adjustment score to reward or penalize houses that fall below or above the average home size, but the neutral score is pegged to the average for Scottsdale, 3,000 to 3,500 square feet, considerably larger than the national average for the US of about 2,400 square feet. Once the scored residence meets the mandatory measures, points are awarded for measures in the rating categories noted above. Residences must accumulate 50 to 90 points (after size adjustment) to achieve an Entry Level rating; and 100 or more points to earn the home an Advanced Level rating.

Anthony Floyd of the City of Scottsdale describes his organization's program:

> We started the program in 1998, and it has evolved over time. Our program is voluntary, but once someone enrolls, the plans are approved and a green building permit is issued, they are obligated to comply. We recently increased the number of required points — it's nearly double what it had been. Entry level is 50 points, and Advanced is 100 points through the program.
>
> About 35 percent of all new homes in 2005 and 2006 have been part of the program. In 2007 we updated our rating checklists, and now we suspect that the percentage is decreasing. In our program, we now have 28 mandatory items, which makes it basically the equivalent of ENERGY STAR. For example, homes now have to have an on-demand hot water circulation pump if the water heater is 20 feet away from closest fixture [so they don't use so much water waiting for the water to get hot]. Half of the toilets in a home are required to be low-flow (less than 1.3 gallon flush). We also have a house size-adjustment: the larger the house the more points you need.[37]

Green Building Ratings from Local Non-profits

EarthCraft House

One of the better programs in the country operated by a non-profit is EarthCraft House, started in 1999 by the Southface Energy Institute in Atlanta, Georgia, in partnership with the Greater Atlanta HBA. EarthCraft has been around for many years and is now widely accepted throughout the Atlanta metro region. Recently, it has expanded its reach into neighboring South Carolina, and farther north into North Carolina and Virginia. According to Southface, in Atlanta and the metro area, over 4,000 Earth-Craft House single-family homes and over 1,800 EarthCraft multi-family units had been certified through the end of 2007. Developers working with EarthCraft House to promote environmental policies on a larger scale have created seven EarthCraft Communities in the Greater Atlanta region.[38]

To achieve EarthCraft House certification, homes must meet ENERGY STAR certification criteria and exceed minimum scores on diagnostic tests for air infiltration and duct leakage. In addition, each house must achieve a minimum of 150 points from a scoring sheet. Select and Premium status are awarded to homes that meet additional criteria and achieve 200 and 230 points, respectively. All EarthCraft certified homes are also awarded ENERGY STAR certification. What I like about EarthCraft is that it gives positive guidance to builders, in great detail, based on sound regional building science principles.

Laura Uhde, director of residential green building services at Southface, describes her program:

> The main thing to educate a consumer on is making sure they look for a green program certification on the house that at a minimum requires visual inspection and testing by a third party on all homes (and does not allow for sampling). They should also look for programs that are consistently recognized for making updates. We update our program at least annually to continually raise the bar and make it more challenging for the builders so they stay on top of the market.
>
> Every single EarthCraft House is inspected and tested. That means every house meets certain criteria and certain standards for energy efficiency. At a bare minimum, the homes are 15 percent better than the 2004 energy code. In reality, they're probably 20 to 40 percent better on average. The buyers also get the assurance of quality construction. For example, the flashing on a window is a common weak spot on a house, and if you don't have somebody that's working with your builder on that, how do you know what they're doing behind the walls? Insulation is another issue. Every EarthCraft House gets graded on insulation criteria.
>
> We've had testimonials from clients who have purchased Earth-Craft Houses who have children with asthma or other health problems. One child stopped having to go to the hospital for his monthly breathing treatments. Their health has drastically improved and the only thing that changed in their lives was their house.[39]

Jackie Benson, a partner in Milesbrand, Atlanta, who works with the Earth-Craft House program, talked about its benefits:

When we created EarthCraft, our first goal was to redefine a quality home. We felt like the EarthCraft House program did that. It helped redefine it for a builder who uses the word "quality" over and over again. It was also a way to help the consumer understand the word "quality." Secondly, green is extremely misunderstood and political. We really want to stay away from that issue and get back to the craft of building a home. So the word "craft" related to Earth was sort of automatic that went together for us. It's helping craft a better Earth; it's being environmentally conscious, at each step in building, of what a home takes from the Earth. I think we all agreed at the time that green was probably not the best term.

Buyers have to educate themselves so they can ask the tough questions when they go to a community to look at homes. They need to know what "green" means. They need to understand more about comparing one builder's "green" to another builder's "green."[40]

Monte Hewett Homes builds each of its homes to EarthCraft standards. Dina Gundersen, director of marketing for the company, commented:

We promote the EarthCraft certification to homebuyers in every possible way we can. It's in all of our marketing collateral, it's all over the website, and I'm constantly speaking about it. We have customer testimonials that we share with prospective buyers. For example, we have testimonials from "move-up buyers" — someone moving from a smaller home into a larger home — and their energy bill is the same. In fact, that's a personal experience that I had myself — moving from a smaller home into a Hewett home. In going from 2,200 square feet to 4,500 square feet, my energy bill is the same. The house has three heating and A/C units, and my energy bill is practically the same as it was in my other home.

I started at Monte Hewett in late 2003 about the time we were starting to push the program and tell homebuyers about it. Since then, the number of people that are asking about the program has grown significantly. The energy efficiency of our homes is one of the huge points of differentiation when we are explaining the difference between us and the community down the street. We tell them that our homes are third-party certified by EarthCraft, and we list the major things that we put in our homes that other builders don't. One of those things is blown-in cellulose insulation. We can realistically say that our homes are EarthCraft and ENERGY STAR certified and that they are going to save at the bare minimum between 30 and 45 percent.[41]

Build It Green, California

Build It Green is a California non-profit that promotes healthy, energy- and resource-efficient building practices in California. Build It Green has developed GreenPoint Rated, a regional home rating program corresponding to Build It Green's Green Building Guidelines. Homes are verified by Certified GreenPoint Raters — experienced building industry professionals who have completed extensive technical training and passed written and field exams. GreenPoint Rated was developed specifically to address the needs of California's residential new construction and remodeling industries and provides builders and consumers with a gauge of how well a building performs above California building codes.[41] In order for a home to be GreenPoint Rated, it must score 50 points overall and meet minimum points thresholds in the following four categories: energy, water, resource conservation, health/indoor air quality.[42] Other requirements include diverting 50 percent of the construction and demolition waste and incorporating the GreenPoint Rated checklist in the building plans. Specific topics addressed include site, foundation, landscaping, building envelope and structure, exterior finish, insulation, plumbing, HVAC, renewable energy, building performance (including ENERGY STAR with Indoor Air Package), finishes, flooring, appliances and innovative measures including a homeowner's manual.

Brian Gitt, executive director of Build It Green, describes his program:

> From a buyer's perspective, it's all about comfort, health and reducing the cost of home ownership overall. That means reduced maintenance costs and reduced utility bills. In addition to reducing costs, it's also about comfort. A well-designed green home is going to be more comfortable than a comparable home because you've got a tighter building envelope, a better-balanced HVAC system, and you're not going to have leaks around the windows and doors. You're just going to be more comfortable in your home overall, and therefore, you're going to have happier people in it. In addition to comfort, health and indoor air quality is an emerging trend that is driving decisions around interior finishes such as cabinets, paints, adhesives and flooring. However, from a customer standpoint, I think comfort is probably number one. That's even above, I would say, reduced costs of homeownership. Because when you buy a new home, you're spending a lot of money on it, and you expect to be comfortable and cozy in your new home.
>
> We're also getting a lot of positive feedback from builders. An example of this is Meritage Homes' development in Vacaville (halfway

between Sacramento and the Bay Area). It's just 40 to 50 homes, and they're finding that — this is not hard scientific data, it's just anecdotal from the sales staff — they are seeing a significant increase in foot traffic and interest because of the green elements. There's a competing project right across the street that has the same type of product, same neighborhood, same schools and more and less all of the other elements are the same, but yet it's not a green project. Meritage feels they are getting significantly more in terms of interest and foot traffic and sales because of how it's being marketed and how it was actually built. I think, in general, most builders will say if everything else is equal, having a home Green Point Rated is certainly an advantage.[44]

Florida Green Building Coalition

As of September 30, 2007, under the Florida Green Home Designation Standard, the Florida Green Building Coalition (FGBC) had certified 1,227 homes, with 573 (nearly half) coming from one builder, WCI communities, in North Venice. The FGBC Green Home Designation Standard certification program requires a minimum of 100 points (with no specific energy-savings requirements) under Version 5.0, in effect until June 30, 2008.[45] A third-party organization accredited by the FGBC performs the certification assessment. With no prerequisites and no minimum energy performance required for certification, this is not as strong a certification as other available standards. The only real surprise for me is that more Florida builders are not using it.

Canada ENERGY STAR

This program is currently available in Ontario and Saskatchewan. There is also a Canadian government national program called R-2000 that sets an even higher standard, but most builders are not using it at this time. Michelle Cote, an account manager with the EnerQuality Corporation in Toronto, the delivery agent for ENERGY STAR in Canada says:

> With ENERGY STAR in Ontario, we simplify our messages quite a bit for consumers. Everyone has seen an ENERGY STAR label on a computer or refrigerator or other appliances; there are something like 42 product categories. Now you can get an ENERGY STAR label for a house. The label signifies best in class. People are able to recognize a product as best in class if it's got an ENERGY STAR label on it; now, the same works for the house. An ENERGY STAR-qualified home is 30 percent more energy-

efficient than a home built to the Ontario building code [this is twice the level of energy savings required of an ENERGY STAR home in the US].

Our three key messages are: Every home is government-backed, performance-tested and third-party-verified. The third-party evaluators go out and pass or fail the home [with ENERGY STAR in Canada, it's only pass or fail; there's no in-between.] It's not a performance rating. Either they've met the requirements or they haven't. Once a house is qualified as ENERGY STAR, the third-party verifier has tested the home and labeled it and so the homeowner can look for the blue ENERGY STAR label on their electrical panel.

ENERGY STAR for new homes in Ontario has completed two years of the pilot project. The first year [2005] of ENERGY STAR, we labeled 96 houses. Last year [2006] we labeled almost 1,250 houses. When the program started there were 48 builders; now we have over 260. These builders have taken the choice to be leaders in building above code, in a voluntary program, and they're making it happen.

For buyers in Ontario, I encourage people to visit the website because there's a lot of good information to help them understand ENERGY STAR.[46] My advice for someone who's looking for an energy-efficient green home is to look for the label. With that label comes peace of mind. It's that security blanket that people are looking for when purchasing a house.[47]

Environments for Living
(GE ecomagination and Masco Contractor Services)

The Environments For Living® (EFL) program uses the principles of building science to help builders construct homes that are more energy-efficient, comfortable, durable, healthier and safer than conventional homes. Originally developed by Masco Contractor Services, in 2007 General Electric's ecomagination[SM] program announced that it would include EFL in its homebuilder certification program. The EFL program establishes requirements for tight construction, fresh air ventilation, improved thermal systems, right-sized HVAC equipment, balanced air pressure, internal moisture management and combustion safety. As of the end of 2007, homebuyers could find homes certified and guaranteed by EFL in Arizona, California, Colorado, Florida, Nevada, North Carolina and Texas.

The EFL program includes requirements in seven key areas:

- Tight construction — providing a tight shell and air-sealing the thermal envelope

- Fresh air ventilation — bringing fresh air into the home in a controlled manner
- Improved thermal systems — installing improved insulation systems and, in some homes, more energy-efficient windows
- Right-sized HVAC –right-sizing and installing HVAC systems to improve the performance of equipment and minimize duct leakage
- Pressure balanced — installing air returns, transfer grilles and/or jump ducts to help make sure all rooms are pressure-balanced, to manage air flows and achieve balanced temperatures (comfort) throughout
- Internal moisture management — using vapor barriers and vapor retarders to help allow moisture inside building assemblies to dry, and making sure all fans vent directly to the outside
- Combustion safety — adding carbon monoxide detectors and making sure all combustion appliances within the conditioned space of the home are sealed or power-vented, to address backdrafting and buildup of carbon monoxide.

EFL conducts a plan review for each new model to help builders determine the steps required to meet the program specifications. The program is performance-based and does not require builders to use a particular manufacturer's product. EFL evaluates built homes through random testing by trained and certified contractors.

Builders may choose from four levels of participation, Silver, Gold, Platinum or Diamond class. At each level, there are progressively more stringent requirements for construction and performance. Gold and Platinum levels result in homes with at least 30 percent less energy use than the 1993 Model Energy Code and qualify for ENERGY STAR designation. The Platinum level also earns a designation under the US Department of Energy's Building America℠ program and exceeds the International Energy Conservation Code 2000 standard by 30 percent. Diamond Class homes must meet all of the program's Platinum-level requirements and exceed the Platinum level in one or more of several key components of green building, such as energy-efficiency, water conservation and advanced indoor air quality.

The EFL program provides two limited guarantees: energy use and comfort. These are offered for two years with an option for the builder to extend for a third year. Energy use refers to the estimated annual amount of energy needed to heat and cool a home, not to actual money spent. If actual use exceeds the estimated amount, the homeowner is refunded 100 percent of the cost difference based on local energy prices. The comfort guarantee, offered

Figure 5.11. Each home in the Caserro Ranch neighborhood in Sparks, Nevada, is certified by ENERGY STAR, Environments for Living (Platinum level) and American Lung Association's Health House program.

at the Gold, Platinum and Diamond levels, promises that the temperature at the location of the thermostat will not vary more than three degrees from the center of any conditioned room for that zone. To date the program has issued more than 4,000 guarantees.

"Homebuilders have a tremendous opportunity to take advantage of building science," says Rick Davenport, director of building science for Masco Contractor Services, the sponsor of EFL. "A number of builders who have adopted this systems approach and joined the Environments for Living program have reported gains in customer satisfaction and fewer call-backs, among other benefits."[48]

At this time, EFL has limited use by homebuilders. By searching on its website, you can find builders and developments offering the EFL guarantee, but there are not a lot. For example, in all of California, as of the end of 2007, there were only 6 builders and only 10 developments participating in EFL. In Florida there are only 10 builders and 19 developments.[49] So, the likelihood of finding an EFL development is not as high as finding a homebuilder following the NAHB or ENERGY STAR guidelines.

In May 2007 General Electric's ecomagination[SM] program announced it would team up with EFL to offer their certification, along with GE's ENERGY STAR appliances and other energy-related products.[49] Whether this partnership will serve to expand the EFL program to more states and more builders was not clear as of the end of 2007. As of October 2007, GE claimed that seven large communities in the US, ranging from Idaho to Florida, and consisting eventually of 25,000 homes at full build-out, had agreed to become part of the new program.[51]

American Lung Association Health House Program

We interviewed Robert Moffitt, director of the American Lung Association's green building rating program, Health House. There's lots more information on the Health House website, but this is what he stressed as the most important points about the program:

The Health House program is one of the oldest green building programs in the nation. It started in 1993. We have a set of guidelines that a builder uses to create strategies to build a more energy-efficient and healthier home. Energy efficiency, durability and indoor air quality are the main aspects of the program. Our Health House homes are third-party verified by a certified energy rater. Some things are different about a Health House. We require capillary breaks on the footings, sealed combustion equipment, enhanced flashing for rainwater control, radon venting, advanced air sealing, and source control of VOCs.

For our program, the builder must hire a third-party verifier, which costs $1,000 to $1,500. As far as equipment and direct construction costs, we've always said it may cost three to five percent more to meet our standards. However, if you put that three to five percent in your mortgage, you'll get double the extra monthly payment back in energy savings.

We work on prescriptive assumptions. We know that radon is a problem [in various parts of the US]. It's been identified as the second leading cause of lung cancer in the US. An estimated 20,000 people a year die from long-term exposure to radon. [So we make sure radon doesn't get into the home.] Exhaust fumes are another good example. We know if we test for what's called communication between garage and the home, we can limit the introduction of carbon monoxide into the house when cars are started and vapors from gasoline and things that are typically stored in the garage.

[We recommend to buyers] that they use a third-party-verified green building program, such as Health House, and that they work closely with their builder and the home rater so they're part of the relationship. That way they can understand the decisions that are being made while the builder is following the guidelines.[52]

This is a good program. However, at the time I prepared this book there were very few builders in the US building to Health House standards.

Bringing It All Together —
Building Science and Third-party Certification at Civano

Al Nichols is a professional mechanical engineer who has been involved with the Civano development in Tucson, Arizona, since its inception in 1990. When his engineering firm was commissioned to write an energy code for the Civano project. All building plans must be reviewed for energy code compliance before construction. A number of local experts joined together to create a workable code which was later deemed the Tucson Sustainable Standard. Nichols is also a homeowner at Civano and has his engineering office there. Here's his perspective about the proper use of building science, third-party review and the right way to design energy-efficient homes. (Tucson is in the Sonoran Desert, a climate that in the summer regularly gets at least 60 days a year of temperatures over 100°F and in the winter often gets freezing nights into the mid-twenties from December through February.)

> If there isn't a third-party review, then you pretty much get what the builder wants to give you. Building codes require inspections that check for life safety, but they don't check for things that make the building energy-efficient. It's not that the inspectors don't want to; they simply don't have enough time do it.
>
> ENERGY STAR, Tucson Electric Power (TEP) Guarantee Home and other programs all start with a review of the house drawings. They will first make sure that the air conditioner is properly sized for the house — if it's undersized, or particularly if it's oversized, which is the biggest crime, you don't get the efficiency because of its short-cycling [turning on and off rapidly]. Without having properly sized equipment, you're dead in the water to start with. In the drawing review, they will also review the insulation.
>
> The next level is testing the infiltration and tightness of the house by using a blower door and duct blaster tests. Knowing that someone is going to come out and do a blower door test on the house puts the builders on notice. It's the same with the air conditioning guys. They always ask, "Is this a TEP Guarantee Home?" Because they have to test the air tightness of the ductwork, they sometimes charge more to do it right.

Third-party review is important, because someone comes in and tests to see if your house is tight and if it has a fresh air supply. It's the stick, if you will. Everyone wants the carrot. "Let's just make it optional," but you need the stick.

TEP comes out before the drywall goes on and evaluates the insulation. They ensure that it was installed correctly. If you don't put in the insulation correctly, you can lose half of your insulation value. There's another example of a third-party test.

In Civano, annual heating and cooling requirements are nearly 50 percent less than the 1995 Model Energy Code. We've compared homes built prior to the implementation of the model energy code and then homes that were built after the model energy code. It's pretty dramatic, considering that the cost increase [to get this level of savings] is minimal.

In our 2006 report on this project, we compared the sales price in Civano Phase I and the sales price of homes in Civano Phase II and the sales price of homes in nearby Mesquite Ranch (built to minimum energy code). What we found was the Phase II homes built by Pulte, a vertically integrated builder, are selling for 2 percent more — $3 per square foot more for the Phase II homes versus Mesquite Ranch. Civano Phase I homes sell for $30 per square foot more — about 15 percent more — and most of that has to do with the architecture of the place. When we originally tried to justify the extra initial cost of the homes here, we said it is less than 5 percent for the energy standards and the rest of it is the New Urbanist design.

There are about another 120 homes being built and those will complete Civano Phase I. In Phase II, Pulte built 500 or so homes. They're now building Phase III, 800 homes. All Civano homes exceed ENERGY STAR because there is a mandatory solar component. I estimate that 98 percent of homes out here have solar hot water heaters and some of them have PV.

After putting in CFL lighting wherever possible, the next level is better windows. Most builders can pass code and get away with fairly ordinary aluminum frame, low-e glass, double-pane glass. But in the Civano homes, if your glass isn't at least R-3, you won't pass. So that drives you to wood or vinyl frames [instead of aluminum] to get that thermal break.

You've got roof, walls, windows and mechanical systems. Starting with the roof, prescriptively what does pass is at least R-38. At least R-20 has to be in the walls, and we require R-3 with low-e, heat-rejecting coating for the windows. We require that the mechanical systems in Civano be above the national standard. We recently changed the requirement so that we require SEER-14 air conditioners. Where the code allows for gas heater efficiency to be only 80 percent, we require 90 percent.

The word "affordable" has to be used every time you talk about this. If it's not affordable, it's just a waste of time and energy. By running the insulation up the roofline and back down through the wall, the building becomes significantly more airtight than a traditional attic with a blown-in or fiberglass batt insulation. That is significant, and it keeps the building much tighter because there aren't any leaks going out through the top.

Our newest guidelines say that you have to produce 550 kWh of renewable energy per year per bedroom using solar. That involves, for example, a four-by-ten-foot solar panel for water heating, if it's the right type, for up to four bedrooms. You can do PV instead as long as you produce the minimum requirements. We also adopted LEED commercially. Commercial buildings must achieve a minimum of LEED Silver and derive 5 percent of their energy requirements from solar.

Done correctly, energy-efficient green homes are hardly more expensive than conventional homes. You can get someone like Pulte who knows how to do it. We've shown that the penalty is about $3 per square foot, and you can negotiate that much when you buy a house. We see between $600 and $1,000 plus annual savings compared to conventional homes; besides, they're so much more comfortable, and you've got peace of mind because you've had third-party review. That's a key element — that it's got some sort of certification. The third-party review is attractive because it's a guarantee of a well-built and well-designed home.[53]

CHAPTER 6

Where Can I Find a Green Home?
Single-family Home Developments

You've probably been waiting for this information. You're excited, committed and ready to go. Where can you find a homebuilder that will offer you a green home? Together, we're going to take a brief representative (but necessarily incomplete) tour of more than 50 of the many green home developments that are already out there. In this chapter, our tour focuses on detached and attached (low-rise) single-family homes. In chapter 7, we'll turn to high-rise condominiums. If I don't list a particular homebuilder or region that interests you, try using the information in earlier chapters to do your own search. Be aware that the green home movement is growing very fast in popularity among builders; you'll find more green homes and green homebuilders in your area each year. And by now, you know how to evaluate their offerings. In the Resources section, I also give you many good information sources to help you with your search. Now, sit back, relax with that quad-shot, skinny, *venti* caramel latte you've bought with your future monthly energy savings and join us as we explore the possibilities.

ENERGY STAR Builders

The first place to start is with the thousands of builders already participating in the ENERGY STAR program. The government's ENERGY STAR (energystar.gov) website allows you to search for particular builders by state. Figure 6.1 shows the states with the highest percentage of ENERGY STAR homes in 2007, the latest year for which complete data are available. These are the states where you have greater odds of finding such homes. There may be other homebuilder certification programs that do all of the things required by ENERGY STAR, but if they're not independently tested and certified, you're not getting all the peace of mind you should. At the end of this chapter, as an aid to your search for a green home, you will find a list of the top ENERGY STAR builders in each state.

You want an ENERGY STAR home not only to save you energy, but also to be healthy, comfortable and low-maintenance. ENERGY STAR's website lists builders in 18 states who employ four "must-have" features "behind the walls." And, remember, you typically can't look behind the walls of the new home you're buying.[1]

1. Air sealing and insulation that works, to control air leaks, cold spots and mold.

Figure 6.1. Leading states with ENERGY STAR homes, 2007

State	ENERGY STAR Certified Homes, 2007	Percentage of New Housing Starts
Arizona	7,501	20%
California	12,978	12%
Connecticut	719	13%
Hawaii	1,725	39%
Iowa	2,828	34%
Massachusetts	1,401	15%
Nevada	8,387	46%
New Jersey	5,926	46%
New York	2,947	14%
Oklahoma	2,254	19%
Rhode Island	420	19%
Texas	40,146	34%
Utah	2,671	15%
Vermont	720	25%

US EPA [online], energystar.gov/index.cfm?fuseaction=qhmi.showHomesMarketIndex, accessed February 26, 2008

2. Ducts that don't leak, so that all the conditioned air you're paying for actually gets delivered to the living space.
3. Advanced windows for comfort, to reduce drafts, fading of fabrics and loss of energy. Otherwise you may be too warm in summer and too cold in winter.
4. Independent testing and inspection to ensure quality construction, especially with blower door and duct blaster tests.

If you can't get satisfaction on these four measures, you probably should keep looking.

States with between 3 percent and 11 percent ENERGY STAR-rated homes (of total homes built) in 2007 included the following: Colorado, Delaware, Idaho, Indiana, Kentucky, Maryland, Michigan, Minnesota, New Hampshire, New Mexico, North Carolina, North Dakota, Ohio, Oregon, Virginia, Washington and Wisconsin.

NAHB National Green Building Program

Chapter 5 describes the many builder organizations that are promoting green buildings. With the advent of a national program from the National Association of Homebuilders in early 2008, I expect homebuilders' green home offerings to improve in quality and frequency. Nevertheless, if you're not being shown an ENERGY STAR home, keep looking. Even if you are, ask to see the rating system checklist the builder is using. In any case, I'd ask for a Silver or Gold NAHB rating from the builder.

LEED for Homes

In chapter 5, I called LEED for Homes the "gold standard." If your builder is offering a LEED-certified home, grab it (assuming it meets your other family and financial requirements). You'll be getting the best green home on the market, one that meets ENERGY STAR with the Indoor Air Package, and one that's certified by a completely independent third party. If I were you, I'd look first for at least a LEED certification from the builder. Because there are only 10,000 residential units registered in the LEED for Homes pilot program, you're going to have to do your research on the US Green Building Council's website for this program.[2] You can also try contacting the LEED for Homes "providers" (local raters) listed on that website. If you can't find a LEED-certified home, try to get one that has a more complete green certification than just the ENERGY STAR label.

Local Certification Programs

Chapter 5 includes a number of established local utility and non-profit programs that are fine-tuned for the region's climate and that have proven themselves over time to have integrity. Check them out carefully, to make sure they still require ENERGY STAR and offer other green building features. Wherever possible, ask for the highest-rated homes in each program.

Pacific Northwest

New Tradition Homes

There are many exemplary developments in the Pacific Northwest (Oregon, Washington, Idaho and western Montana). One that stands out is New Tradition Homes in Vancouver, Washington, described by Steve Tapio, quality control manager and building science team leader for the company:

> Affordability is so important, but yet we still want to build a better home. So the question is how do we build a better home with better equipment in it and still keep it affordable? It's a challenge, and yet we feel that we're doing a good job at it. With the input from the building scientists and the other consultants that we're dealing with, we're able to find the most cost-effective and affordable products that are more energy-efficient, better and make a sustainably built home that's going to last.
>
> Our definition of "green" may be a little bit different from what other builders think of as "green." Some builders think that if they use bamboo flooring and wool (low-VOC) carpeting that they are building green houses. I would say, rather than just looking at products that you put into the house, we should be looking at how the house is built. Is it built so that it's weather resistant, durable and going to last 100 years rather than 50 years? If a house is built to code or in some cases, substandard practices, it will probably have a lot of water-intrusion issues especially in the maritime climate here in the Pacific Northwest.
>
> We look at the heating and ventilation of the house. We put in high-efficiency furnaces, which other [local] builders are not putting in. We seal all of the duct work in the houses, and we do the performance testing on the HVAC system. We put in ENERGY STAR-rated appliances and correctly installed insulation. Rather than putting it in per code, we put it in according to the ENERGY STAR standard, which doesn't reduce the R-value. We make sure it's installed correctly with no gaps, voids or compressions so it performs correctly.

For the exterior wrap, we use a Tyvek® product that's called Drain Wrap. It's a sort of corrugated product that allows for some drainage channels behind the siding so that when moisture gets behind the siding — which it will, regardless of type of siding you put on — it will have a drainage plane that it can travel down and leak out the bottom rather than getting stuck behind the siding (and therefore creating moisture problems). We use finger-jointed wood products in the house, which use scrap pieces of wood. We use some intermediate and advanced framing techniques where we're using less wood in the house.

All of our homes are built to Earth Advantage standards and are ENERGY STAR-rated. All of our homes are third-party certified, which proves that we're not involved in greenwashing — where we claim that we're doing all of these things and claim that we're building a better house, but that's just our word. Why should the buyer just take our word for it? After all, we have sales people that are trying to sell you something. We've all been sold something before that's maybe not quite what the salesperson told us it was. So we want to have a third-party involved to give credibility to the product.[3]

Southwest Washington, New Tradition Homes

An Earth Advantage builder, New Tradition Homes has communities in Vancouver, Washougal, Battle Ground, Pasco and Richland where all of the homes are ENERGY STAR qualified. In partnership with Washington State University and the US Department of Energy's Building America program, the company built test homes in the Serena Estates subdivision. The homes are being monitored and evaluated for energy efficiency and indoor air quality over a period of two years. New Tradition Homes aims to build homes that provide homebuyers with significant long-term savings, improve indoor air quality and quality of life and appeal to energy-conscious consumers. "We believe that this is a better way to build homes. It is our hope that other builders will also recognize the value of bringing high-quality, affordable homes that are energy-efficient and environmentally conscious to the market," said Kelly Helmes, Vice-President of New Tradition Homes.[4]

Seattle, Washington, High Point Neighborhood

A winner of the Urban Land Institute's Global Awards for Excellence, Seattle's High Point neighborhood, when complete, will encompass 1,600 homes all meeting or exceeding 3-Star Built Green standards. The narrow streets and porous sidewalks reduce rainwater runoff and direct it to planted areas where it will be filtered before it reaches a salmon habitat stream nearby. Ninety percent of the old-growth cedar from a rundown public housing development built during World War II was recovered and reused, and 150 trees were preserved on-site. Located 10 minutes from downtown Seattle and 20 minutes from the airport, the High Point community is made up of a variety of housing types, emphasizing front-porch architecture, tree-lined sidewalks, 100 acres of parks, neighborhood shopping, community services and access to the local trail system.[5]

Seattle, Washington, Ashworth Cottages, Pryde + Johnson

The LEED Platinum-certified Ashworth Cottages in Seattle, Washington, are designed to reflect and complement the architecture and heritage of the surrounding neighborhood and to build community. The project is located in a revitalized urban space, and more than 90 percent of the construction waste was recycled. Each of the 20 single-family homes includes a custom-designed heat-recovery ventilation system, an on-demand hot water system, efficient fixtures, dual-flush toilets, locally sourced materials and zero-VOC paint. "The Pryde + Johnson design team took an integrated approach to building Ashworth Cottages targeting the highest green standards and LEED certification from the onset," said Curt Pryde, principal at Pryde + Johnson.

Renton, Washington, Shamrock Heights, CamWest

Built by CamWest Development, the fourth-largest builder in the Northwest, these homes are all Built Green Washington (4-star level) and ENERGY STAR-certified. With 117 lots on ten acres, including a lake and a greenbelt area, this community on the southern end of Lake Washington is selling well.[6] Carolyn L. Gladwell, Vice-President for sales and marketing at CamWest, says:

> As a builder, I hope that green building practices and materials will become mainstream. Green shouldn't have to be more expensive. With enough customer demand, large building material and appliance manufacturers will figure out ways to produce green products at the same price as other products, in turn making the choice an easy one for builders. Green building is healthier for the environment; green homes and communities create a healthier way of life for all of us.[7]

Figure 6.2. Located about 18 miles from Seattle, these homes in the Issaquah Highlands neighborhood are built to ENERGY STAR and Built Green Washington standards.

Issaquah, Washington, Issaquah Highlands

Upon completion, there will be more than 3,000 homes in the Issaquah Highlands community. The housing types include single-family detached homes, townhomes, condos, carriage houses, lofts, duplexes, mixed-use urban row homes and custom estates. All of the residences are built to Built Green standards and are ENERGY STAR-certified. The community developer designed streets, paths and amenities to encourage walking, bicycling and public transit use.[8]

Ada County (Boise), Idaho, Hidden Springs

Located about ten miles northwest of Boise, Hidden Springs is a master-planned development with 840 residential units on about 1,844 acres of land, 1,000 acres of which is protected open space. For-sale residential units range up to 2,400 square feet, with custom homes up to 6,000 square feet. Developers estimate project completion by December 2008. The master developer encourages the 13 approved individual builders to build ENERGY STAR homes. From 2004 through 2006, the project sold 467 homes.[9]

Salem, Oregon, Pringle Creek

Home of the Northwest's first LEED Platinum home, upon completion the Pringle Creek Community will feature walkable neighborhoods, a meandering creek and wetlands, a vibrant community plaza of preserved and re-purposed historical buildings, community gardens and open green space for all to enjoy. All new homes will be constructed with 100 percent FSC-certified lumber. New and existing community buildings will be built or revitalized to LEED standards. Several buildings have been relocated or re-cycled, as a result, more than 200 tons of concrete and 100 tons of wood and steel have been recycled through environmental stewardship efforts.[10]

Bend, Oregon, NorthWest Crossing

Located in central Oregon's high desert near Bend, every home in North-West Crossing is required to be Earth Advantage-certified, a program that addresses building issues such as energy efficiency, recycling, building materials, landscaping, and water and indoor air quality. Following the traditional neighborhood development concept, NorthWest Crossing's interconnected street, sidewalk and trail system encourages residents to rely less on vehicles. Upon completion, the community will include more than 1,200 homes.[11]

Northern California

Rocklin, Whitney Ranch, Newland Communities

Newland Communities is the developer of the 1,200-acre master-planned Whitney Ranch in Rocklin, near Sacramento. Eric Clifton, Vice-President of sustainable business development for Newland, speaks of his company's commitment to green building:

> A large number of builders are building fairly energy-efficient homes; however we're trying to push things further with programs like GE's ecomagination, EFL and LEED. We also have a technology company called Onteriors that we work with to educate the buyers on audio-visual loads, satellite irrigation and lighting control in order to help our residents further reduce the power and water consumption in each and every home. One of the big drivers for this service is plasma TVs; they generate a lot of heat, which requires more air conditioning, and they use 60 percent more power than an equivalent LCD set.
>
> Newland has a few builders that are starting to address solar, but we don't have a full program today. We're working towards a two-kilowatt

PV system on each home. People tend to focus on photovoltaics, but we're also looking into solar thermal for hot water, which provides just as much (or more) of a benefit at a much lower price point in terms of energy efficiency and overall benefit.

We are always looking for ways to help consumers conserve water and that will eventually transition into future building guidelines as well as certification programs to support this effort. However, we've taken water conservation one step further and have mandated WeatherTrack®, satellite irrigation control in our Houston and Tampa communities.

A healthy home is part of our vision; one that falls under our cornerstone Healthy Living Systems. In our research, we found that the two biggest driving interests of buyers are indoor air quality and "time famine" (lack of time in people's lives). To address time famine, we look at transportation issues, working from home, setting up a remote office facility, easy recycling, making energy efficiency practices easy and other areas that make day-to-day life simpler.[12]

Rocklin, Carsten Crossings, The Grupe Company

The 144 homes in the Carsten Crossings neighborhood in Rocklin all were built with the commitment to be LEED-certified. The homes include Sun-Tile™ PV roof tiles, expected to provide up to 70 percent of the home's electrical power needs. The 2,500 square foot Oakgrove model was awarded LEED certification early in 2007. Overall annual utility savings are estimated at $1,400.[13] As of December 2007, there were 49 LEED-certified homes at Carsten Crossings.[14]

The builder has dubbed its energy-efficiency efforts "GrupeGreen." The GrupeGreen homes at Carsten Crossings exceed California's strict Title 24 mandated standards. The solar electric systems are fully integrated with the roof shingles. Homes range from 2,168 to 2,755 square feet and are priced in the high $400,000s. "We are excited about being LEED certified," said Mark Fischer, Grupe's Senior Vice-President of operations. "The Grupe Company believes that a deep respect for the land and the environment is always the first step in building a timeless community. That philosophy has led us to offer the exclusive GrupeGreen homes with energy-saving standard features at Carsten Crossings."[15]

East San Francisco Bay area, Lennar (multiple communities)

Homes in Lennar's SOLAR*plus* East Bay communities include a 2.1 kilowatt solar system; high-efficiency appliances; dual-pane, low-e-coated windows;

James Yudelson

Figure 6.3. Each of the 67 homes in the Sonata at Dublin Ranch, one of Lennar's SOLAR*plus* communities, is equipped with a roof-integrated solar electric system. Lennar introduced its solar program in February 2007, committing to solar power for all new residential developments across the San Francisco Bay Area.

a SEER-14 A/C unit and a 92 percent efficient AFUE furnace. In the more than two dozen SOLAR*plus* communities in the Sacramento, Bay Area, Central Valley and Southern California areas, the solar and energy-efficient features will save homeowners as much as 60 percent on their electric bills and reduce carbon dioxide emissions by the equivalent of taking 620 vehicles off the road. Using PowerLight's SunTile® system, the roof-integrated technology blends seamlessly into the homes' design. "By harvesting the region's abundant sunlight and including solar power as a standard feature, Lennar and its customers are contributing significantly to California's energy independence," said Howard Wenger, executive vice-president of PowerLight.[16]

Dublin, Sonata at Dublin Ranch, Lennar

Priced from about $750,000 to about $850,000, the 67 single-family detached luxury homes on Sonata at Dublin Ranch are part of Lennar's SOLAR*plus* program. The roof-integrated solar electric system is a standard feature on each home. SOLAR*plus* homeowners can view their home's energy production and consumption online. Homes range from 2,200 to 2,850 square feet.

Sacramento, Provence, DR Horton

In the Provence community, home builder DR Horton is introducing solar sustainable homes priced within reach of most first-time homebuyers, topping out in the high $240,000s. The solar power system on each of the 187 homes will produce an average of 2,400 kilowatt hours a year. DR Horton also expects to be the first Sacramento-area production homebuilder to qualify for LEED Silver certification. Provence homes will qualify for the Sacramento Municipal Utility District's SolarSmart program, which reduces homeowners' utility bills if their solar systems produce more energy than they consume. "DR Horton is unique in that it's a large-scale builder that is offering state-of-the-art green technology within reach of the average homebuyer. Right now, that's the most intelligent thing we're trying to do as an industry," said Mark LaLiberte, with Building Knowledge Inc., a green home practices consulting group.[17]

Danville, Ponderosa Colony at Alamo Creek, Ponderosa Homes

The ComfortWise™ energy-efficient homes in the Ponderosa Colony at Alamo Creek in Danville exceed California energy standards by at least 15 percent. The homes include R-13 insulation in the exterior walls, R-38 insulation in the attic areas, water-conserving Kohler shower heads and dual-flush toilets, a recirculating hot water pump for faster hot water delivery, dual-glazed windows and radiant-barrier OSB roof sheathing. Tankless water heaters and solar photovoltaic panels are available as upgrades on some homes.[18]

Redding, RiverCrest, DR Horton

The homes in DR Horton's RiverCrest community are built to Environments for Living standards. The builder guarantees occupant comfort (temperatures throughout the house will not vary more than three degrees from the thermostat setting) and offers a three-year maximum heating and cooling usage guarantee. The homes exceed California's Title 24 energy code, as well as ENERGY STAR efficiency levels. Every home is independently tested for air tightness, duct tightness and pressure balances.

Watsonville, Vista Montaña, Clarum Homes

Priced for first-time buyers (and move-up buyers who are priced out of neighborhoods closer to Silicon Valley), each of the 257 Enviro-Homes™ in Vista Montaña come with a solar electric system as a standard feature. Clarum Homes was able to reduce the estimated energy consumption of the homes by more than 50 percent by participating in the US Department of Energy's Zero Energy Homes initiative and by working with the National Renewable Energy Laboratory (NREL). All of the homes are ENERGY STAR rated, ComfortWise qualified and California Green Builder certified. Other sustainable features of the homes include engineered lumber, recycled decking material and water-saving plumbing and landscaping. Recycled-content carpet, bamboo flooring, cork flooring and low-VOC paint are offered as options.

Southern California

Victorville, Victory Homes

Strong winds, little rain and temperatures that range from freezing to 110°F make the high desert city of Victorville, California, a challenging place to call home.[19] Local builder Victory Homes decided to try the California Green Builder program not only to construct homes to withstand the elements, but to use it as a sales tool. "It's really to our advantage to market a home that uses less energy and water than our competitors," says Austin Richey, Vice-President of construction for Victory Homes. "It really matters to our customers who are buying their first home because it will let them keep more money in their pocket."

Victory Homes was one of the first to use the California Green Builder certification, developed by California's Building Industry Association (BIA). "It wasn't even on anyone's radar three years ago," says Richey. "We worked very hard with the BIA to get this program established." He says ramping up his company's recycling efforts was one of the biggest challenges under the program that requires diverting 50 percent construction waste from landfills. Unlike many of the coastal areas of California, Victorville and its local trash haulers didn't have recycling experience. "We essentially introduced the concept to the market, and we continually work with our contractors to make sure they understand how to sort the construction materials."

Another big change was a shift to water-conserving landscapes that eliminated all lawns from the yards, but still featured beautiful plants appropriate for the high-desert climate. Richey says the change in landscaping and installation of low-flow fixtures saves 20,000 gallons of water annually in each home.

While Victory Homes has only been building green for a few years, the company took home the 2006 Golden Nugget Grand Award for a Green Builder Residential Project — beating out other builders from 14 western states. The judges said Victory Homes are meeting the unique challenges of

Figure 6.4. Landscaping at Victory Homes is well suited to the arid conditions of California's high desert. The company also makes green construction affordable for people buying their first home.

constructing entry-level homes in a market that is just beginning to understand what it means to be green.

Orange County, Terramor at Ladera Ranch, Rancho Mission Viejo
Terramor is a village within the 4,000-acre master-planned Ladera Ranch development. The goal was to reduce energy and water use by 20 percent each, measured against comparable homes, a goal that has been met. Many of the homes have photovoltaic systems, tankless water heaters, moisture sensors for irrigation control and drip irrigation systems. Sixty-five percent of construction waste was recycled. One survey indicated that 88 percent of residents were willing to pay $1,500 per year extra for the green features, especially energy conservation and onsite PV power production. The development is quite dense, consisting of 1,260 units on 300 acres, with 110 acres left as open space. Prices ranged from $275,000 to nearly $875,000.[20]

Orange, Depot Walk, Olson Homes
Designed to reduce private vehicle usage, Depot Walk is located two blocks from Old Towne Orange and less than a block from the Orange Metrolink station (the commuter heavy rail system in southern California). Located on an infill site, significant infrastructure was already in place, and no green or open space was disturbed to build Depot Walk. Certified at LEED for Homes Silver, the 32 two-story condos are equipped with solar PV, Forest Stewardship Council certified wood, tankless water heaters, dual-flush toilets and bamboo flooring. I visited this development in the summer of 2007 and can attest to the attractiveness of the residential units and the presence of rooftop solar PV systems.

Irvine, Woodbury East, John Laing Homes

Woodbury East includes 617 attached and detached homes that feature water-efficient plumbing and low-flow irrigation. Buyers will also have the opportunity to choose bamboo flooring, rooftop solar panels and form-aldehyde-free cabinets at an added cost. The development is being built under the City of Irvine's new green standards (which are not as stringent as ENERGY STAR, LEED or other standards.) To receive a Green Building certification by the City of Irvine, builders must achieve a minimum of 50 out of the 100 points. I also visited this development in the summer of 2007; it's a very walkable community and attractively laid out.

San Diego, Pacific Highlands Ranch, Pardee Homes

Belonging to Pardee's LivingSmart program, the homes in Pacific Highlands Ranch are designed to provide homebuyers with the opportunity to add state-of-the-art environmental, energy conservation and health and safety upgrades. ComfortWise certification, high-SEER A/C units, ENERGY STAR appliances, low-flow fixtures and photovoltaic systems are available. Surrounded by 1,300 acres of preserved natural habitat, the community offers its residents a convenient opportunity to enjoy a multi-use trail system for hiking and biking and an open country feel.

San Diego, Del Sur

The developer of Del Sur, a master-planned community in north San Diego, has mandated that at least 20 percent of the community's 2,500 homes incorporate solar energy systems. Some neighborhoods are exceeding the minimum, installing photovoltaic technology as standard in 40 percent of homes or more, and nearly all Del Sur residences have the option to incorporate solar power to generate electricity. Tankless water heaters and weather-based satellite irrigation systems are mandatory in most homes, potentially saving up to 40,000 gallons of water per home per year. The community also requires that at least 50 percent of all landscaping be drought-resistant. The Ranch House, a community information center, was awarded a LEED Platinum certification. With an initial goal of 50 percent construction waste diverted from local landfills, the Del Sur builders — Standard Pacific Homes, Davidson, Shea Homes, William Lyon Homes, McCullough-Ames and Laing Luxury — have consistently exceeded Del Sur's mandatory recycling requirements, successfully diverting over 92 percent of construction waste. Del Sur was recognized as a Sustainable Community of the Year by the Building Industry Association (BIA) of Southern California.

Bill Timmerman, courtesy of Modus Development

Figure 6.5. The ultra-modern-designed Galleries of Turney, a LEED for Homes certified community of eight detached town-homes, is located minutes away from major shopping, restaurants, parks and commuter services. A "rainscreen" façade system of corrugated zinc paneling and a fiber-cement skin that floats over the home shield it from the harsh effects of the Arizona sun.

Southwest

Phoenix, Galleries at Turney, Modus Development

The LEED-certified homes at Galleries at Turney feature eight detached two-story residences located only blocks from Phoenix's busy Biltmore area. With nearly 2,000 square feet, each is an expression of modern living — large open spaces with 12-foot ceilings and cutting-edge, contemporary design. In addition to high-efficiency Bosch appliances, the homes also utilize efficient plumbing fixtures, low-e windows and doors, low-VOC paint and high-efficiency heating and cooling systems. The developer emphasized site orientation of the individual units to shade hardscape elements and reduce the heat-island effect.

Figure 6.6. Located in Tucson, Arizona, the Civano community is a *Sunset* magazine award-winning, 820-acre traditional neighborhood development where all homes reduce potable water use by 60 percent, heating/cooling energy use by 50 percent and overall energy use by 30 percent compared with typical local houses. Civano features multiple energy-efficiency approaches: R-28 structural insulated panel walls, R-38 roofs and reflective roofing materials to reduce absorbed solar radiation, tightly sealed duct work and high-efficiency air conditioning systems.

Dan Byrnes, a buyer at the Galleries at Turney comments:

> I am proud of being able to make a personal statement through exercising purchasing power. Change takes place in the world because of economics more than any other single factor. To my mind, the Galleries at Turney has raised the bar in Arizona not only for sustainability and efficiency but for socially responsible residences. The project demonstrates that it is possible to be environmentally friendly and still be modern, exciting and functional. With the Galleries, I did not have to sacrifice any of my desires [for a residence] to achieve a result that benefits society overall.[21]

Tucson, Civano, Pepper Viner Homes

Richard Barna is construction manager at Pepper Viner Homes, building the final homes in Civano, Phase I, in Tucson. He describes their approach to building green homes in the hot, dry Sonoran desert:

It's a no-brainer that a house should work better if it's designed as a system. The building business has been left in the Dark Ages, and there's a lot of technology, knowledge and building science that just hasn't been integrated into production building. Our goal is to try to integrate it and be smart about how we build our houses.

We use Shaw carpet; it isn't recycled — there isn't enough recycled carpet available (because it's a new thing), but it is recyclable. With carpet, that's about as good as you can do right now. Every carpet that goes into our homes is recyclable. Shaw built a factory in Georgia where they are taking that recyclable material and starting to create new carpet out of it. The carpet is all low-VOC, as is our paint.

There are a lot of problems all over the country with mold and air quality in general. A lot of it is because the houses are built tighter nowadays. If there is a leak or any moisture gets into the wall system, it can't get out and then you have a problem. Here in Tucson, most everything is a stucco product. Typically underlayment for it is black tarpaper, and that stuff doesn't breathe. So we switched 100 percent to Tyvek®, which is used in a lot of the country, but here we're using it in a stucco application. It is tighter for air and water intrusion, but if moisture gets in there, it lets it breathe out. We have also tested the new Tyvek roofliner under our metal roofing. We think durability of our weatherproofing is very important.

When people started making tighter houses, they were ending up with bad air because there weren't air changes inside the house. Air changes used to happen naturally because the houses were leaky. Now that houses are built much tighter, we have mandatory fresh air intake into the system. It comes in through ductwork to the outside. Air comes in, is filtered and then goes through the system so it's constantly turning over fresh air in the house. That's mandatory with the new ENERGY STAR indoor air-quality requirements.

All appliances in the homes meet ENERGY STAR guidelines. Nearly every light bulb is a compact florescent bulb. In our standard house for the Civano subdivision, we use solar hot water heating with a gas backup. We have a gas water heater in the house, but the water comes through the solar system first.

In 2006 we decided that every future project will, at a bare minimum, meet ENERGY STAR, but actually we've taken that a step further. For example, the Civano project goes way beyond and qualifies for the EPACT federal tax credits, which means it's documented by the energy rater as saving more than 50 percent in heating and cooling costs. We get a federal tax credit on every house we build. It gives us $2,000 back, and that helps pay for more things that we can put in the house. Our approach has been to reinvest that money — get it, reinvest it and try and make the house better.[22]

Tucson, Armory Park del Sol, John Wesley Miller Homes

Photovoltaic and solar thermal systems with on-demand water heater backup systems are standard on all of the models in the Armory Park Del Sol neighborhood in Tucson. Each home comes with a five-year guarantee for maximum heating and cooling bills from Tucson Electric Power, as well as energy-efficient appliances and water-saving features. This high-density community won the NAHB 2007 Livable Communities Award, Governor Janet Napolitano's 2007 Arizona Innovation Award and the 2005 NAHB Energy Value Housing Award.

Las Vegas, Sun City Anthem, Pulte Homes

Sun City Anthem is a 55-plus, age-restricted community located outside of Las Vegas on 812 acres. Homes there range from 1,246 square feet to approximately 3,175 square feet and are priced from $230,000 to $1,050,000. The ENERGY STAR certification requires good insulation and low-e windows. A cocoon-type insulation in the attic keeps the air conditioning and heating system inside the insulated space, further improving efficiency.

Santa Fe, Evergreen, Homewise

Each home in Santa Fe's Evergreen community is at least 30 percent more energy-efficient compared to homes built to code. The builder, Homewise, strategically placed the homes to increase winter solar gain and installed energy-saving appliances. Each home is ENERGY STAR-qualified and features low-VOC paint, low-flow fixtures, a recirculation pump on the hot water heaters (to save water) and blown-in cellulose insulation. All of the landscaping is xeriscape using bark, gravel and native plants. Once established, the yards should not require any watering.

Reno/Sparks, Caserro Ranch, DR Horton

The homes in Caserro Ranch in Sparks are American Lung Association Health House Certified as well as Platinum-level Environments for Living and ENERGY STAR. The builder, DR Horton offers a three-year heating and cooling guarantee, as well as a comfort guarantee (temperatures

throughout the house will not vary more than three degrees from the thermostat setting). Tyvek® exterior wrap was installed to mitigate water intrusion, and every home was tested for air tightness, duct tightness and
pressure balancing.

Salt Lake City/South Jordan, Utah, Daybreak

Daybreak consists of more than 4,000 acres about 20 miles south of Salt
Lake City. By 2017 the developer expects to build more than 13,000 residential units with about 9 million square feet of retail, industrial and commercial uses. About 30 percent of the land is open space. All homes are expected
to be ENERGY STAR certified, which would make it by far the largest community in the US with all homes having this level of energy savings. Some of
the community, school and commercial buildings will be LEED certified as
well. Almost 9,000 single-family homes are planned, ranging from 1,300 to
4,000 square feet, along with nearly 3,000 for-sale townhomes. Through the
end of 2007, the developer expected to sell 2,500 lots, out of an expected total exceeding 13,000. While dawn has certainly broken on Daybreak, there's
still a long way to go until sunset.

West

Denver, Stapleton Community

Stapleton is a master-planned community located on the site of Denver's
former municipal airport. The master developer, Forest City Stapleton,
sets the green home building standards for the individual homebuilders.
Melissa Knott, director of sustainability for Forest City Stapleton, describes
the company's approach:

> The philosophy at Forest City Stapleton is to keep evolving our sustain-
> ability program no matter what the application, whether it is commer-
> cial, residential or retail. We want to keep seeing those standards and
> those levels of performance increase over time, as Stapleton is a 20-to-
> 30-year project. In terms of residential development, we work in part-
> nership with the builder teams. We provide technical and marketing
> support so that the builders can achieve higher-performance homes
> and are able to share that information with potential homebuyers. Our
> approach is a partnership where we work together so that the builders
> understand how and why certain techniques are better than others. Sta-
> pleton will continue to evolve standards over time. In the early days of
> Stapleton, we started with the Built Green Colorado program. In the last

two years, we've moved to the ENERGY STAR program. I'm quite certain that we'll make another change in the next couple of years. We don't set a standard and then have performance remain at minimum levels, but we keep trying to evolve the level of performance and efficiency that we ask the builders to achieve.

The clear benefit to the homeowner is a high-quality home that is very energy-efficient, saves money over time and is built from the best materials. The more a builder improves their building techniques, the more it's a clear win for the buyer in terms of quality, investment, health and durability.

Homes at Stapleton are tested by a third-party home rating company so that the home is verified to be performing to the required levels. Part of the reason for having third-party verification is not only to assure the homebuyer of the home's quality but also for the protection of homebuilder. The builder can be sure that they are actually getting the performance in a home that they designed and paid for. It's a protection of their investment that they can convey to the homebuyer. Third-party verification is another set of eyes that reinforces the quality standards that the builder was intending to achieve. That additional quality control for the builders is also more protection for the buyers.[23]

Denver, Stapleton, New Town Builders

New Town Builders is one of the homebuilders at Stapleton.[24] Taking a practical approach to green construction is the secret behind New Town Builders' success in the highly competitive Denver market. "Our mission has increasingly become focused on how we deliver great, environmentally responsible homes and neighborhoods without asking our purchasers to pay a premium," says Gene Myers, President and CEO of New Town. "We see it not only as the right thing to do, but also as an important niche for us to fill."

Myers is a big believer in certification programs that emphasize what's called a systems-approach to construction, where aggressive air-sealing combined with a strong insulation package make his homes quiet, comfortable and 50 percent more energy-efficient than many of his competitors. New Town Builders is one of only a few companies certifying its homes under Built Green Colorado, Environments for Living and ENERGY STAR.

The builder is also on the lookout for new approaches to constructing an even better house. "We're just really committed to research and development," says Myers. In addition to doing a demonstration house for the EPA

Figure 6.7. The homes constructed by New Town Builders in Denver's Stapleton project feature traditional neighborhood design details combined with green elements, such as drought-tolerant landscaping and energy-efficient design.

on its new indoor air quality standards, New Town Builders is taking part in the national pilot program for the LEED for Homes certification program. But what may be the company's most innovative idea is building its homes in a prefabricated factory that's located next to the construction site.

"We've partnered with a company called Cohen Brothers Homes who has a patented whole housebuilding system," says Myers. "We are building houses in one piece, in an enclosed environment, and then rolling them out onto their foundations. We hope to get some good market acceptance on this because these houses are really built better, because they're not exposed to the weather during construction like the conventional stick-built house."

While Myers admits that many of his customers don't always understand the extra measures his company takes to build a better house, he says the many letters his office receives from homeowners who say they love their new home and their new neighborhood make it worth it. "You start to feel validated about your values when you realize that what you thought was important to customers actually is."

Westminster, Colorado, Bradburn, New Town Builders

New Town Builders' Bradburn community is a 125-acre village with traditional neighborhood design and smart-growth values. Located 16 miles from Denver in Westminster, the community is oriented around a pedestrian-friendly village core with shops, restaurants, offices and residences. A variety of housing types are represented, including individual homes, townhomes, live/work lofts and row apartment homes. There are nine community parks, two recreation areas, access to 45 miles of trails and a major employment center.

Denver, McStain Neighborhoods, Various Projects

Founder and "mission adviser" Tom Hoyt has a very simple philosophy:

> At McStain Neighborhoods, we really try and look at the long-term, and that comes from being a mission-driven operation to begin with. When a homebuyer is making a decision about what they're going to spend their money on, my advice to them is to try and buy a home that is going to be the best long-term investment from a dollar standpoint. When you do that, and if you really do it right (think long term versus dollars today), you're probably also making the best sustainability decision at the same time. Too often we look at first costs instead of our long-term costs.[25]

Dallas, Saratoga, McGuyer Homebuilders, Inc.

Steve Hayes, division president for McGuyer Homebuilders, Inc. in Dallas, describes the company's EcoSmart program:

> Our EcoSmart program helps us to provide our customers with a healthier, cleaner, more energy-efficient home. It ties together the things we're doing with ENERGY STAR, Green Built North Texas and some of the components that we think we're doing that are better than other volume builders in the market. We created "EcoSmart" because we didn't want to say that we're a "green" builder. That word has become so ambiguous that people don't know what it means. So we created EcoSmart and made sure we branded ourselves with ENERGY STAR and Green Built North Texas to show that this isn't something that we're saying, we have two highly respected entities backing us.
>
> Our homes, under our signature brands — Pioneer Homes, Plantation Homes and Coventry Homes — do cost more to build. At the same time that we're doing this program, we do understand we also have to stay competitive in price. We think that we're able to do both. Our operations have to be tighter to offset the costs of our EcoSmart features, but we think it benefits our customers and us as well.

McGuyer Homebuilders, Inc

Figure 6.8. Texas-based McGuyer Homebuilders, Inc. builds all of its homes under its signature brands — Pioneer Homes, Plantation Homes and Coventry Homes — to the Green Built North Texas standards.

We know our homes are 15 percent more efficient than homes built between 2000 and 2006, and we know our homes are at least 30 percent more efficient than a home built before 2000. We can give buyers specific numbers as far as the cost of electricity bills and the amount of savings and how that allows people to buy a house that may cost a few thousand dollars more. The homeowner will break even quickly, and as the cost of electricity continues to rise, they will be able to save more. It's just a matter of sitting down and looking at the numbers.[26]

Horseshoe Bay, Texas, Skywater, Lakes and Hills Development

Skywater is a 1,000-home master-planned community on 1,600 acres located about 70 miles west of Austin in the famed Texas Hill Country. The 3,000 square foot Stone House (expected to be LEED Gold-certified in 2008) will function first as the sales office, then as a community center. The first homes are expected to be built in 2008. The developer has set aside more than 40 percent of the land as permanent open space. The Summit Rock golf clubhouse, to open in the summer of 2009, will also seek LEED Gold certification. The first phase of the project includes three neighborhoods, with approximately 200 homes on 650 acres. Skywater is the largest master-planned community to focus on encouraging all homes to seek LEED certification through design guidelines and careful attention to orientation and placement on each lot.

Norman, Oklahoma, Ideal Homes

Named "America's Best Builder" in 2007 by the National Association of Home Builders, Ideal Homes offers heating and cooling cost guarantees for its Signature line of homes. Each includes blown-in insulation; high-performance, low-e windows; SEER-14 air conditioners; technologically advanced fresh-air ventilation systems; and third-party testing and validation. For more than 15 years, various research groups have turned to Ideal Homes to test the latest and most innovative building technologies. "From helping families understand the homebuying process so they can make good decisions to safeguard their future, testing emerging technologies and incorporating the best ones into our homes as quickly as possible, to supporting our communities by giving our time and our resources to improve quality of life, we believe companies like ours can and do make a difference," says Vernon McKown, Ideal's founder and co-owner.

South and Southeast

Atlanta, Glenwood Park, Green Street Properties

I visited Glenwood Park in August of 2007 and saw a very fine mixed-use community, with 91 townhomes, 99 single-family detached homes, 138 condominium units and a small (72,000 square foot) commercial and retail sector, all within easy public bus service of downtown Atlanta. Frankly, the only drawback for me was the noisy presence of Interstate 10 just on the northern periphery of the development. There are three builders at Glenwood Park, and they are all committed to achieving the local EarthCraft certification for each residential unit. The average residential unit is about 2,400 square feet, with a total of 328 units on 28 acres; the condominium units range from 600 square feet to 2,200 square feet, making them accessible to first-time homebuyers, as well as families with children and individuals with home offices. The price range — $141,000 to $950,000 — ensures a wide variety of family sizes, incomes and occupations, ideal for an urban infill, mixed-use community.[27]

Kimberly Miller, one of the homeowners at Glenwood Park, speaks of her experience living there. She's an experienced homeowner, having owned six previous homes.

The biggest difference for us living in this home is that we have cut down on water usage to take care of landscaping because we recycle our water. We're getting a definite bonus from having the solar panels; there's a significant chunk taken off our electric bill because we sell power back to Georgia Power. It is so quiet (indoors) because of the extra insulation.[28]

Atlanta Metro, Vickery, Hedgewood Homes

One of the builders at Glenwood Park, Hedgewood Properties, has developed an outstanding suburban community, Vickery, which I also visited. Vickery is very much an instant community, with an elementary and middle school within easy walking distance, a fairly large commercial and retail town center and a full range of housing types and styles. What I particularly liked was the developer's plan to build adjacent homes to look different from each other, which makes the streetscape interesting and varied. As many of you know, there are a lot of new communities where you'd have trouble finding your own home late at night, if you were slightly impaired, so alike are all the residences.

Atlanta/Smyrna, Sherwood Park, Monte Hewett Homes

Situated among pockets of greenspace and a neighborhood pool, Sherwood Park is made up of 57 townhomes and 36 single-family homes. Alley-entry garages, sidewalks, park benches and woodland borders give the entire community an atmosphere of sanctuary and respite, while the conveniences and establishments of the town of Smyrna bustle nearby. Three-story townhomes were priced from $400,000; luxury single-family homes from $500,000. Like all homes built by Monte Hewett, the homes in Sherwood Park meet EarthCraft House construction standards for energy-efficiency, environmental impact and clean indoor air.

Venice, Florida, Venetian Golf and River Club, WCI Communities

With 663 acres of the more than 1,000 acres of landscape devoted to golf course, lakes, wetlands, conservation areas and a 70-acre nature park, the Venetian Golf & River Club was designed for the nature lover. WCI Communities constructed more than 500 homes at Venetian Golf & River Club to meet the Florida Green Building Coalition guidelines. Key green building principles include: passive design, natural materials, indoor environmental quality, energy-efficiency, water-efficiency, water quality, construction waste management, site preservation and landscape planning.

WCI Communities

Figure 6.9. The Venetian Golf & River Club is a Green Development Design Standard certified community according to the Florida Green Building Coalition.

Harmony, Florida, Harmony Development Co.

Located about 40 minutes south of Orlando, Harmony Florida is a master-planned, environmentally intelligent community with energy-efficient homes. There are eight architectural models to choose from, with 1,305 to 6,216 square feet of living space and priced from $180,000 to $1.7 million. Home designs include villas, townhomes, single-family homes and large custom-built manors, all arranged in well-integrated local neighborhoods. Every home in Harmony is built to be ENERGY STAR-compliant, fitted with highly energy-efficient appliances, high-performance windows, tightly sealed duct systems and efficient water heaters. Strategically located within easy reach of every home are parks, full-service restaurants, unique outdoor attractions, hiking trails, lakes and the Town Square.

North Charleston, South Carolina, Oak Terrace Preserve, Noisette

There are about 20 houses built or being built in this neighborhood (as of summer 2007). Ultimately there will be 300 single-family homes and 60 or 70 townhomes. The community itself is built using the New Urbanism premise of a lively streetscape, so these are alley-fed houses. It's also very dense housing, with the average lot 4,000 to 5,000 square feet (8 to 10 units per acre). The homes are all EarthCraft certified.[29] This builder specializes in "back-to-the-basics" proven methods to build a good house that's more energy-efficient. They use a whole-house concept for design, with a smaller air conditioning system because of a really tight building envelope with a high R-value. Their goal is to compete at the same price point as a normal house but deliver one that is more durable, while saving considerable money on a homeowner's energy bill.

Wilmington, North Carolina, Briar Chapel, Newland Communities

At Briar Chapel there will eventually be about 3,000 homes. The master developer, Newland Communities, decided to go with a building science approach that had a green backbone, implementing Environments for Living Platinum level for all homes. The recreation and information facilities will be LEED-NC certified. The community in that area is very earth-friendly, according to Eric Clifton of Newland.[30] "The local residents originally tried to stop the development until they found out we were building sustainably." At Briar Chapel, the individual builders will also be required to choose between the NAHB/National Green Building Program and North Carolina HealthyBuilt Homes programs.

Eastern Seaboard

Front Royal, Virginia, Oden Ridge, Dodson Homes

Dodson Homes is two-generation family business with a hands-on approach. Every home in the Oden Ridge community in Front Royal, Virginia, is built to ENERGY STAR standards. Starting in the low $300,000s, each home will use up to 30 percent less energy than a standard home. Dodson Homes uses a comprehensive quality checklist that includes blown-in cellulose insulation in the attic, an air-stop package, sealed ducts, low-e windows and Tyvek® housewrap.

Glastonbury, Connecticut, Glastonbury Heights, Toll Brothers

Located just minutes from downtown Hartford, Glastonbury Heights is a community of Toll Brothers estate homes situated on wooded home sites in the heart of the Connecticut River Valley. All appliances are ENERGY STAR rated, and ENERGY STAR CFL lamps are used throughout the homes. Toll Brothers uses high-performance insulated windows featuring a 0.34 U-factor (R-3) with dual-pane low-e glazing and argon gas between the panes, which reduces unwanted heat transfer. All exterior penetrations to the home are silicone-sealed. Furthermore, caulking is used where all exterior wall plates meet the subfloor to reduce drafts from the outside. The

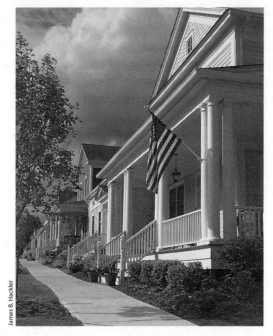

Figure 6.10. New siding materials such as fiber cement combined with special exterior paints mean homeowners at Warwick Grove, New York, won't need to worry about painting their homes for another 15 to 20 years.

direct-vented furnace burns 92 percent efficient. The homes also use water heaters that are 92 percent efficient.

Tuxedo, New York, Warwick Grove, Leyland Alliance

While the architectural details of the new homes in New York's Warwick Grove echo the historic buildings down the street in the village of Warwick, the construction materials and techniques are very much in the 21st century. "It's blending the best available technology and science in a way that we're respecting the environment while creating a real place for people to live," says Lou Marquet, Vice-President of the Leyland Alliance, the builder and developer of Warwick Grove.

Instead of using typical lumber that can warp over time, Warwick Grove uses engineered wood joists and finger-jointed studs that ensure the lines to the homes' 10-foot ceilings; they're also a more sustainable product because engineered wood can use smaller trees and more of the tree than traditional lumber. Another environmental feature of the homes is unvented crawl space where the crawl space's walls are insulated, rather than the floor, which Marquet says helps increase the home's energy efficiency without increasing construction costs. Other energy-saving measures are tankless water heaters, low-e windows and locating the ductwork for the heating and air conditioning system inside the home's conditioned space. "I don't think there's enough consideration given to the savings that you can get if you build a better envelope for the house, I like to think of it as a thermos bottle," says Marquet. "When you encapsulate all your energy equipment inside the conditioned space of the house, the savings are great."

Marquet says what may be the most remarkable environmental feature of Warwick Grove is an innovative bridge with a series of reinforced grates that allow natural light to illuminate the creek and ground underneath the bridge. The natural light encourages wildlife such as the threatened Bog Turtle to feel safe in passing from one wetland to another. Designed by conservation biologist Dr. Michael Klemens, the "Leyland Bridge" is serving as a new model for the New York Department of Environmental Conservation for developments in similarly sensitive areas.[31]

Midwest

Grand Rapids, Michigan, Brookside, Legacy Homes
Located in Ada Township near Grand Rapids, Brookside started four years ago. The original plans included natural open space and green building practices; as the project unfolded, the builder decided to certify the whole neighborhood under the Michigan Green Built program. The neighborhood is situated inside ten acres of conservation. There are 15 lots in total, with 9 or 10 of the homes already built.[32]

Troy, Michigan, Cedar Pines of Troy, Wake Pratt Construction
A Michigan Green Built Community, the homes in Cedar Pines of Troy use an estimated 52 percent less electricity, 54 percent less natural gas and 46 percent less water than traditional homes. Each home is Michigan Green Built and ENERGY STAR certified. Rainwater harvesting, dual-flush toilets, advanced framing techniques, cellulose wall insulation, bamboo flooring and recycled carpet are a few of the green features found in the 17 homes, priced from the high $400,000s.

Maumee/Toledo, Ohio, Deer Valley, Decker Homes
Awarded the Green Energy Ohio (GEO) business of the year, Northwest Ohio's Decker Homes builds 100 percent of their homes to ENERGY STAR

standards. The solar shingles on the demonstration home in the Deer Valley subdivision near Toledo produce about 30 percent of a home's total energy demand. The home also includes a tankless water heater, high-efficiency gas furnace, ENERGY STAR windows, compact fluorescent lighting and a tight building envelope. Each Decker-built home is ENERGY STAR certi-fied, comes with a Home Energy Rating Certificate and is built to exceed the Model Energy Code by at least 25 percent.

Grayslake, Illinois, Prairie Crossing

Prairie Crossing is located about 40 miles north of downtown Chicago. Started in 1987, the development was one of the first in the US to make sus-tainability a core value and planning approach, with a considerable amount of land devoted to conservation. With 359 homes and 36 condominium units on 135 developed acres, the community is not very dense having only three housing units per acre. The single-family homes were built according to the standards of the federal Building America program (aimed at saving 50 percent on annual heating and cooling bills), while the condominium units were built to ENERGY STAR standards, aiming for LEED certifica-tion. Completed in 2007, the project has about 72,000 square feet of mixed-use commercial and retail buildings associated with it.[33]

Canada

In Ontario ENERGY STAR-qualified homes are approximately 30 percent more efficient than homes built to the current minimum Ontario Building Code. The average ENERGY STAR upgrade package costs the homebuyer approximately $5,000, or $34 per month based on a 6.65 percent mortgage (25-year amortization). ENERGY STAR-qualified homes cost less to own since each delivers energy savings (30 percent) in dollars that are greater than the incremental mortgage cost ($34 per month) from upgrading. This means ENERGY STAR homebuyers enjoy positive cash flow on their in-vestment from the beginning.[34]

Since 2006 ENERGY STAR for New Homes and the EnerGuide for New Homes, both created with the Ontario Home Builders Association and the Canada Energy Efficiency Alliance, have effectively replaced R-2000 in Canada's most populous province. On a national basis, the most recent tally is 2,925 ENERGY STAR Canada certified homes,[35] while for R-2000, the most recent tally is 12,160 certified homes in Canada, but few in recent years.[36]

Calgary, Alberta, Acqua + Vento, Windmill Development

The Acqua+Vento condominium development in Calgary was the first multi-family residence to receive LEED Platinum certification in North America. Designed for two sites in a downtown redevelopment area, both three-story condominium buildings take an aggressive approach to environmental objectives. The project's sustainable design initiatives include an enhanced building-envelope design, stormwater collection, graywater recycling, dual-flush toilets and photovoltaics.[36] Each unit is 50 percent more energy-efficient than the Model National Energy Code of Canada and consumes up to 60 percent less water than a typical condo. In each unit, you will find a heat-recovery ventilator; radiant floor heating; R-22 insulation; double-glazed, low-e argon-filled windows; ENERGY STAR appliances; dual-flush toilets; low-flow fixtures and recycled kitchen counter tops.

Langley, British Columbia, Creekside at Yorkson

Creekside at Yorkson in Langley is Canada's first Built Green community. The community developers incorporated strategies to preserve the quantity and quality of water in the local aquifers and to enhance fish habitat creation. The Built Green and ENERGY STAR-certified homes include ENERGY STAR lighting, low-VOC paints and carpets, low-flush toilets, ENERGY STAR appliances, water-wise landscaping and programmable thermostats.

Vancouver, British Columbia, Koo's Corner

Completed in 2002, Koo's Corner is a six-unit townhouse project in Vancouver's historic neighborhood of Strathcona. The project's green features include heat-recovery ventilators, solar thermal water heaters, graywater heat recovery, reclaimed materials and low-VOC finishes and adhesives. This infill project was previously a car repair shop and parking lot. It is located in an older neighborhood, home to artists and creatives, and close to Vancouver's Chinatown district. The units range from 720 to 1,170 square feet and $185,000 to $280,000.

Tillsonburg, Ontario, Gentrac Building Corporation

The Merlot model green home in Tillsonburg, built by Gentrac Building Corporation, includes a 785-watt solar array. The system is "grid-tied" for the purpose of net metering and also has a backup power system, which can supply about three days of power. The 1,530 square foot model green home also features nine-foot ceilings, hardwood and ceramic flooring throughout, granite counter tops and cove moldings, among other luxury items. All of the homes in the subdivision will be ENERGY STAR qualified, and buyers will have upgrade options that include solar power and R-2000 certification.

Ottawa, Ontario, Urbandale Construction

Not only does Urbandale Construction build every home to ENERGY STAR standards, but starting in 2007, all of the Ottawa builder's single-family homes met R-2000 requirements. Urbandale's Smart Choice homes use an estimated 30 percent less energy than homes built to Ontario's standard building code. The company's R-2000 homes include low-VOC paints, Green Label carpets, a fresh-air ventilation system, recycled materials and upgraded HVAC systems and windows.

Mississauga, Ontario, Erin Mills, the Daniels Corporation

Named 2006 ENERGY STAR builder of the year, the Daniels Corporation builds affordable quality homes in their FirstHome Communities. One such FirstHome Community is Erin Mills in Mississauga where the 153 townhomes are priced from the mid $100,000s. Each home is ENERGY STAR qualified, which because of the energy savings will allow qualified homebuyers to arrange a 35-year mortgage amortization and receive a 10 percent mortgage insurance premium rebate.

A State-by-state Listing of Leading ENERGY STAR Homebuilders

Because ENERGY STAR is such a dominant rating system among homebuilders, this section helps you find some of the more prominent homebuilders in each part of the country who participate strongly in this program. These names are only current through the end of 2006, the last full year of reporting by the ENERGY STAR program before this book was written. They include the top ENERGY STAR builders in each state, listed in order of the total number of homes built to ENERGY STAR certification standards. I have excluded military housing, public/affordable housing and Habitat for Humanity projects from this list, since you are not likely to be a candidate to buy these residences.

Pacific Northwest and Alaska

Alaska: Hall Quality Builders; Spinell Homes; J&M Homes
Idaho: Holton Homes; Capitol Building Co.; Shiloh Development
Montana: McCall Development (Billings); only 12 homes total

Oregon: DR Horton (Portland); Palmer Homes; Tom Walsh and Company
Washington: Shea Homes Trilogy; Fort Lewis Communities; Sundt Construction; American Eagle Communities

California, Hawaii, Nevada and Arizona

Arizona: DR Horton; Pulte Homes; Beazer Homes (many other large builders)
Northern California: Pulte Homes; DR Horton; KB Home; Centex
Southern California: Pulte Homes; Pardee Homes; KB Home; Irvine Company; Shea Homes
Hawaii: Actus Lend Lease; Gentry Builders; Betsill Brothers Construction
Nevada: Pulte Homes/Del Webb; KB Home; Pardee Homes; Lennar

Texas, Colorado and the Southwest

Colorado: Engle Homes Colorado; McStain Neighborhoods; Oakwood Homes
New Mexico: Artistic Homes; Thurston Equity Corp.; Charter Building & Development
Texas: Lennar (Houston); Perry Homes JV; MHI/McGuyer Homes; KB Home; Pulte Homes; DR Horton (and a host of other builders with more than 1,000 certified homes)
Utah: Ence Homes; Coral Canyon (Suncor); Destination Homes
Wyoming: Too few to mention

Midwest

Arkansas: Carpenter Construction (all others are very small)
Illinois: Cambridge Homes; Hi-Tech Housing; Saddlebrook Farms
Indiana: Pulte Homes; Centex; Weiss Homes; Southlake Development
Iowa: Regency Homes; Jerry's Homes; Skogman Homes
Kansas: Stitt Energy Systems (none other with any volume)
Michigan: Bosgraaf Homes; Eastbrook Homes; Holwerda Homes; Lombardo Companies
Minnesota: K. Hovnanian; College City Homes; Centex Homes
Missouri: none with more than 10 homes certified
Nebraska: Spring Valley Homes; Schultz Construction; Brighton Construction Co.
North and South Dakota: none with more than 10 homes certified
Ohio: M/I Homes of Central Ohio; Pulte Homes; Beazer Homes (Columbus)

Oklahoma: Ideal Homes; Home Creations; Rausch Coleman Homes

Wisconsin: Veridian Homes; Schmidt Brothers; Lexington Homes; Premier Builders

Northeast

Connecticut: The Metro Construction Company; Toll Brothers; Vigliotti Construction

Maine: none with more than 10 homes certified

Massachusetts: The Green Company; Oaktree Green; Thorndike Development

New Hampshire: Starter Building and Development; North Branch Construction; R.J. Moreau Communities

New Jersey: K. Hovnanian Homes; Ryan Homes; RPM Development; DR Horton

New York: Ryan Homes; Robert Marini Builders; Benjamin-Beechwood

Pennsylvania: R&L Construction; Fine Line Homes/Harrisburg; Pulte Homes

Rhode Island: Starwood/Tiverton; Women's Development Corp.; Northwind Partners

Vermont: Homestead Design; Yandow Dousevicz Construction Corp; Smugglers Notch Corp.; Sheppard Custom Homes

Mid-Atlantic

Delaware: Frank Robino Companies; Carl M. Freeman Companies; Benchmark Builders

District of Columbia: Bozzuto Homes; Bunting Construction; Van Metre Condominiums

Maryland: Bob Ward Companies; Pulte Homes; Grayson Homes

Virginia: Clark Pinnacle Family Communities; Dodson Homes

South and Southeast

Alabama: Hunter Homes

Florida: Cambridge Homes; On Top of the World Communities; Masterpiece Homes; Beazer Homes

Georgia: Haven Properties; Hedgewood Properties; Waterford Homes

Kentucky: Arlinghaus Builders; Actus Lend Lease; B.O.L.D. Homes

Louisiana: no builder with more than 10 certified homes

Mississippi: Florence Gardens

North Carolina: Lennar Carolinas; Anderson Vanguard; Cimarron Homes
South Carolina: Brentwood Homes; Hogan Properties Construction
Tennessee: Goodall Homes & Communities; Grassmeier Homes; Robinson Properties
West Virginia: none

CHAPTER 7

Where Can I Find a Green Condominium?

Many of you want to live in cities, not suburbs or exurban areas. You might be single (of any age), a couple without children, a couple with very young children, or a baby boomer empty nester looking for more access to cultural activities and city life. You may want to live close enough to where you work to actually walk there, or take a nearby bus or streetcar to work. You might like to live close enough to things to bicycle there. There are a host of reasons why people are returning to the cities for the first time in 50 years. You might also want to reduce your environmental footprint by driving a lot less. In 2003 we gave up our second car and decided to do just the things I'm saying here. It's now 2008, and my wife and I still have only one car, even though I'm living in a very spread-out western city. Not everyone has this option, but more people are making the choice to relocate downtown or near downtown in major cities across the US and Canada.

One of the fastest-growing aspects of green homes is the rise of urban condos and apartments that are certified green buildings. We're beginning to see them in New York City, Seattle, Portland, Los Angeles, Boston, San Francisco, Chicago and other major cities that are attracting the knowledge workers of this century's economy. Many of these are rental units (in fact, most of the completed green projects in Manhattan are rentals), but more for-sale condominiums are being built. The speculative excesses of the housing boom hit the condo market especially hard, but developers are now seeing that LEED-certified condos have a promising market advantage. In fact, for much of 2007, one could see very high-end condos advertised in full-page ads in each Sunday's *New York Times Magazine*, with fancy names like The Brampton, all with the notation, "LEED Registered."

I mentioned earlier my experience of living in a LEED Gold-certified apartment building in Portland, Oregon, about two years ago, before I moved to my current home in Tucson, Arizona. Several features of this project really made a difference to me: the bamboo floors, the tight building envelope that made the units very quiet and comfortable, and the low-VOC cabinets, carpets and finishes that meant no new-home smell when I moved in as the first tenant. Best of all, the apartment was non-smoking, a requirement for LEED residences. Occupying 50 percent of the second floor was a green roof that provided a parklike setting above the city streets. This showed me that the LEED certification could indeed result in a healthier, more comfortable living unit.

Portland, Oregon, South Waterfront Development

The same developer that built my LEED Gold apartment also created the first LEED Gold-certified condos on the West Coast in 2003. Since 2005 that developer, along with partners, has been building a series of high-rise condo towers along the Willamette River just south of downtown Portland. This new urban area, with retail, health care, commercial, office and residential uses, built on the site of former shipyards, is called the South Waterfront, or SoWa in the local parlance. Figure 7.1 shows one of the towers, recently certified LEED Gold. They are examples of excellence in design and a lower environmental and energy footprint. In fact the developer built a condominium tower, the 16-story, 61-unit Casey, that aims to be the first such LEED Platinum-certified project in the US. Residents began moving into the Casey in December 2007. "The Casey is a bright green building, which means it sacrifices nothing in terms of either sustainability or lifestyle," says Mark Edlen, managing partner of developer Gerding Edlen Development. "This will be our third completed LEED Platinum building; we're pushing beyond Platinum to develop buildings over the next four years that generate more energy than they use and consume more waste than they produce." Gerding Edlen Development has a total of 40 LEED-certified and pending projects including four Platinum, 23 Gold and 13 Silver, more than any other

Figure 7.1. The South Waterfront Central District in Portland, Oregon, offers "healthy 20-minute living"; the goal is to have everything residents need no more than 20 minutes' walk away. The project, the largest and most expensive redevelopment effort in Portland's history, is transforming a former 130-acre industrial brownfield along the Willamette River south of downtown into a $1.9 billion high-rise neighborhood, as dense as parts of Manhattan, where all of the buildings will be LEED certified.

private developer in the country. The firm is an innovator of cutting-edge, sustainable techniques and is driving change in building codes and standard practices from Los Angeles to Seattle.[1]

Seattle, Florera

Located near Seattle's Green Lake Park, the Florera has the goal of LEED Silver certification for its 59 condos. Fifty percent of the building's energy will be purchased from renewable energy sources. An 18,000 gallon cistern will collect and store runoff stormwater, which will be used for irrigating the courtyard and rooftop gardens.

Charlotte Austin is a student who, along with her mother, bought a unit at the Florera in Seattle. She describes her reaction to finding a really green home to live in:

My mother purchased the unit, actually, with the intention that either one of us could live there. We were looking for a place with a central location; a good community spirit; a clean, bright, happy living space — and, of course, maximum livability. We were attracted to Florera for

Dockside Green

Figure 7.2. Upon completion, Dockside Green in Victoria, British Columbia, a mixed-used harborfront development, will have 26 buildings and about 2,500 people. Not only will all buildings be certified LEED Platinum, but the entire development will be "greenhouse gas positive" by producing more energy than it consumes.

several reasons. At the most basic, of course, it's a great value, feels like an inviting place to call home and is in one of Seattle's best neighborhoods. But honestly, I think the environmentally friendly aspects were probably a deciding factor.

We didn't begin the search with anything specific in mind — we just wanted to see what the options were. Certainly LEED certification wasn't initially a criterion. But after investigating the environmental integrity of Florera, it was hard to get as excited about anything comparable. In the end, it was probably the thing that tipped us over the edge. We're thrilled. I haven't even moved in yet, and I brag about it all the time!

Victoria, British Columbia, Dockside Green

A new 15-acre master-planned community redevelopment waterside project in Victoria, Dockside Green aims to be largely self-sufficient, where waste from one area will provide fuel for another. It will bring many green and sustainable community concepts together, including smart growth, New Urbanism and LEED. Scheduled for first occupancy in January of 2009, the

1.3 million square foot project will include townhomes and condominiums, live/work spaces, a hotel, retail, offices and light industrial uses. Residents will have access to a vehicle-sharing program, a mini-transit system, walking and cycling trails, waterways and onsite amenities. The developer has committed that all project elements will be LEED Platinum certified.[2]

Los Angeles, South Park

In Los Angeles, the South Park development is the first downtown residential development built in the past 20 years, with four planned condo towers. South Park's first complete tower, Elleven, was certified LEED Gold in 2007. Located on the corner of 11th Street and Grand Avenue, this 13-story, 397,000 square foot, mixed-use residential project incorporates lessons the developer learned in Portland, but is designed for southern California. Starbucks is the anchor retail tenant, part of 5,800 square feet of ground-floor retail that activates the street edge. The five townhouses facing 11th Street are designed to accommodate live-work units, adding additional pedestrian-level vitality to the area. There are 124 loft-style residences and a terrace garden, including some private terraces, on the third level above retail and parking. Floor-to-ceiling windows in all units provide spectacular views of downtown. Elleven, the first of a three-phase project, sold out in just two days, well before construction was complete. This building was the first LEED Gold condominium building in California.[3]

Toronto, L Tower

In June of 2007, developers of L Tower, the 55-story Daniel Libeskind-designed condo adjacent to the Hummingbird Centre in downtown Toronto, announced they would aim for LEED Gold certification. Although there are a number of green building guidelines in Canada, including Toronto's own Green Development Standard, LEED has been gathering momentum. For the developer, the LEED Gold process started with a discussion of bike racks when L Tower partners were considering only the lowest level of LEED recognition.[4]

Toronto, Radiance @ Minto Gardens

The 33-story, 377-unit Radiance @ Minto Gardens, LEED Silver, was completed in 2004.[5] According to one analysis, since occupancy began in late 2004, Radiance has used about one-third less energy than similar-sized buildings and has saved its residents about $200,000 a year in common-area energy costs and about $55,000 in water fees.[6]

John Horner, courtesy of Office dA, Burt Hill and Pappas Enterprises

Figure 7.3. The roof of the LEED Platinum-certified Macallen Building in South Boston is covered with flowering plants that will collect rainwater runoff for landscape irrigation. To maintain high indoor air quality, smoking is not allowed anywhere in the building.

North Vancouver, British Columbia

The Silva, a 16-story condominium building completed in 2005, became Canada's first LEED-certified residential building. Project highlights include an attractive living roof designed to capture stormwater; a 50 percent reduction in water use; healthy interior finishes and a number of energy-saving features.[7]

Boston, Macallen

The Macallen Building, a 140-unit development in South Boston, opened its doors to residents in June of 2007. It received a LEED Gold certification, the first in Boston for any development project. The project's unique design is a sloping building, ranging from 6 to 12 stories; there are three levels of below-ground parking and ground-floor retail stores. Owing to its green roof, the Macallen expects to save over 600,000 gallons of water each year. Energy-conscious design expects to reduce overall annual energy use by 30 percent, compared with a similar condo tower built just to meet local codes. The entire building is non-smoking; unique to the Macallen are HVAC systems in each unit that pull fresh air from the outside directly into each unit to maintain optimal indoor air quality. The two-building project has an outdoor heated pool on an 18,000 square foot plaza and an onsite health club.[8] I visited the Macallen in January of 2008 and was really impressed by the high-design quality of the place.

New York City, Riverhouse at Battery Park City

Scheduled for occupancy in 2008, the Riverhouse in Battery Park City is a green condominium tower that is expected to achieve LEED Platinum certification. This 31-story, 264-unit building is considered to be the first finished green luxury condominium in New York City. In addition to 470,000 square feet of condominiums, the site includes 30,000 square feet of retail, the neighborhood's first public library, a health club and an indoor children's playroom, as well as 35,000 square feet of parking. Condominium amenities include filtered air and water, non-emitting carpets and paints, acoustical treatments, triple-glazed windows and roof-top gardens.[9]

The developer aims to achieve New York's first residential LEED Platinum designation, with such features as louvered photovoltaic cells on the roof that maximize solar energy by tracking the sun, ENERGY STAR appliances, a master light switch, dimmers and efficient lighting fixtures, heat pumps with programmable thermostats and triple-pane windows that will make Riverhouse 25 to 30 percent more efficient than the New York code requires. And heliostats, mirrors mounted on a building across the street, reflect sun onto the public park that lies between the building's wings, making it a bright gathering spot.[10]

New York City, The Lucida

Scheduled for occupancy in late 2008 and owned by Extell Development Company, the Lucida is a new 18-story, 110-unit mixed-use building with retail spaces and high-end residential condominiums. It's the Upper East Side's first LEED-certified green residential building. The heating and cooling system consists of water-source heat pumps serving residential units. Indoor air quality is enhanced with filtered outside air centrally supplied into residential units. Energy conservation comes from a variable-speed pumping system, high-efficiency motors, variable-air-volume central air-handling units, a central building automation system and high-efficiency residential heat pumps. The project expects to receive LEED certification.[11]

Figure 7.4. Aptly named Reflections, both of the 17-story towers are clad in a triple-glazed curtain wall that reflects the sky and scenery, allowing the buildings to blend in with their surroundings. The 267-unit LEED-certified project has views of the Minnesota Valley National Wildlife Refuge to the south and the downtown Minneapolis skyline to the north.

Minneapolis/Bloomington, Reflections

In 2007 Reflections at Bloomington Central Station, a multi-unit housing complex developed by McGough Companies, was awarded LEED certification for new construction (LEED-NC). This certification made Reflections the first LEED-certified housing complex in Minnesota and places it among the first LEED-certified, for-sale, multi-unit residential projects in the United States. Consisting of two 17-story glass towers and completed in the fall of 2006, the project contains 282,012 square feet of condominiums and 152,582 square feet of parking. The LEED certification at Reflections was based on a number of green design and construction features, including a high-performance, glass curtain-wall exterior that mitigates noise, provides daylighting and is well insulated to reduce energy costs. Located near light rail, the project is the first residential phase of a 54-acre transit-oriented development. It is also the first suburban development in the region linked to light rail transit. Site development aims to filter stormwater before it flows into the Minnesota River, and landscaping aims to cut irrigation water use by 50 percent.

St. Louis, Gustine Townhomes

The Gustine Townhomes were awarded Gold status under the HBA of St. Louis and Eastern Missouri's Green Building Program and 5+ stars under the Department of Energy's ENERGY STAR program. Two of the four townhomes were built using SIP (Structural Insulated Panel) construction; two were stick-built to allow the builder, Sage Homebuilders, to compare the performance of the two techniques. The three-bedroom, 2,148 square foot homes also include green elements, such as 96% efficient furnaces, PEX manifold plumbing systems (to reduce running time for hot water to arrive at the faucet), tankless water heaters, bamboo flooring, low-VOC paints and native plantings.

Nation's Capitol Region

The Washington DC metro area is home to an ever-expanding number of high-rise condo projects with LEED certification granted or pending, including the following:[12]

- Fairmont Condominiums, Arlington, VA
- 220 Wisconsin Avenue Condominiums, Washington, DC
- Turnberry Tower Condominiums, Arlington, VA; new 26-story downtown Rosslyn high-rise condominium building
- The Alta Condominiums, Washington, DC; the first LEED-certified residential building in DC in 2007
- Palatine Condominiums, Arlington, VA; new 11-story condominium building
- The Hawthorn Condominiums, Arlington, VA; new 9-story condominium with commercial space and parking below, completed 2006
- West Lee Condominiums, Arlington, VA; new 4-story condominium with commercial space and parking below, completed 2006
- The Monroe at Virginia Square Metro, Arlington, VA; new 9-story condominium building with parking below, completed 2006

Atlanta, Oakland Park

Oakland Park is a new 65-unit condominium development that opened in 2007, with units ranging from 688 to 1,244 square feet and priced from $190,000 to $450,000, overlooking historic Oakland Cemetery. The project has attained LEED Silver certification. Consistent with the principles of New Urbanism, Oakland Park is located in a redeveloping corridor where high-density, mixed-use projects are replacing low-density development. The property is located within walking distance to public transit,

Joe Perry, courtesy of Melaver

Figure 7.5. Aiming for LEED certification, Oakland Park features 65 one- and two-bedroom residences in a high-density neighborhood in Atlanta. Low-VOC paint, bamboo flooring, dual-flush toilets, recycled and locally sourced material as well as large operable, low-e windows are included in each unit.

restaurants and shops. Bamboo flooring, Green Label Plus low-VOC carpeting, operable picture windows, EcoCycle recycled porcelain tile, ENERGY STAR appliances, dual-flush toilets and low-VOC paint are a few of the interior features.

Palo Alto, California, Vantage

A 2.0 kW photovoltaic system is included as a standard feature on every unit in the Vantage neighborhood, making it the largest solar-powered residential community on the San Francisco Bay Area Peninsula. The 76 towvnhomes built by Warmington Homes are certified Gold according to Build It Green's Green Points rating system. Located in Palo Alto, the homes range from 1,200 square feet to 1,600 square feet and cost from $850,000 to $1.2 million.

Green Condo Rating Systems

Once a building goes beyond four stories, the only viable green home rating system that works today is the LEED for New Construction (LEED-NC) certification program. It also works for most commercial projects but has been adapted for the peculiarities of the residential market. To get an idea of what goes into a high-rise green home project, let's take a look at the LEED certification for the Elleven project in Los Angeles. Certification

Figure 7.6. The Vantage townhomes in Palo Alto are Gold-certified under the Build It Green, Green Points rating system.

under LEED-NC version 2.1 was granted by the US Green Building Council in September 2007.

To get a LEED Gold ranking, this high-rise condo project did a lot of things right. Let's take a more detailed look at the information revealed in the LEED scorecard.

- Sustainable site development was emphasized. The site is a high-density development, located on a former contaminated site (brownfield) close to downtown, with all manner of transit services nearby. The development provides secure bicycle storage and preferred parking for hybrid vehicles. It treats all stormwater coming from the site, reduces urban heat-island effect with underground parking; uses an ENERGY STAR-compliant roof surface with a green roof and takes effective measures to reduce light trespass from the site.
- Water use for landscape is reduced by 50 percent, typical for an urban infill site, and efficient water fixtures in the condos cut estimated water use by 20 percent.

- Energy use is reduced by 40 percent compared with the then-applicable (1999) standard, the energy-using systems are commissioned by an independent third-party, no ozone-depleting chemicals are used in the HVAC system and the project buys 35 percent of its energy needs from green power sources.
- Construction operations recycled more than 75 percent of all waste and took effective measures to protect indoor air quality (such as wrapping duct work during building).
- Materials used in the project contain a total of 10 percent recycled content, and 20 percent of the materials came from sources within 500 miles.
- Indoor environmental quality is protected with low-VOC paints, sealants and carpet; all residents have individual temperature and lighting controls for all occupied spaces; thermal comfort systems monitor temperature and humidity and there is abundant daylighting in 75 percent of all spaces, with views outdoors from 90 percent of all spaces.
- The project takes innovative measures to promote green housekeeping (such as having a list of approved household chemicals) to protect indoor air quality; all onsite parking is underground to reduce the heat-island effect, and there are educational materials for all residents on green building.

CHAPTER 8

How Can I Pay for a Green Home?

Show Me the Money!

This chapter aims to show you how to pay for some of the features of a green home that may be more costly or represent options or upgrades for which you have to pay extra. The key consideration for buying any green home is to reduce your annual utility bill by 15 percent, 25 percent or more, through a combination of efficiency measures and solar power systems. Let's review some of the ways in which you and the homebuilder can reduce energy use:

- Efficient building envelope: building with greater R-values and a very tight envelope, making ventilation purposeful rather than accidental.
- Efficient glass: buy the best possible windows, with at least double-pane glass, thermally broken frame and low-e coatings. Get a triple-glazed window if you live in a really cold climate. If you can get someone to offer it, go for a double-pane window filled with argon, an inert gas.
- Efficient HVAC system: get a SEER-14 or better air conditioner if you live in a warmer climate. If you plan to stay warm in winter, get the most efficient AFUE boiler or gas heater you can afford. Remember, in most climates in the US and Canada, you'll use a lot more energy for heating than cooling.

- Energy recovery or heat recovery ventilation system: this will help you recover warmth or "coolth" from outgoing air and allow you to get fresh air into the house without a big energy penalty.
- Efficient appliances: we're not talking about SUB-ZERO® refrigerators here, but your refrigerator should be high on the ENERGY STAR scale; after all, it's a heat pump that runs 24/7, unlike any other appliance in the house.
- Efficient lighting: this means CFLs in every high-use area, and even hyper-efficient LED lighting in various places that you might use a lot, such as under kitchen cabinets.
- Efficient water heater: another appliance that runs basically 24/7 unless you get a tankless variety that more builders are offering. Pay up for one if you have a large family.

Now some of these measures might cost more, while others might reduce cost. For example, a more efficient building envelope will reduce heating and cooling energy demand, which should allow the builder to reduce the size (tonnage) of the air conditioner or heat pump, while still increasing its efficiency. Some builders might charge a premium for the energy-efficiency package, while others will simply consider it good business and figure out how to reduce cost elsewhere in the home. Many studies of consumer "willingness to pay" for energy efficiency indicate that you are willing to pay anywhere from $2,500 to $10,000 for a well-documented package of energy use-reduction upgrades, especially those that will result in healthier indoor air quality, more comfort and fewer hot spots or cold spots.

What are the benefits you might claim? First, the direct energy savings might range from $500 to $1,000 per year, or more. Second, there may be direct utility payments. Ask your builder about local electric and gas utility programs that might offer rebates for upgrading to higher-efficiency appliances, HVAC, water heating and lighting systems. Third, look for utilities such as Tucson Electric Power that offer "guarantee" programs to protect you against excessive heating and cooling bills, by capping your total annual bills. Some builders also offer similar guarantees.

Credits and Incentives

Next, look to federal tax credits from the Energy Policy Act of 2005 (EPACT) that is currently good for solar and conservation investments through the end of 2008. (Watch for Congress to act sometime in 2008 to extend this credit until at least the end of 2009 or 2010.) This law provides for 30 percent tax credits (up to $2,000 maximum credit) for each solar thermal (heating/hot water) and solar electric (photovoltaic) system.

Remember this about federal tax credits: they reduce your taxes by one dollar for each dollar of credit. This is far better for you than tax deductions, such as mortgage interest and property taxes, which reduce your taxes by only your marginal tax rate. In other words, if your marginal tax rate is 25 percent, then a federal (or state) tax credit of $100 is worth $100 to you, but a tax deduction of $100 is only worth $25 to you. (If you are subject to the Alternative Minimum Tax [AMT], this analysis may not hold.)

The EPACT provides a 10 percent credit for buying qualified energy-efficiency improvements. To qualify, a component must meet or exceed the criteria established by the 2004 International Energy Conservation Code (including supplements) and must be installed in the taxpayer's main home in the United States. The following items are eligible:

- Insulation systems that reduce heat loss/gain
- Exterior windows (including skylights)
- Exterior doors/metal roofs (meeting applicable ENERGY STAR requirements)

In addition, the law provides a credit for costs relating to residential energy property expenses, which might help offset some upgrades to the property after you move in. To qualify as residential energy property, the property must meet certification requirements prescribed by the IRS and must be installed in the taxpayer's main home in the United States.

The maximum credit for ALL taxable years is $500 — no more than $200 of the credit can be attributable to expenses for windows. That's not a lot of money, but why pass it up?[1] Under the IRS rules, manufacturers need to certify that specific measures are eligible. Homeowners should obtain a copy of this certification from the manufacturer, installer or retailer when buying these products.[2]

Purchasers of highly efficient heating, cooling and water heating equipment can take tax credits of up to $300 for purchasing qualifying equipment, as detailed below. These credits are available for systems placed in service from January 1, 2006, through December 31, 2008. There is a $500 cap on the credit per home, including the amount received for insulation, windows, air and duct sealing as described above.

What types of equipment qualify and for how much?

- High-efficiency gas, oil and propane furnaces and boilers: $150
- High-efficiency fans for heating and cooling systems: $50

- High-efficiency central air conditioning units, including air-source and ground-source heat pumps: $300
- High-efficiency water heaters, including heat-pump water heaters: $300

Where must the equipment be used? Under guidance issued by the IRS, equipment is eligible if installed in a home occupied by a taxpayer as their principal residence at the time the equipment is installed. This implies that equipment in new homes is generally not eligible since in new homes equipment is generally installed prior to occupancy. However, efficient equipment in new homes will help that home qualify for the new home tax credit. If you add this equipment after moving in, you could probably claim the credit, but it will be cash out of your pocket.[3]

Under the same law, if the home achieves a 50 percent reduction in projected energy use for heating and cooling, using the 2004 International Energy Conservation Code (2006 amendments) as a baseline, there is a $2,000 tax credit to the builder. At least 20 percent of the energy savings must come from building envelope improvements. This is a major incentive for the homebuilder to give you a very energy-efficient home. So if your builder is claiming 50 percent reduction in heating and cooling costs, some of the extra costs for conservation upgrades are probably being offset by this federal tax credit.[4]

The federal Tax Relief and Health Care Act of 2006 extended the tax credit deadlines in the 2005 EPACT from the end of 2007 until the end of 2008. In late 2007 Congressional leaders announced plans to extend the credits beyond 2008, but we'll have to wait to find out!

In December 2007 Congress passed the Energy Independence and Security Act of 2007 (EISA) which provided for upgraded appliance efficiency standards and a phase-out of 100-watt incandescent bulbs in the 2012 to 2014 time frame. You should really be looking carefully at how many light fixtures in your new home can accept compact fluorescent bulbs (including the vanity, chandeliers and other areas where CFLs might look out of place) and then replacing them.

Finally, many states offer incentives and direct payments for solar energy systems and energy conservation.[5] State incentives can include income tax credits, property and sales tax abatements, direct rebates, grants and loans. Figure 8.1 shows the number of programs that states offer in each category of incentive. There are too many here to mention individually, so you'll have to do the homework for your state. Many of these incentives may not be applicable to new homes, or may be income-restricted, but you'd benefit by

Figure 8.1. Number of state incentive programs for conservation and renewables

Type of Incentive	Income Tax Credit	Sales Tax Rebate	Property Tax Abatement	Grants	Loans	Rebates
Conservation	13	6	4	53	211	612
Solar	32	26	46	62	93	224

North Carolina Solar Center [online], dsireusa.org/summarytables/FinEE.cfm?&CurrentPageID=7&EE=1&RE=0, accessed December 27, 2007

finding out. Many tax credits have a fairly low ceiling for total credits; check the overall net cost of various systems before deciding. (In chapter 10, I give an example with a solar water heater added.)

For example, in Tucson, Arizona, the local electric utility, Tucson Electric Power, offers a $3,000 per kilowatt payment for photovoltaics, and there is a 10 percent Arizona State tax credit (capped at $1,000) and a 30 percent federal credit (capped at $2,000). For my 1.5 kW, $12,000 PV system, I would receive $7,500 in total payments and credits, so that I only incur a net system cost of $4,500. That's a pretty good deal!

Using Energy Savings to Pay the Mortgage

Once you've taken any direct payments or tax credits for your energy-efficiency and renewable investments, it's then useful to look at how the extra cash from energy savings (we're neglecting water savings here, because they tend to be less than 10 percent of energy savings) can pay off a slightly higher mortgage (assuming your green home costs a little more, which it may not). Figure 8.2 shows an example of how energy savings can pay off a slightly higher mortgage. In this example, an ENERGY STAR home's annual mortgage costs have increased by $108 ($9 per month), but energy savings are $480 per year ($40 per month), so the net annual savings would be $372. Just Google "Energy Efficient Mortgage," and you'll be able to get updated information as more lenders introduce such products over the coming year or two.[6]

Figure 8.3 shows a method that you can use to figure out your own costs and benefits. This calculator deals only with principal and interest costs and excludes taxes and insurance. In this example, we've added $5,000 to the cost of a $300,000 home, assumed a 20 percent down payment and a conventional 6.5 percent, 30-year loan. The savings from the $5,000 investment are assumed to be $60 per month, which is probably a low number.

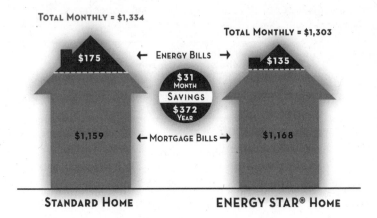

Figure 8.2. Energy savings can help offset higher home mortgage costs for ENERGY STAR homes. *Adapted from Building America's Best Practice Series, Volume 1*

The table shows that the total savings are $35 per month, or $420 per year. If your lender requires your mortgage to be no more than 35 percent of your monthly income, for example, this savings is like adding $100 to your monthly income, without fudging the W-2! If your marginal personal tax rate is 20 percent, then saving $35 per month is like getting a raise of $175 per month. These are not huge numbers (after all $35 per month is just the cost of getting 10 lattes at Starbucks), but they are nice to have, and they increase every year, as utility prices go up.

Energy-efficient Mortgages

The appraisal world still hasn't caught up to the fact that energy savings add value to your home. And with the subprime mess likely to be with us for a while longer, it may be tough even for credit-worthy borrowers to qualify for loans, as lenders tighten underwriting standards. Nevertheless, there are signs that lenders are recognizing energy savings in two ways:

- If you're on the edge of qualifying for a loan, some lenders will allow you to add the energy savings to your income. This so-called energy-efficient mortgage (EEM) is starting to pop up, and the Federal Housing Authority (FHA) does offer one. Lenders may also offer their own and also provide a VA EEM for veterans.
- FHA EEMs allow lenders to add 100 percent of the additional cost of energy-efficiency improvements to an already-approved mortgage loan (as long as the additional costs do not exceed $4,000 or 5 percent of the

Figure 8.3. Calculating the value of energy efficiency

	"Conventional" Home	Energy Efficient Home
Purchase Price	$300,000	$305,000
Down Payment @ 20%	$60,000	$61,000
New Appraisal	—	$305,000
Loan Amount	$240,000	$244,000
Interest	6.5%	6.5%
Principal and Interest (30 years level payment)	$1,517	$1,542
Average Gas and Electric Bill (monthly)	$150	$90 (40% savings)
Energy Savings (monthly)		$60
Monthly Total	$1,667	$1,632
Monthly Overall Savings	—	$35

value of the home, up to a maximum of $8,000, whichever is greater). No additional down payment is required, and the FHA loan limits won't interfere with the process of obtaining the EEM. VA mortgage limits on energy upgrades range from $3,000 to $6,000.[7]

In other words, if you have an already approved FHA loan, you can add costs for energy-efficiency upgrades and not increase your down payment requirement. This allows you to keep your spare cash for the inevitable "hidden" costs of buying and moving into a new home.

The only missing element from this rosy picture is the appraisal industry. Because appraisals are typically based on "comparable" sales in the area or price per square foot, there's no easy way for appraisers to take the energy savings into account, unless the bank you're using specifically tells them to, or makes the adjustment itself. Some lenders are beginning to do just that, particularly if your home is ENERGY STAR certified and you can furnish the HERS rating for the home. In that case, the bank will likely assume that the cost of the improvements will pay for themselves and issue a larger mortgage for the same down payment, in the amount of the added energy-efficiency costs.

The Canada Mortgage and Housing Corporation (CMHC) has a program that offers homebuyers a 10 percent CMHC mortgage loan insurance premium refund and extended amortization periods of up to 40 years without surcharge when you use CMHC-insured financing to purchase an energy-efficient home.[8]

Resale Value

A study in the late 1990s used statistical methods to show that energy savings could add $20 to home value for every $1 of annual energy cost reduction.[9] In other words, saving $500 per year in energy costs could increase home value by $10,000. Interestingly, studies in the commercial market for office buildings are beginning to show similar value increases of $16 to $20 for every dollar increase in "net operating income" from energy cost reductions, so this notion might not be so far-fetched for the residential sector.

When you go to resell your home, you're always competing not just with other pre-owned homes on the market, but with all new ones. If you guess that homebuilders will be rapid adopters of green building, energy-efficiency measures over the next few years, wouldn't you want to have a home that's also certified by a major national program such as ENERGY STAR, NAHB, LEED or EFL? That should give you a competitive edge in the resale market, everything else held equal.

CHAPTER 9

Choosing Green:

Evaluating Home Builder Offerings

I f you've gotten this far in the book, you know just about everything you need to know about choosing green. Now the ball is in your court. Melissa Knott, director of sustainability for Forest City Stapleton in Denver, offers this advice for homebuyers:

> I encourage buyers to educate themselves. The builders need to explain the features in their homes and the buyers need to understand them. Buyers should educate themselves so they can ask smart questions about the house and the features within the house. It's also important to compare the builders that a buyer is considering. My philosophy is that the more that we can educate the buyer market as well as the builder community, the more we will continue to see more progress in high performance homes and green building. We need buyers to ask more questions [about energy use and sustainability], not just get excited about granite countertops, and also get excited about their monthly utility savings. One challenge is that a lot of the sustainability features are hidden in the walls, attic or the basement. But these features will ultimately impact the comfort, durability and cost to operate a house. Buyers should get

interested in these issues, ask questions, become educated and ask for information about sustainability features when they're buying a house.[1]

J. R. Kramer, a homebuyer at the Oak Terrace Preserve project in North Charleston, South Carolina, suggests:

> Do your homework and look at what is truly sustainable as far as energy efficiency. It's stewardship, common sense and making sure you're getting the product that you're promised.[2]

Doing Your Homework

I'm assuming that you'll do a lot of preliminary screening of homes on the Web, so we've included an extensive resource section at the end of this book. You can start by going to the ENERGY STAR website (energystar.gov) and looking for homebuilders who are building to those standards. Their names are listed by state, so it's easy to check out before you get in the car and start driving around. If you have options, the first thing I'd recommend is not to go to any development that doesn't feature ENERGY STAR or other green home certifications that require ENERGY STAR. Chapter 5 has an extensive discussion of certifications that require ENERGY STAR including the NAHB programs, LEED and others.

You might also want to keep up with this fast-changing field by subscribing to one of the magazines listed in the Resources section and by reviewing a lot of the consumer websites that discuss green homes. Give yourself a couple of months, if you can, before you go house hunting, to really dig into the literature and information resources on green homes. You'll need to be an informed and persistent buyer, because many of the salespeople in the model homes or sales offices most likely won't have a clue what you're asking about.

One of the first ways to educate yourself is to find out if a certified home has been labeled by an independent third-party or whether it's self-certified by the homebuilder. You will want to watch out for greenwashing (making environmental claims without justification). For example, it has been known that a builder might certify one home in a subdivision, perhaps the model home, then claim all of the homes as "green homes."[3] If the sales consultant in the model home or sales office doesn't have the answers, make sure they get them for you before you get emotionally committed to a particular home or particular subdivision.

Richard Michal, an engineer, consultant to homebuilders, and former project manager for a major homebuilder, offers some simple advice:

> Buyers should look for energy-efficiency standards and certification. Green homes should be certificated under a recognizable program and preferably a national program such as ENERGY STAR. Buyers who are looking for a green home should start their search on the Web. If developers and builders are committed to sustainability, they are going to market it.[4]

Let's suppose that the builder has certified the home you're interested in buying according to one of the green home rating systems we discussed in chapter 5. You should ask for a copy of the rating scorecard, to see how the home has been rated: is it the highest or lowest or some intermediate ranking in that particular rating system? Then, look at the specific credits or points that the builder has claimed, or been awarded, to see if the things that are most important to you are included in the rating. For example, if you or someone in your family has severe allergies, or asthma, you're probably more concerned about indoor air quality than energy savings and even more concerned about low-VOC paints and carpets. If those issues haven't been addressed by the builder and certified as having been included in the home ranking, you may want to pass on the home. Of course, if the home is being built specifically for you, you can still negotiate to have these key issues addressed.

Many of these requests are absurdly simple and cheap for a builder to include, particularly if your home hasn't been built yet, so don't hesitate to ask for them and don't agree to pay a lot more for them. And get in writing that you'll get proof that everything was done according to this understanding, including labels from the paint cans used and "cut sheets" or other manufacturer's literature from the carpet supplier. If it's important to the sale, the builder should be willing to comply. Richard Michal says:

> Through my consulting work with homebuilders, I discovered a lot of things builders are doing that are green, but they are not taking credit for them. For example, in one development, we discovered that with only an additional $100 cost increase per house, we could build a whole series of homes to the American Lung Association's Health House standards. It required relatively simple, low-cost changes such as using

low-VOC paint and carpet and a few minor changes to other materials and processes.[5]

Alternatively, if you're determined to have solar power in the home, you will want to look at those developments that include solar as a standard feature or as an easily upgradable option. You'll also want to read the codes, covenants and restrictions (CCRs) for the subdivision to make sure that you can install or add to a solar power or solar water heating system in the years ahead. I did this when I moved to my current home in Arizona; interestingly, Arizona law requires CCRs to accept solar energy systems.

Testing Your Own Preferences for a Green Home

In chapter 3, you heard what other people consider important about living in a green home. Now it's time to evaluate your own preferences. We're all different, and one person's reasons just may not work for you; in fact, they probably won't suffice at all.

Figure 9.1 shows some of the many possible reasons for choosing a green home. I've included it so that you could test your own preferences before you set out on your homebuying adventure. A lot of choices will vary by region. For example, in the Northeast, home energy costs (which rely heavily on heating oil) are almost double what they are in Oregon and Washington, primarily because the Pacific Northwest and British Columbia have had an abundance of historically cheap hydroelectric power. The Southwest is predicted to be entering a time of "permanent drought" because of climate change and global warming, so you might have much more concern about water use. If you are a strong environmentalist, you might consider the carbon footprint of a home and include transportation energy use as well as home energy use in your rankings. Finally, if you or someone in your family has allergies or asthma, you might rank indoor air quality the highest.

Since living in a new home is always an exercise in "different strokes for different folks," this table helps you assess your personal preferences, so you can evaluate homebuilders' options before you set out to buy a home. You might even want to make a couple of copies of it and make a couple of passes at it before settling on a family set of preferences. If you have kids old enough and knowledgeable enough, you might invite them to participate.

Here's how to use this table. Rank everything that might be important to you and your spouse or significant other. Establish your joint preferences by talking these things out. Each family is going to be different. Think about features that are good for both you and the environment. Think about how

Figure 9.1. Assessing your preference for green home features/benefits

Green Home Features/Benefits	(a) Personal Preference (Rank in order of importance; 1 = most important)	(b) Spouse/S.O. preference (rank in order of importance; 1 = most important)	Importance to our Family: [(a) + (b)]/2 (lower score is more important)
Energy savings (third-party documented)			
ENERGY STAR appliances			
Water saving appliances			
Low-VOC paints and finishes			
Indoor air quality package			
Low-VOC carpets			
Recycled materials such as carpets and countertops			
Certified wood cabinets and other sustainable materials			
Solar electric power (standard and/or allowed by CCRs)			
Solar water heater			
Close to transit stops			
Walk to work, school or shopping			
Utility guarantee of energy performance (if available)			
Quiet and comfortable (usually associated with energy-efficient, quality construction)			
Open space or parks in the neighborhood			
Other (your choice)			

different features might affect the resale value of your home. And decide if you might want more visible features such as a solar electric system (good to show to neighbors and visitors) or if you might not want the prospective maintenance issues of a feature such as a solar water heater (such as pump replacement). Then take your top three features and use those as a starter

Figure 9.2. Evaluating competing builders' green offerings

Issues	Your Preference (Example)	Builder A (Check ✓)	Builder B (Check ✓)	Builder C (Check ✓)
Certified green, independent third-party	1			
ENERGY STAR certification	2			
E. S. w/indoor air quality Package	3			
Estimated total annual heating and cooling costs	4			
Solar power included	5			
CCRs allow solar	6			
Utility incentives	7			
Tax incentives	8			
Healthy finishes	9			

for choosing which green home developments to look at, including those which might offer one of your choices as an upgrade.

Obviously, if you're buying a starter home, your choices are probably going to be more limited than if you're buying in the upper ranges of local production homes, but my goal is for you to go into the home buying process with a clear understanding of what you want. It's the old saying, "If you don't know what you want, anything will do."

Evaluating Builders' Green Offerings

This is the tricky part of the whole process, as you may well know. How do you compare one builder's offerings against another's? Let's assume that you've already narrowed down the choices, by considering price, location, neighborhood amenities, home size and any other variables of concern to you. Using the preferences you've assessed in Figure 9.1, Figure 9.2 gives you one way to approach the problem. Check off the features offered by each builder according to your preferences. You'll probably come up with others. Taken together, our two tables should help you make a better decision. Figure 9.2 allows you to compare three different homes; as a practical matter, that's probably all you'll end up evaluating seriously, because most people find it hard to choose from among greater numbers.

Figure 9.3. Galleries at Turney LEED Certificate.
Courtesy of Modus Development

What Does It Take to Become Certified Under LEED for Homes?

The Galleries at Turney, an eight-unit, two-story detached townhome development in Phoenix, became LEED-certified (the first of four certification levels) in 2007. To illustrate the process and outcome of LEED certification, here are some of the things this project did, based on the checklist completed by the home energy rating company, Sonoran LEED for Homes. The rater certified 45 points out of 108 available credits, close to the 50 points required for LEED Silver certification.

Mandatory items for this project included the following:

- Site development minimized site disturbance, landscaped appropriately with native/adapted plants and limited erosion during construction
- The irrigation system has a sub-meter and third-party inspection of the main shutoff valve, to avoid wasting water
- To promote indoor environmental quality, the space and water heating systems have closed exhaust and carbon monoxide monitors
- The project meets appropriate standards for outdoor air ventilation and local exhaust
- Supply air distribution and filtering meets best-practices standards; all ducts were sealed off during construction, to exclude dust or moisture
- The garages have no return air ducts (to the house), and all surfaces between the garage and the home are tightly sealed, to keep auto exhaust out of the house
- Material-efficient framing techniques were used, and any tropical hardwoods used were FSC-certified

- No more than 2.5 pounds of construction waste per square foot of home; in this case, less than 4,000 pounds of waste were generated
- This is an ENERGY STAR-certified home with a preconstruction durability plan and windows that meet ENERGY STAR requirements, saving at least 15 percent of annual energy use
- Insulation was HERS Grade I, and the envelope tested at less than 0.35 air changes per hour (8 air changes per 24 hours)
- Duct leakage tested less than 5 cubic feet per minute to the outside per 100 square feet of ductwork
- HVAC systems were sized per the ENERGY STAR required "Manual J"
- Each homeowner received an operating manual and a walkthrough of all major systems.

Those are a lot of good things and represent only the prerequisites! As a smaller home (1,600 square foot townhome), the project received 10 bonus points, since energy use is correlated with home size. Here are some of the additional measures adopted by Galleries at Turney to earn LEED certification.

- ENERGY STAR appliances were provided
- Located within a half-mile of existing infrastructure, the project sits on an urban infill site
- The project location is within a half-mile of public transportation and extensive community resources, and is located within a half-mile of green space
- The average density is greater than seven units per acre (less than 6,000 square foot lot size)
- Because of its location in Phoenix, no turf was used, and landscaping was chosen to minimize water demand
- Permanent erosion controls were installed, and biological pest control methods will be used in site maintenance
- Rain-sensing controls and high-efficiency irrigation systems were chosen and installed to limit irrigation water use
- Timers and automatic controls were added to bathroom fans to promote exhaust of excess moisture
- Advanced framing techniques were used to reduce the amount of wood in the home, and a significant amount of the materials used in the home came from within 500 miles
- The project selected environmentally preferable products to install in the home.

There's a lot more that could be written about the project, but the result was a resource-efficient, quiet, comfortable home with potentially great resale value.

Financing the Purchase

Chapter 8 mentioned how to evaluate the benefit of energy savings and solar power production, in terms of what they might do to increase your ability to qualify for an energy-efficient mortgage. There's no point anymore in having a preferred lender; you really have to shop around for an institution that will respect and support your desire for a green home. Also look for lending institutions that might offer reduced points or reduced interest rates for certified green homes or ENERGY STAR homes. With more than 200,000 such homes built every year, most lenders should consider this a large enough market for which to craft special loan products. As many of the fly-by-night mortgage brokers go out of business because of the home-building recession, and with the remaining lenders hungry for quality home loans, the odds should steadily increase in your favor in 2008 and 2009, so ask for it!

CHAPTER 10

After the Sale:

What Can You Do
to Make the Home Greener?

The reality is that most of us are going to have to compromise on some issues even when we buy a green home. We've suggested that you carefully review the builder's green home checklist and note those items that you wish had been put in the home, but weren't.

Hopefully, when you move in, the home will be energy-efficient and comfortable, with good fresh air ventilation and a carefully pressure-tested and balanced clean duct system. Still, there will be green items you want in the home that the builder either won't or didn't include. So it will be up to you to take further action to green your living space. This chapter briefly presents some of those choices and opportunities. It assumes that you have reserved some money for upgrades after the sale. This means you might be doing something "un-American" like buying a home you can actually afford, leaving some financial breathing room. If there is one lasting benefit from the financial crisis of 2006 and 2007, I think it is that we have all learned that we need to be more conservative in our homebuying choices. Instant gratification can turn so quickly into instant mortification, as our individual circumstances change or as ARM rates reset to higher levels.

So first of all, don't "un-green" your green home by doing things that might make it less healthy. Here are some things to watch out for.[1] According to the experts, there are seven steps to a healthy home. A healthy home is:

- Dry: there's no excess moisture sources anywhere, including humidifiers, and fans wherever water is used.
- Clean: cleanliness is next to godliness for sure, and a clean house is not inviting to dust mites, spiders, etc. (This means to clean/change your HVAC filter often.)
- Well-ventilated: fresh air needs to get into the house, even in winter or summer, and stale air needs to leave as fast as unwelcome guests.
- Combustion-product-free: this means that anywhere something is burned, such as natural gas or wood fires, you must get the stale air out of the house right away.
- Pest-free: you don't want uninvited nature in the house.
- Toxic-chemical-free: if it smells like a chemical or a perfume, it probably shouldn't be in the house, so get rid of the Lemon Pledge and all that other stuff you can buy at the supermarket and look long and hard for natural substitutes.
- Comfortable: there shouldn't be unwanted drafts or dramatically cold or hot windows.

How you live in your home affects each of the seven steps. As the authors of this report comment, "Comfort, no pests and good indoor air quality go hand in hand." I can tell you from my own experience that what your mother may have taught you about good housekeeping isn't necessarily so. First of all, get rid of all — or most — of your housekeeping chemicals. If you must use some of them, keep them in the garage and then ventilate the heck out of the house when you do use them. Fortunately, in our house, my wife has severe chemical allergies, so any cleaning product with a chemical odor or perfume just isn't used.

Saving Water

You should have bargained with the builder for a small monetary credit against the conventional toilets that are typically installed, so that you can change out the conventional flush toilets (1.6 gallons per flush) to dual-flush (0.8/1.6 gallons per flush). If you weren't able to get that done when the home was built, try replacing the toilets during the first year with something like Kohler's new Persuade or other manufacturers' dual-flush offerings. Typically, a local plumbing wholesaler with a retail showroom can

Figure 10.1. Kohler's Twin Touch flushing technology on each Persuade toilet could save up to 4,000 gallons of water per year for a family of four. *Photo courtesy of Kohler Co*

order these for you. You can usually call up a local thrift store that supports a nonprofit, as we did, and they'll come out and gladly take the toilet away and sell it to someone. You'll be saving about 2.4 gallons per day per person (assuming three light flushes vs. one heavy flush), so with two people in the home, that's 1,750 gallons of water saved per year, with no sacrifice of health or comfort.

Since far more water is used outside the home in irrigation than inside the home, you should also be looking at the landscaping package. If you were lucky and your local homeowners' covenants allowed it, the builder was able to install drip irrigation and drought-tolerant native and adapted plants for landscaping, with a minimal amount of turf. Most Americans are just learning the joys of not mowing the lawn every Saturday and anointing it with fertilizers and weed killers on a regular basis. Try to bargain for a better landscaping package; perhaps you can even trade a drip system with more extensive shrubbery for a new lawn the builder might offer.

There is also the opportunity for rainwater harvesting.[2] It's a fairly easy job to cut an opening in the downspouts from your home's gutters and divert the rainfall into barrels or tanks. Depending on the location of the home and the landscaping needs, you might want to collect rainwater, get a small pump and use the stored water for irrigation. You can collect a lot of rainwater in a hurry from even a half-inch rainfall. Imagine you have a 2,400 square foot home so that half the roof is 1,200 square feet. Using half the roof, a half-inch of rain will deliver 50 cubic feet (374 gallons) of water to a storage barrel. You can line up a series of 400-gallon (for example, 4 feet tall and 4 feet wide) rain barrels in a side yard, then camouflage them with vegetation, drawing out the water as needed for watering a vegetable garden or trees and shrubs. If you have a summer with occasional rain, then you can pretty much avoid irrigation. On the West Coast, with dry spells from May through October each year, holding enough rainwater for a summer's irrigation might take too much storage space, so you'll have to settle for reducing consumption somewhat. In the Southwest, with storms mostly in July and August, you'll have a lot of irrigation needs from April through early July that will have to be met with stored winter rainwater (two inches in Tucson, or about 1,600 gallons in my case) until it runs out.

While we're on the subject of landscaping, you might remember the discussion of passive design techniques from chapter 2 and ask the builder to put shade trees near the south- and west-facing windows, especially deciduous trees that are either more mature (larger) or fast growing, so that you can avoid the high summer sun coming in those windows while still allowing the lower-angle winter sun to penetrate. (In Arizona, Florida, south Texas and other really hot summer regions, you'd be well advised to put shading on east-facing windows as well, since rooms on that side of the home really heat up by mid-morning.) You'll also be saving on replacing drapes or other window coverings that will fade rapidly if exposed to the summer sun. If this type of tree-planting didn't happen during the home construction, try to get those trees put in during the first year of ownership, so they'll have a chance to grow up and shade those windows before too many cooling seasons have passed. You might want to buy larger, more mature trees to jump-start the process. You'll save money on cooling, and the home will be more comfortable as well during the summer.

Saving Energy

When buying the home, you have maximum bargaining power, particularly as long as homebuilders are struggling for sales, a situation that will last probably well into 2009, as they try to work out "excess inventory overhang" and other financial issues. Try to get upgrades of a higher SEER-rated air conditioner (I recommend upgrading to a SEER-17) and higher-efficiency boilers, furnaces and water heaters, along with the most energy-efficient appliances that are part of the standard package. It's not uncommon to find close to 95 percent efficient furnaces and boilers, instead of the 80 percent efficient units you may find as the default.

You can't easily change the structure of your home, but you can ask for vinyl or wood-framed windows instead of aluminum to increase the energy efficiency and comfort of even dual-pane, low-e windows. If you're in a region with a severe winter (and even with global warming, these winters are likely to persist for the life of the house), ask for triple-pane, low-e coated windows, and see if you can get them, particularly in a house that is going to be built after you commit to the purchase. (This may require some design changes to the window openings.)

If you don't have one, consider buying a programmable thermostat, an easy upgrade that will cut your energy use. And of course, keeping filters clean and equipment well-maintained represent important ways to lower your energy bills.

Producing Energy

Now it's time to get the solar energy systems you need. If you followed my advice in the previous chapter, you found a home in a subdivision where the CCRs don't discriminate against rooftop solar power systems. In that case, supposing the builder didn't offer a solar package, try to get an experienced local installer to put solar in while tax and utility benefits are still prevalent. For example, I installed a 1.5 kW solar PV array and a solar water heating system early in 2008 in a Tucson home I bought in 2006, that was originally built in 2000. Here's what I'll pay, on a net basis:

Figure 10.2. Benefits of residential solar installation, assuming you can use all of the tax credits

Total system installed cost	$16,500[3]
Less tax and utility benefits:	
Federal tax credits	($3,500)[4]
Arizona tax credit	($1,000)[5]
Tucson Electric Power Rebate	($4,500)[6]
Net cost to homeowner	$7,500

I'm estimating $375 per year in savings on energy costs, so the payout is still 20 years at current energy prices. However, more important than the five percent tax-free return on investment, I'll be making a visible and positive statement about the benefits of solar power that I hope will convince many of my neighbors to do the same. Your own local situation may be different; not all utility payments are as generous as mine, but some states such as Oregon and New York may offer even more generous tax credits for solar power, and the federal tax credits for solar PV and hot water are good nationwide.

Figure 10.3. Portland General Electric (PGE) clean power purchase options

Option	Renewable Power Source	How the Option Works	Customer Cost
Green source	100 percent renewable power from new wind, geothermal and biomass sources.	100 percent of your monthly usage is offset with renewable resources.	Your regular PGE energy rate plus an additional $0.008 per kWh.
Clean wind	100 percent renewable power from new wind power sources.	Available in 200 kWh units (each unit represents about 20 percent of your monthly usage).	An additional $3.50 per 200 kWh unit — you can purchase as many units as you wish.

Portland General Electric [online], portlandgeneral.com/home/products/renewable_power/Default.asp?bhcp =1, accessed December 30, 2007

Buying Green Power

One final thought on producing energy. Suppose you don't want to install solar power, can't get the homeowners' association to go along or can't afford it right now. You can still buy green power from most utility companies, by paying a monthly premium of $5 to $15, depending on the amount you buy and the sources. For example, Tucson Electric Power offers two GreenWatts packages: 99 percent wind/1 percent solar, or 90 percent wind/10 percent solar, with two different prices. For my home, I pay $15.50 per month for 200 kWh of clean power. This is quite expensive compared with the program offered at Portland (Oregon) General Electric (PGE). It offers two options: a broad-ranging renewable power source or a "clean wind" program, at the above costs. Both sources represent renewable-power plants that became operational after July 1999.

So if you use 9,600 kWh per year (800 kWh per month), under the first option you'd pay $76.80 per year and under the second option you'd pay an additional $168 per year, but you'd be supporting only wind-power plants. Interestingly, in 2006 PGE had the second-highest total national consumer purchases from its green power program, surpassed only by Austin (TX) Energy, and had the fourth-highest (percentage) participation rate in the country.[7] However, as of late 2007, only 500,000 customers nationwide were participating in green power programs, so there's still a strong need for your involvement.

Downsizing Your Ecological Footprint

According to experts in ecological footprints, humanity as a whole uses the equivalent of about 1.23 Earths annually for its activities.[8] In fact, based on 2003 data, the average American uses more than five Earths, the average Canadian more than four Earths.[9] In other words, the average American consumes 400 percent more resources than what the planet can regenerate from its annual solar income. The problem is, we've only been issued one Earth. We support our lifestyle today by mining the planet's renewable and non-renewable resources, a situation that can't last indefinitely. For the long-term health of the planet, reducing our energy use particularly will reduce our global ecological footprint.

Thinking about the overall health of the planet's life-support systems, you can see that there's more to living a healthy lifestyle than just reducing the energy and water use of your home. Hopefully, you've been able to find a home in a walkable community, or you've bought a condo in an urban in-fill project, so that you can take public transit to work or walk to many of your daily errands. If not, you can do other things to reduce your ecological footprint, or the total impact of your daily activities. Here are some suggestions.

What You Can Do at Home

Recycling

You've probably read lots of articles about becoming more environmentally conscious around the home. At my house, we recycle everything we can, even the inner cardboard rolls from paper towels and toilet paper! But there are all kinds of new recycling opportunities to consider, including batteries, fluorescent bulbs and consumer electronics.

Traveling

If you travel a lot, you can buy carbon offsets from a number of organizations that have sprung up to offer them. With your offset money, these groups buy wind-power capacity, plant trees and invest in solar power. When I went to Australia in 2007, I bought Green Tags from the Bonneville Environmental Foundation to cover the carbon dioxide emissions from 15,000 miles of air travel.[10]

Buy a Hybrid Car or Use Biodiesel in Your Car or Truck

If your current car is ready for replacement, consider buying a hybrid car, or even not replacing it if you can manage without it. There are still models with lots of wonderful federal tax credits left, and you'll amaze yourself and your friends when you push the mileage monitoring button and see 35 to 40 miles per gallon fuel use. If you typically buy 500 gallons of gas per year, you'll now be buying about 300, not only saving money but beginning to reduce your ecological footprint. In 2007 I bought a Honda Civic hybrid and got a $2,100 federal tax credit. It's a great car, and gas mileage to date is about 39 miles per gallon.

What You Can Do at Work

Subsidize Transit Use

If your company doesn't use hybrids or support employees' public transit use, get the company leaders on board to do this. Many cities and states have programs that offset the costs of transit subsidies.

LEED Certify Your Office

If your company is going to move to new office space, insist on a LEED-CI registered (and certified) project for the tenant improvements. If you company plans on a new building, start talking up the idea of a LEED-certified building.

Get Creative with Sustainability

Through an arrangement with a manufacturer, one building engineering firm (and a former employer of mine) with about 150 employees in Portland offers a program to subsidize the installation of dual-flush toilets in employees' homes, each saving about 4,000 gallons of water per year.[11] The same firm has bought four Honda Civic hybrids for travel to client meetings and job sites and subsidizes 60 percent of the cost of public transportation for employees, which has led to nearly 80 percent participation in the program.

Of course, one of the easiest things you can do is to set up a recycling program at work, including paper, corrugated cardboard, glass, plastic and metal. As part of this program, buy mugs for everyone with some inspiring message and get rid of all Styrofoam coffee cups. There will be less trash and a subtle message at every meeting.

Large Companies Go Green

If you work for a large corporation, you might be surprised at how many incentives will be offered in the coming years for you to "go green." For example, early in 2007, the Bank of America offered a $3,000 cash rebate to any of its 185,000 employees who bought a hybrid car.[12] Many companies are offering transit subsidies, participation in local car-sharing programs (so you can get home in the event of an emergency), showers and bicycle lockers for bicycle commuters and similar measures to keep you from driving to work alone in a car.

Greening the Government, School District or University

If you work at a government agency, university or school district, see what you can do to affect its design, construction, remodeling and purchasing policies. There's nothing an elected official, planning commission member or senior civil servant likes more right now than to look good by instituting a sustainability policy. The mayors of over 800 of America's largest cities and more than 300 college and university presidents are on-board to take action to slow climate change.[13] They're going to be looking to their staffs to come up with practical proposals to implement this commitment. Even if you're a student, many college and university student bodies are taxing themselves to pay for the extra costs of running the student union on renewable energy or of building a new student recreation center or student union as a green building.

CHAPTER 11

What's in Store for Green Homes

S uppose you're just not ready to buy a new home now, but you're interested in buying a green home in the future. Where are we headed? Here are a few educated guesses. First of all, I predict that the green home market is going to grow rapidly and become a dominant part of the homebuilding market by 2010.

Richard Michal, a former homebuilder and a consultant to homebuilders, says:

> In my opinion, green building, especially residential green building, is not a question of if, but when. This is the future. In my consulting work with builders, I recommend that they get ahead of the curve and use green building measures. There is still time to take advantage of positive public relations. The alternative is to wait for the regulations and then have to play catch-up. I think a lot of the energy-efficiency, water conservation and indoor air quality measures will eventually be mandated. The secret to sustainability is 90 percent efficiency. Remember the mantra: Reduce, reuse and recycle? This should also apply to building and construction and is ultimately good for business. All builders, and businesses in general, want to reduce waste and minimize costs. Everyone

is hot to trot about technology. Technology, such as photovoltaics, is a great tactic but I consider technology last. Instead I think homes should be designed to reduce energy demand by increasing efficiency.

Looking out to 2010

Looking to the end of 2010, we could see as many as a million ENERGY STAR, NAHB, LEED and other green-rated homes under the various programs outlined in this book. My guess is that there will be a few strong regional programs, such as Earth Advantage in Oregon, EarthCraft House in Atlanta, Austin Energy and Tucson Electric Power. There will likely be only three national programs: ENERGY STAR, the National Association of Homebuilders National Green Building Program (scheduled to start up in 2008) and the US Green Building Council's LEED for Homes system. General Electric's ecomagination^{SM} support of the Environments for Living program might find some marketplace acceptance, but I doubt it. So my advice is to keep your eyes on these three national rating systems and possibly one strong local program. As always, "Think blue, then green," meaning ENERGY STAR certification should always be your bare minimum for even considering a new home investment.

The next likely change is in the environment for financial and tax incentives. I hope to see continued federal support for solar power systems, for builder energy-efficiency investments and probably for other forms of energy conservation, although the 2007 energy bill from Congress did not extend these provisions beyond the end of 2008. Local governments and utility programs will also add to the mix. Utilities in many states will be pushed harder by state regulators to offer a large variety of conservation and solar incentive payments. States may extend existing energy tax credits and property tax abatements to green homes, with new tax benefit programs each year, so it pays to keep checking.

These programs and incentives will all have a net effect of encouraging builders to offer more energy-efficiency measures in homes and more solar-powered homes. As local governments start to pursue climate-friendly incentive programs, you can expect them to give incentives to builders to build green homes, especially by offering accelerated development and permitting approvals to green-rated housing developments.

The likelihood of stronger Congressional action on global warming means that by 2010 there could likely be a national building code for energy efficiency that will raise the baseline for all homes to be at least 15 percent more efficient than the ENERGY STAR homes of today, i.e., 30 percent more efficient than a typical 2004 model home. More builders will figure out how to meet these accelerated and aggressive goals without incurring additional costs or raising home prices. This is where all the good work in building science will come to the rescue. As several of the interviews in this book have clearly indicated, we know how to build better homes; *it's up to you, the homebuyer, to demand that type of performance from anyone from whom you choose to buy a home.* If you speak loudly and forcefully, at the point of sale, they will respond.

The environment for home loans and appraisals is also likely to change, with almost all major lenders (at least, once we get out of the subprime mortgage default crisis) offering energy-efficient mortgages, some with small reductions in loan rates, others with greater consideration of energy savings in determining your ability to meet mortgage payments (especially for first-time buyers who might be stretched a little thin.) Look for "green home loans" to become a major marketing tactic of home mortgage lenders in the years ahead.

For you, the homebuyer in 2010, these changes will likely add up to having more choices among green homes, among neighborhoods and price ranges and housing styles, in more regions of the US and Canada, and with more of today's options offered as standard features by builders eager for your business. You should expect annual savings from $500 to $1,000 on home energy bills in almost every situation. Of course, some builders will construct to the 50 percent more-efficient performance level, and your savings will increase accordingly.

Zero-net-energy (Z0NE) Homes

If I had to make a somewhat surprising bet, it would be that there will be more standard homes offered that will have zero-net-energy use, incorporating 2.5 kW to 5.0 kW solar power systems, along with solar water heating and a host of energy-efficient appliances. I call these "Z0NE" homes, for Zero-net-energy. These homes will likely have "smart" monitoring and control systems that will allow you to know instantaneously (inside the home) which appliances and gadgets are on at any given time, so that you can control your energy use much more efficiently. In the warm to very hot climates of the Sunbelt, we're likely to see automated and programmable shades and shutters that help keep the sun out during the hot summer periods, cutting your air conditioning load. These same devices work in winter as storm windows, cutting your heating bills as well. There will also be much more-efficient air conditioning units (look for SEER-17 to become the norm in

Clarum Homes

Figure 11.1. Clarum Homes built four zero-net-energy demonstration homes 85 miles north-east of San Diego in the Sonoran Desert, one of the hottest places in the US. Four different combinations of energy features and three types of wall systems were used. The builder plans to collect data and study the results to determine the cost-effectiveness of sustainable technology for affordable, entry level and one-move-up homes.

many warm to hot climates) and builder-adopted elements of building science, such as placing ducts only in conditioned spaces.

The concept of zero-net-energy buildings and neighborhoods is quickly capturing the attention of many green building designers and even some homebuilders. A zero-net-energy building would be one that provided all of its own energy on an annual basis from onsite renewable resources or off-site renewable energy purchases. In this way, it would still be connected to the grid, providing power when it had a surplus and drawing from the grid when it needed power, such as at night or in the winter.

This ZONE home approach typically involves using solar energy for electricity and water heating and possibly for space heating, employing such design measures as passive solar design, natural ventilation, operable windows and other means for space cooling (with some electric power assist). In practice, a completely energy-independent building is quite achievable at the household level and with small buildings. Much depends on the local microclimate; indeed, if one thinks about it, all homes in the world were zero-net-energy before the Industrial Revolution, powered only by renewable fuels such as wood; so there are many sources of indigenous architecture for inspiration!

In the high desert east of San Diego, California, in partnership with the federal Building America program, Clarum Homes has built four zero-net-energy demonstration homes in the town of Borrego Springs. These are constructed with green building products, generate their own electricity with photovoltaic (solar electric) systems and reduce energy consumption by up to 90 percent with other energy-efficient features such as on-demand hot water heaters, radiant roof barriers, energy-efficient HVAC, tight duct-work, increased insulation and low-e window systems. The project's goals are threefold:

- Design and build highly energy-efficient sustainable production hous-ing for the entry-level and one-move-up market, including achieving up to 90 percent energy reduction in cooling energy use
- Build energy-efficient homes with highly sustainable characteristics while meeting earthquake Zone 4 structural requirements (the toughest standards)
- The 2,000-square-foot homes all have exterior shade screens for the hot desert sun and a 3.75 kW solar PV system. Three different wall systems are being used, along with three cutting-edge cooling systems.[1]

Based on a number of demonstration homes being built, operated, tested and evaluated around the US, we can expect to see more production build-ers incorporating the results of these projects into what will become their standard green homes of 2010.

A single-family home in Paterson, New Jersey, certified at LEED for Homes Platinum level in 2006, shows how one home can move toward the goal of zero-net-energy. Called the BASF Near-Zero-Net-Energy home, it includes expanded polystyrene insulation, polyurethane foam sealants and cool metal roof coatings to reduce typical energy use by 80 percent.[2]

In December 2006, the UK government announced a program for zero-carbon new homes: by 2016 all new homes in UK are to be zero-carbon emitters, with a 25 percent improvement on energy use on current build-ing regulations by 2010 and a 44 percent improvement by 2013. A 100-home project near London, the BedZED (Beddington Zero-Energy Develop-ment), set a goal of becoming carbon-neutral, cutting carbon emissions by 56 percent through energy-efficiency measures and an onsite solar photo-voltaics system.[3]

On a larger scale, in March 2006 the World Business Council for Sus-tainable Development announced that it is forming an alliance to develop zero-energy buildings. They have an ambitious target: by 2050, all new buildings in the world will consume zero-net-energy from external power sources and produce zero-net-carbon-dioxide emissions while being eco-nomically viable to construct and operate.[4]

How likely is this to happen? It's up to you, the homebuyer or prospec-tive buyer, to visit the large number of Z0NE demonstration homes that are likely to be built by more adventurous builders over the next few years,

Gridley & Graves

Figure 11.2. The BASF Near-Zero-Net-Energy home in Paterson, New Jersey, is a prototype for the USGBC's LEED for
Homes rating system. The home is 80 percent more energy-
efficient than a conventionally built home, owing to radiant
floor heating, a 2.5 kilowatt solar electric system, a 4-kilo-
watt solar thermal system and energy-efficient design.

in cooperation with local utilities and often state and local government
energy-efficiency programs.

Here's what one builder in the Denver Metro area, McStain Neighborhoods, does to push the envelope of new technology, according to founder
Tom Hoyt:[5]

> One of the most significant ways in which we stay on top of technol-
> ogy is doing what we call a Discovery Home. We bring all of the experts
> together and ask, What is out there that we haven't tried and should?
> We pick a particular neighborhood that we're building in and do a Dis-
> covery House where we incorporate a bunch of new technologies. We
> screen the big list down to a number of things and try a bunch of stuff
> there and see what works. We'll find out if a contractor really can build
> it economically and effectively. Although we sell the Discovery Homes,
> we retain the right to monitor them over a two- or three-year period. So
> we're testing for effectiveness and durability.
>
> For example, in the last Discovery Home, we were looking for a bet-
> ter way to construct insulated structural slabs and allow for hydronic
> heating potential in the slabs while avoiding mold issues. These have

been important issues in our marketplace because we have expansive clay soils here, and you have to be very careful about how you do basement slab work. We pioneered a whole new foam support system for slabs which have traditionally been done out of cardboard and wood. They would rot underneath the slab and potentially create mold problems. The new system was clearly superior and did not encounter construction issues, so we put it into production and it's part of all our homes now.

Let the Sun Shine In!

Solar power technology is headed for major influence on our world. Consider for a moment that the total weight of silicon used in solar cells in 2008 is expected to surpass the silicon used for all of the world's microprocessors; in other words, solar power is becoming cheaper, more ubiquitous and more accepted with each passing year. Consider that utilities in many states will have to meet accelerated "renewable portfolio standards," which will effectively mandate that by 2020, 10 to 20 percent of their total annual electricity generation must come from sun and wind. This will mean that utilities will be offering major incentives to builders to put solar power systems onto south-facing rooftops of most new homes, even in colder, cloudier parts of the country, such as Portland and Seattle, Detroit and Boston, Minneapolis and Bozeman. You are likely to see larger and cheaper solar systems on new homes, each with the potential to put power back into the grid on weekdays when you're at work or play, the kids are in school and there are few appliances working except your ultra-efficient ENERGY STAR refrigerator (also running 24/7.) By 2010, tens of thousands of green homes are likely to have solar PV as a standard feature, as well as solar hot water systems.

A Final Word

We started out this journey by showing you the importance of buying a green home, then helping you figure out what that meant and then showing you where you might find one for sale. The last chapter encouraged you to think more broadly about your personal situation and how you might create a healthier, lower-environmental-impact lifestyle. As many have remarked, sustainability is not a destination, but a journey. We're all in this together. I wish you the best of luck on your own green home-buying journey and hope you will succeed at it. I hope also that you will continue to show the leadership and take the actions needed by your family and your community for a more ecologically responsible society.

Glossary

Advanced framing: Home construction techniques designed to reduce the amount of lumber used and waste generated in the construction of a wood-framed house. Advanced framing techniques improve a home's energy efficiency and create a structurally sound home with lower material and labor costs than a conventionally frame house. Additional construction cost savings result from reduced waste disposal, which also helps the environment. Advanced framing actually replaces lumber with insulation material to maximize the wall area that's insulated, which improves the whole-wall thermal resistance or R-value.

Annual fuel utilization efficiency (AFUE): The ratio of annual output energy to annual input energy, measures efficiency of gas furnaces and boilers. The higher the percentage, the greater the efficiency of the appliance; for example, standard furnace efficiencies run from about 75 percent to 82 percent, while higher-efficiency furnaces have 90 percent or over AFUE.

Bamboo flooring: A member of the grass family, a bamboo plant can mature in as few as three years, making it a rapidly renewable material. Extremely hard, strong and attractive, bamboo is frequently used as a wood substitute in flooring. Much of the bamboo imported into the US and Canada comes from China.

Blower door test: A device for testing the airtightness of a home, a blower door test determines the air infiltration rate. A powerful fan is mounted to the frame of an exterior door and pulls air out of the house, lowering the air pressure inside. An air-flow meter measures the amount of outside air that flows into the house through any unsealed cracks and openings.

BTU (British thermal unit): A basic measure of thermal energy. The term BTU is used to describe the heat value of fuels as well as the power of heating and cooling systems. Technically, a BTU is the amount of heat required to raise the temperature of one pound of water by one degree Fahrenheit. A typical home gas bill comes in therms, each of which represents 100,000 BTU.

Building envelope: The building envelope is the "skin" of a home. A major factor in the energy efficiency of the home, the building envelope is responsible for proper ventilation, protection from the outside elements and moisture control. It consists of the structural materials and finishes that separate the inside of the home from the outside, including windows, walls, doors, roofs and floor surfaces.

Building science: The study of how a building's systems function together under various environmental conditions in an attempt to achieve an ideal balance of comfort, health and safety. Building science assesses heating and cooling systems, energy efficiency, ventilation and humidity control.

Carbon footprint: The measure of the impact human activities have on the environment in terms of the amount of greenhouse gases produced, measured in equivalent units of carbon dioxide. One use is to conceptualize an individual's or organization's impact in contributing to global warming. There are many online tools to calculate your personal carbon footprint.[1]

CCRs: Codes, covenants and restrictions (CCRs) are guidelines that define the rules of subdivisions for both the homeowners association and the homeowners. Read the CCRs to make sure they don't prohibit solar panels or rainwater harvesting systems; some states (such as Arizona) now forbid them from unduly restricting solar panels.

Cellulose insulation: Insulation made from recycled newspaper. Cellulose insulation is treated either with sodium borate, boric acid or ammonium sulfate. All have been deemed safe for humans and make the insulation fire-retardant.

Certified wood: Wood certified as sustainably grown and harvested by the Forest Stewardship Council. Forests are critical to maintaining life on Earth, and certification helps to protect ecosystems from destructive logging practices. All FSC-certified wood carries a "chain of custody" that tracks each piece of wood from the forest to the consumer.

Cistern: A receptacle designed to catch and store rainwater, usually from a roof or some other catchment area. Cisterns can be placed underground, at ground level, on elevated stands outdoors and even on rooftops. The harvested water typically goes to non-potable uses such as irrigation.

Compact fluorescent lamps (CFLs): Energy efficient alternatives to standard light bulbs, CFLs use about one-third the power (watts) for the same amount of lighting output (lumens) and typically have a longer life than incandescent bulbs. If every household replaced its most commonly used incandescent light bulbs with CFLs, electricity use for lighting could be cut by two-thirds. Doing so would lower our annual carbon dioxide emissions in the US by about 125 billion pounds. This action alone could halt the growth of our carbon dioxide emissions, at least for a period of time.[2]

Cork flooring: Harvested from the bark of the cork oak tree, cork is considered a rapidly renewable material because it has a much faster rate of renewal than hardwoods. Cork can be harvested every nine years from the same tree. It also does not contain vinyl and other synthetic materials that release toxic fumes (VOCs). Most cork used in the US and Canada comes from Portugal.

Construction waste recycling: The separation and recycling of recoverable waste materials generated during construction and remodeling. Some materials can be recycled directly into the same product for reuse; others can be reconstituted into other usable products. An estimated 8,000 pounds of waste are typically thrown into a landfill during the construction of a 2,000 square foot home.

Double-glazed windows with low-e coating: A window with two layers of glass separated by an air space. The glass and the space between them trap some of the heat that passes through. Low-e coatings are microscopic layers of metallic oxide bonded to the surface of window glass that prevent heat and ultra-violet rays from passing through the glass. Note that without adequate "thermal breaks," even these windows will not work very well. In hot climates, the low-e coating works to keep heat out of the house; in cold climates, it helps to retain heat in the house.

Duct blaster test: A method to test for air-tightness of the ductwork. Using a calibrated fan to pressurize the duct system, the rate of airflow out of the ducts is used to determine the duct tightness. Leaky ducts can be a significant source of energy inefficiency in homes.

Dual-flush toilet: A toilet that offers two flushing options in terms of the amount of water used, typically either 1.6 or 0.8 gallons. The user can choose a small flush for liquid waste or a big flush for solid waste.

Energy-efficient mortgage (EEM): An EEM allows borrowers to qualify for a larger mortgage because energy-efficient homes have lower operating costs. Therefore, home-buyers can afford to spend a little more on their mortgage loan because they will likely spend even less on monthly utilities.

Energy modeling: A method of using computer software to simulate the energy use of a home over the course of a typical year. Energy modeling is used to optimize building design in terms of a home's energy use. It can also be used to reduce the size of an HVAC system, by proving that there is less demand for heating and/or cooling than from a typical home.

Energy-(or heat-) recovery ventilation: A method of ventilating a home with minimal energy loss. Unlike a typical bathroom or kitchen vent fan, an energy-recovery ventilator utilizes a mechanical heat exchanger to capture the warmth (or coolness) to preheat (or precool) incoming fresh air before it reaches the furnace (or air conditioner). In winter, a recovery ventilation system can recover and reuse up to 85 percent of the heat from the exhaust air.

ENERGY STAR®: A voluntary, government-backed labeling program that promotes energy-efficient consumer products and homes. Developed in 1992, ENERGY STAR helps businesses and consumers easily identify energy-efficient homes, buildings and products such as major appliances, office equipment, lighting and home electronics.

Formaldehyde (in building and remodeling products): Formaldehyde is a suspected human carcinogen used frequently in the manufacturing of building materials and numerous household products. In homes, the most significant sources of formaldehyde are likely to be sawdust or wood-chip products made using adhesives that contain urea-formaldehyde (UF) resins. Pressed wood products made for indoor use include particleboard (used as sub-flooring and shelving and in cabinetry and furniture); hardwood plywood paneling (used for decorative wall covering and used in cabinets and furniture); and medium-density fiberboard (used for drawer fronts, cabinets and furniture tops).

Graywater: Wastewater that is filtered and reused for irrigation. Graywater comes from dishwashers, showers, sinks and washing machines and makes up 50 to 80 percent of residential wastewater. Some states prohibit re-use of graywater.

Green power: Renewable energy, typically solar or wind power, produced somewhere else and purchased by the home usually through a local utility program. Green power should be certified by recognized national programs such as "Green-E."

Greenhouse gases: Chemical compounds found in the Earth's atmosphere that absorb infrared radiation and trap heat in the atmosphere, including carbon dioxide, methane, nitrous oxide and chloro-fluorinated hydrocarbons. Some greenhouse gases occur naturally while others are created and emitted solely through human activities. Increased emissions of greenhouse gases appear to have increased the average temperature of the Earth over the past half-century. Rising temperatures produce changes in weather patterns, commonly referred to climate change.

Greenwashing: A term used to describe the actions of an organization that tries to make itself appear to be more environmentally friendly than it really is. The term is typically used to accuse corporations of making false claims of environmental responsibility.

Ground-source (or geothermal) heat: A technology that uses the natural heat storage capacity of the earth or groundwater to provide energy-efficient heating and cooling. In winter a ground-source heat pump moves heat from the earth into a home; in summer it pulls heat from your home and returns it back into the ground, cooling the home.

Harvested rainwater: Rain channeled by gutters to a storage tank for use in landscape and vegetable garden irrigation.

HEPA filter: HEPA (high-efficiency particle-arresting) filters remove tiny pollutants from the air flowing through the home's air handler. They are rated up to 99 percent efficient in the removal of most indoor air pollutants.

Indoor air quality: Gases or particles released into the air such as mold spores, radon, carbon monoxide and toxic chemicals are the primary cause of indoor air quality problems in homes. Indoor air quality is directly related to a home's ventilation and moisture management design. Combined with inadequate ventilation, pollutants in the home can lead to poor indoor air quality and can compromise health, safety and comfort.

Infill development: The process of developing vacant or under-used parcels within existing urban areas that are already largely developed, with existing infrastructure. Successful infill developments locate where overall residential densities are high enough to support improved transportation choices and a wide variety of convenience services and amenities.

Insulated concrete form (ICF): Highly insulated, poured-in-place walls that significantly reduce heating and cooling loads. The key concept is to place the insulation on the outside of the concrete in a form and to pour the concrete into the forms. Expanded polystyrene (XPS) is a typical material used for the forms.

Inverter: An electronic circuit that converts direct current (DC) created from PV panels to alternating current (AC). Connected to a photovoltaic system, the inverter allows the solar-generated electricity to be used by standard appliances or to flow directly into the grid.

Kilowatt (kW): A unit of electrical power, typically used for photovoltaics. A 1 kW PV panel will product about six to 10 kilowatt-hours of electrical energy on a bright, sunny, summer day.

Kilowatt hour (kWh): A unit of electrical energy, 1,000 watt-hours. For example, a light bulb rated at 100 watts, burning for ten hours, will consume one kWh of energy, typically costing consumers 8 to 15 cents in the US and Canada.

Light-emitting diode (LED): A tiny light bulb illuminated by a computer chip. LEDs produce about two times as much light (lumens) per watt as compact fluorescent bulbs, with an extremely long lifespan (100,000 to 1,000,000 hours). They emit far less heat than incandescent bulbs or CFLs, so they don't require as much cooling to overcome the heat gain.

Low-e glass: *See double-glazed windows.*

Low-flow faucets and showerheads: Low-flow fixtures reduce water flow by increasing water pressure and mixing air with the water as it comes from the tap. You can purchase low-flow fixtures for as little as $10 each and achieve water savings of 25 to 60 percent from faucets and showerheads.

Native or adapted plant landscaping: Native plants have evolved over thousands of years in a particular region and provide a beautiful, hardy, drought-resistant, low-maintenance landscape while benefiting the environment by providing food and shelter. Once established, landscaping with native plants saves time and money by eliminating or significantly reducing the need for fertilizers, pesticides, water and lawn maintenance equipment.

Net metering: Net metering allows you to get credit, at retail rates, for power produced by a PV system, in effect running your meter backwards. When power generated is greater than your home's consumption, you effectively get a refund!

New Urbanism: A movement in community design based on principles of planning and architecture that work together to create compact, walkable communities. New Urbanist communities consist of both commercial and varying types of residential properties, generally located near a major transportation hub, and are designed to segregate traffic from pedestrian walkways.

Off-gassing: The evaporation or emission of volatile chemicals at ambient atmospheric pressure. Building materials such as paints, stains, sealants, varnishes, carpet, insulation, flooring, kitchen cabinets, countertops, plywood, particleboard and paint strippers can release chemicals into the air causing poor indoor air quality.

Passive cooling and heating: A strategy in home design to increase ventilation and retention of heating/cooling within building components, using thermal mass (concrete, tile or stone) to store/release heat or coolness for later use. Typically these homes also have overhangs to keep out summer sun and well-placed windows to let in winter sun. They may also use deciduous trees and other vegetation for summer shading of windows.

Photovoltaics (PV): Solar panels mounted on the roof (less typically on the ground) to collect solar radiation and convert it to electricity that can be used immediately, using an inverter, or stored in batteries for future use, or fed back into the electric grid.

Post-consumer recycled materials: End-products made up of consumer recyclables, such as office paper, cardboard, plastic bottles and aluminum cans, that otherwise would have been disposed of in a landfill. For example, carpet made from recycled plastic bottles, gypsum wallboard from recycled sheetrock and recycled paper.

Pre-consumer recycled materials: End-products are made up of recyclables generated by manufacturers and processors of materials such as scrap, trimmings and other by-products that were never used in the consumer market; for example, recycled glass countertops.

Programmable thermostat: A thermostat that automatically adjusts the temperature settings at various times throughout the day based on occupancy and usage. Once programmed, the thermostat can, for example in the winter months, automatically decrease the temperature at a predetermined bedtime, increase it in the morning and decrease it again during the day when no one is home. A programmable thermostat that reduces the temperature by 10 to 15 degrees for eight hours a day can save you as much as ten percent a year on heating and cooling bills.

R-value (of insulation): The R-value indicates resistance to heat flow (by conduction). The higher the R-value, the greater the insulation's effectiveness. The R-value is the inverse of the U-value that measures how readily a substance conducts heat.

Radiant barrier: Materials that are installed in buildings to reduce summer heat gain and winter heat loss and therefore reduce energy required for heating and cooling. Radiant barriers typically reflect infrared (heat) radiation and are usually put in roof decking.

Radon: A cancer-causing natural radioactive gas that you can't see, smell or taste, radon comes from the natural decay of uranium. It typically moves up through the ground to the air above and into your home through cracks and other holes in the foundation. Your home can trap radon inside, where it can build up. Proper ventilation is the key to keeping radon levels low inside the home. Radon is found only in selected areas of the US and Canada, so please do check for this potential hazard if you're moving into an unfamiliar area.

Renewable energy: Energy resources, including solar and wind power, that are constantly replenished and will never run out. They can be used directly in residential applications or purchased through utility green power programs.

SEER (seasonal energy-efficiency ratio): A rating method used to evaluate air conditioner efficiency and reduce energy use. The SEER rating correlates to the amount of energy input needed to provide a specific cooling output. A SEER of 13 is code-required, but a SEER of 17 is better.

Solar water heater: A device or combination of devices used to harness energy from the sun to heat water. A solar water heating system usually consists of a hot water storage tank, a solar collector that absorbs solar energy, a pump and controls. Most homes with solar water heaters have a backup system such as electricity or gas.

Sprawl: Suburban and rural home development which leads to the spreading out of cities, mostly over agricultural land. Sprawl leads to a loss of prime farmland, loss of wildlife habitat, increased air and water pollution, increased water and energy use, degraded and noisy surroundings and social fragmentation. There is increasing evidence that sprawl also leads to obesity, as people drive more and walk less.

Structural insulated panels (SIPs): High-performance building panels used in floors, walls and roofs. SIPs are typically made by sandwiching a core of rigid foam plastic insulation between two structural skins of oriented strand board (OSB).

Sustainability: According to the Bruntland Commission of the United Nations (1987), sustainability is "development that meets the needs of the present without compromising the ability of future generations to meet their own needs."

Tankless water heater: Instantly heats water when it is needed without the use of a storage tank. A gas burner or an electric element heats water as it runs from the pipes to the fixture. As a result, there is a constant supply of hot water because there is no need to wait for a storage tank to refill.

Therm: A unit of heat energy equal to 100,000 BTU, typically used by gas utilities to measure the amount of natural gas used in the home.

Third-party certified: A home that has met certain recognized green building standards, as evaluated by a person or organization independent of the homebuilder.

Tight construction: A method of building a house that minimizes the amount of penetrations (gaps, holes and leaks that can occur during framing, wiring and plumbing) in the building envelope and seals those penetrations. Tight construction can improve the energy efficiency, air quality and comfort of a home.

Transit-oriented development (TOD): An approach that aims to create a compact, walkable community that includes both residential and commercial districts centered around a high-quality public transportation system. TODs reduce the need for driving and therefore are part of the global warming solution.

U-Value : Inverse of R-value. Typically used mainly for glass, a U-value of 0.33 is equivalent to an R-value of 3.0. It's used to rate and compare exterior building components. such as windows, doors and skylights, but not exterior walls. U-values rate the energy efficiency of the combined materials in a building component. The units of U-value are BTU/sq.ft./°F/hour.

Vapor barrier: Placed between the interior side of the exterior surfaces and the insulation (and also between the subfloor and the insulation), this impermeable material prevents passage of moisture through walls and floors. Vapor barriers need to be very specific to given climatic conditions. A newer term is "vapor diffusion retarder," since there are few absolute barriers to moisture flow.[3]

Volatile organic compounds (VOCs): Gases that evaporate from building materials and home products, such as adhesives, sealants, paints, varnishes, carpet, furnishings, office equipment and upholstery, can cause acute and chronic illnesses and lead to poor indoor air quality.

Xeriscape: Landscaping design that decreases (or eliminates) water use and requires less maintenance than traditional techniques, such as lawns. Using thoughtful planning, design methods, soil improvements, appropriate plant selection, practical turf areas, efficient irrigation, mulches and appropriate maintenance, xeriscape techniques can produce a beautiful landscape that conserves water and protects the environment.

Zero-net-energy home (also "Net-zero" home): A home with an average net energy consumption of zero over a typical year. A zero-net-energy home is usually connected to the grid and uses energy from the local electric utility when it is consuming more electricity than it is producing. For example, a home with a large-enough PV system may produce more electricity than it uses on most sunny days. The system inverter sends the remainder back to the utility to offset the amount purchased from the utility on cloudy days or at night. That way the grid becomes the "storage battery" for the home.

Resources for Further Study

Books

Most books are outdated shortly after they are published in this fast-changing green building field. Nevertheless, there are a few that have some degree of shelf life, even now. You might find them interesting, some perhaps life-changing.

Kari Foster, Annette Stelmack and Debbie Hindman. *Sustainable Residential Interiors*, New York: Wiley, 2006.
Basing their approach on an integrated design process, Associates III, a leading interior design firm in Boulder, Colorado, with expertise in addressing environmental concerns in homes, presents solutions for the residential interior designer.

Eric Corey Freed. *Green Building and Remodeling for Dummies*, Hoboken, NJ: Wiley, 2008.
As advertised, this new book is a "hands-on, practical guide to the materials and construction methods of green building." You'll find lots more technical and practical detail about green homes than we were able to include in this book.

Jo Allen Gause, ed. *Developing Sustainable Planned Communities*, Washington, DC: Urban Land Institute, 2007.
If you want to understand how developers plan sustainable communities, this beautifully photographed book, with contributions by industry experts, will help you understand if you want a home in such a community. Ten very well-written case studies lend credibility and usefulness to this book.

Jennifer Roberts. *Good Green Homes*, Salt Lake City: Gibbs-Smith, 2003.
While this lavishly illustrated book is oriented more at people who want to build their own home, there's a lot of good information here to help you with your green home search.

Godo Stoyke. *The Carbon Buster's Home Energy Handbook*, Gabriola Island, BC: New Society Publishers, 2007.
One of the few books I've seen that can help a homeowner make sense of all the fuss about reducing one's carbon footprint. It helps to have a bit of a technical bent, as there's lots of detailed numerical information here.

Paul Scheckel. *The Home Energy Diet*, Gabriola Island, BC: New Society Publishers, 2005.
No matter how good a green home you buy, there's always room for reducing energy consumption, especially since nearly half of home energy use comes from appliances

and lights, things you can control. This book systematically walks you through the process.

Alex Steffen, ed. *World Changing: A User's Guide for the 21st Century*, New York: Abrams, 2006.
It's hard to know what to say about this nearly 600-page compendium of everything we know about green solutions, except that you need a copy in your library for reference.

Sim van der Ryn. *Design for Life: The Architecture of Sim van der Ryn*, Salt Lake City: Gibbs Smith, 2005.
The subtitle gives away the book. This is the story of Sim's life work, told brilliantly, movingly and from a very personal perspective. Sim's work has influenced thousands of sustainable designers. If you're thinking about designing your own home after all, this book should give you lots of ideas and insights from a decidedly non-traditional viewpoint.

Alex Wilson. *Your Green Home*, Gabriola Island, BC: New Society Publishers, 2006.
This is a great primer for anyone considering building a new home and wanting to make it as green as possible, probably the best overview of these topics.

Jerry Yudelson. *Green Building: A to Z: Understanding the Language of Green Building*, Gabriola Island, BC: New Society Publishers, 2007.
This is the best introduction to the language of green buildings, written for both residential and commercial uses. Includes introductory material about the importance of green homes and green buildings, as well as 108 well-defined terms. Definitely a great companion to this book, if I do say so myself!

Publications

It's hard to keep up with the proliferation of green home magazines and related publications. Here are a few publications I read on a regular basis and find valuable for staying in touch. Most of these are available both in hard-copy and electronic versions, so if you're averse to having too much paper around, you can keep up with the news via the electronic editions and related online newsletters.

Dwell: At Home in the Modern World, dwell.com
This is the classic modern home magazine focused on high design. Good coverage of green homes with a focus on custom homes and leading-edge ideas. (Maybe you do need that Sub-Zero refrigerator after all!) Well-written and illustrated, a great coffee-table magazine.

Ecological Home Ideas, ecologicalhomeideas.com
A consumer quarterly filled with good ideas for living in a green home.

eco-structure magazine, eco-structure.com
Technically a trade magazine, *eco-structure* is the best illustrated, with a lot of easy-to-read case studies and a broad selection of topics that make it a good way to keep up.

Environmental Building News (EBN), buildinggreen.com
EBN is simply the best-edited and most relevant publication for green builders. The monthly feature stories keep you abreast of emerging issues in green building design,

construction and operations. Quite a bit of coverage of residential design, construction and maintenance issues.

Green Builder Magazine, greenbuildermag.com
This monthly magazine for the members of the National Association of Home Builders is essential reading if you want to know what this audience is learning about green buildings.

Home Energy Magazine, homeenergy.org
A fairly technical magazine on energy-efficient home design and home improvements, this journal is accessible to the serious homeowner as well as anyone with good technical understanding.

Natural Home, naturalhomemagazine.com
This is probably the best consumer magazine for green living in a green home. Very approachable by anyone interested in a healthier, more ecologically sound lifestyle.

Renewable Energy World, renewable-energy-world.com
A lavishly illustrated, technically accurate (without being off-putting) journal from the UK, it covers the spectrum of renewable energy developments. Best of all, it's free.

Smart Homeowner, smarthomeownermag.com
This consumer magazine focusing on innovative solutions for creating healthy, eco-friendly homes is well-written and very accessible.

Solar Today, solartoday.org
This official publication of the American Solar Energy Society is written for a general audience. You can even find it at the checkout counter of natural foods stores, as well as in most chain bookstores.

Sustainable Industries Journal, sijournal.com
Gives great coverage of the West Coast's developments across a wide range of sustainable industries, including green homes. Short articles, easy to read and available in electronic edition.

Ultimate Home Design, ultimatehome.com
This monthly provides great coverage of the emerging field of universal design, to which homebuilders should be paying a lot more attention. Also covers home theater systems, for some odd reason. Short articles, easy to read and available in electronic edition.

Websites

Choosing Green
choosinggreenbook.com
This is the website we've created to keep the information in this book up-to-date. It will debut in the fall of 2008.

Green Building Initiative
thegbi.org
This is the official website for the Green Globes rating system, with a strong residential focus. You may register and download a trial version of the system.

IGreenBuild
igreenbuild.com
This is a good overview website of the business and product side of the green building movement.

National Association of Homebuilders, National Green Building Program
nahb.org and nahbrc.org
At this site, you may download the green home rating system preferred and currently used by most homebuilders and homebuilder associations.

Sustainable Buildings Industry Council (SBIC)
sbicouncil.org
The SBIC is a leading national educational organization focused mainly on green homes and high-performance schools. Its residential green building guidelines came out in a fifth edition in 2007.

US Green Building Council (USGBC), Green Home Guide
greenhomeguide.org.
The USGBC website is the premier website for the green home movement and the LEED for Homes rating system. Launched in November 2007, it has an impressive array of features.

US Environmental Protection Agency, ENERGY STAR program
energystar.gov.
The essential site for learning about ENERGY STAR ratings for products, homes and buildings, with lots of great free information you can use to assess the energy performance of your home.

World Changing
worldchanging.com.
Emerging innovations and solutions for building a brighter green future; an essential site if you want to know what's going to be a mainstream concern in short order.

Local, Regional and National Green Building Programs

Beyond LEED for Homes and the NAHB Model Green Home Guidelines, many other green home rating systems are profiled in this book. For further information about some of the more prominent systems, see these websites.

Arlington County Green Home Choice Program
arlingtonva.us/Departments/EnvironmentalServices/epo/EnvironmentalServicesEpo
GreenHomeChoice.aspx

Austin Energy
austinenergy.com/Energy%20Efficiency/Programs/Green%20Building/Sourcebook/index.htm

Boulder Green Builder Guild
bgbg.org/

Build a Better Kitsap, WA
kitsaphba.com

Build San Antonio Green
buildsagreen.org

Builders Association of the Hudson Valley Green Builder Program
hvbuilder.com/Hudson_Valley_Green_Builder.asp

Build it Green (California only)
builditgreen.org/index.cfm?fuseaction=guidelines

Built Green Colorado
builtgreen.org/homebuilders/default.htm

Built Green Washington Checklists
builtgreen.net/checklists.html

California Green Builder Certification (CA Building Industry Association)
cagreenbuilder.org

City of Boulder Green Points Program
bouldercolorado.gov/index.php?option=com_content&task=view&id=208&Itemid
=489

City of San Jose Green Building Program
sanjoseca.gov/esd/natural-energy-resources/greenbuilding.htm

ConSol ComfortWise (rater for California Green Builder)
consol.ws/comfortwise.html

ENERGY STAR
energystar.gov/index.cfm?c=new_homes.nh_features

Earth Advantage
earthadvantage.com/builders/

EarthCraft
southface.org/web/earthcraft_house/ech_main/ech_guidelines.htm

Environments for Living
eflhome.com/index.jsp?action=fl_progchecklist

Frisco, Texas, Residential Green Building Standards
ci.frisco.tx.us/Projects_Programs/Green_Building/index.aspx?id=155

Florida Green Building Coalition Home Standards
floridagreenbuilding.org/db/?q=node/5360

Florida Power & Light Build Smart Program
fpl.com/doingbusiness/builder/build_smart/buildsmart_program.shtml

GE ecomagination Homebuilder Program
ge.ecomagination.com/site/index.html#echm/details

Greater Cleveland Green Building Coalition
clevelandgbc.org

Green Building Association of Central Pennsylvania
gbacpa.org

Green Building Initiative (National Program)
thegbi.org/home.asp

Green Building Initiative, Central Ohio
biahomebuilders.com

Green Building Initiative, Central Washington
cwhba.org

Green Building Initiative, Columbia, SC
columbiagreenbuilders.com

Green Building Initiative, Dallas, TX
thegbi.org/residential/featured-projects/dallas

Green Building Initiative, Durham, NC
thegbi.org/residential/featured-projects/durham

Green Building Initiative, Houston
thegbi.org/residential/featured-projects/houston

Green Building Initiative, Indianapolis
bagi.com

Green Building Initiative, Interior Alaska
thegbi.org/residential/featured-projects/interioralaska/default.asp

Green Building Initiative, Keystone, PA
thegbi.org/residential/featured-projects/keystone

Green Building Initiative, Little Rock
hbaglr.com/index.asp

Green Building Initiative, Long Island
libi.org

Green Building Initiative, Maryland
homebuilders.org

Green Building Initiative, Missoula, MT
buildmissoula.com

Green Building Initiative, New Mexico
thegbi.org/residential/featured-projects/newmexico

Green Building Initiative, Northeast Ohio
thegbi.org/residential/featured-projects/northeastohio

Green Building Initiative, Rochester
rochesterhomebuilders.com

Green Building Initiative, Southern Nevada
thegbi.org/residential/featured-projects/southernnevada

Green Building Initiative, St. Louis
thegbi.org/residential/featured-projects/stlouis

Green Building Initiative, Utah
thegbi.org/residential/featured-projects/utah

Hawaii Built Green (self-certification checklist)
bia-hawaii.com/subpage.asp?section=70

Health House/American Lung Association
healthhouse.org/build/index.asp

High Performance Home 100
hph100.org/about/
The High Performance Home 100 is a public-private partnership of 100 local governments, associations, corporations and individuals that are working in the Rocky Mountain West to effect market transformation to high-performance homebuilding standards.

Homes Across America
homes-across-america.org/

Kansas City Green Building Program
kchba.org/buildgreenkc/Forms/Forms.shtml

Memphis EcoBuild Program:
mlgw.com/SubView.php?key=about_ecobuild

NAHB Guidelines
nahbrc.org/greenguidelines

New Jersey Housing Resource Center Green Building
state.nj.us/njhrc/owners/develop/dev_green.html

North Carolina Healthy Built Homes Program Checklist:
healthybuilthomes.org/builders_and_developers.cfm

North Texas Green Built
dallasbuilders.com/displaycommon.cfm?an=1&subarticlenbr=400

Portland (OR) Office of Sustainable Development Residential Guidelines
portlandonline.com/osd/index.cfm?c=41591

Scottsdale Green Building Program
scottsdaleaz.gov/greenbuilding

Seattle Green Residential Building
Single-family: cityofseattle.net/dpd/GreenBuilding/SingleFamilyResidential/
BuildingProfessionals/default.asp
Multi-family: cityofseattle.net/dpd/GreenBuilding/MultifamilyResidential/
Overview

Southern Nevada Water Authority. Water Smart Home Program:
snwa.com/html/cons_wshome.html

Telluride Residential Green Building Checklist
town.telluride.co.us/home/index.asp?page=311

Vermont's Building for Social Responsibility Certification and Checklist
bsr-vt.org/vermontbuiltgreenprogram.html

Washington State Dept. of Ecology's Sustainable Building Toolbox
ecy.wa.gov/programs/swfa/greenbuilding/

Western North Carolina Green Building Council
wncgbc.org

Wisconsin Green Built Home
greenbuilthome.org/builder/index.php

Canadian Resources

Canada Green Building Council
cagbc.org
The Canadian counterpart of the US Green Building Council. Lots of great free resources. More members per capita than even the USGBC.

Canada Mortgage and Housing Corporation
cmhc-schl.gc.ca/en/
Lots of quality information and technical resources for cold climates for both builders
and homebuyers/owners.

EnerGuide for Houses
energuideforhouses.gc.ca
Introduction to EnerGuide for Houses, an energy evaluation service developed by the
Government of Canada to improve the comfort and energy efficiency of Canadian
homes. An initiative of Natural Resources Canada's Office of Energy Efficiency.

ENERGY STAR Canada
oee.nrcan.gc.ca/energystar/english/consumers/index.cfm

Natural Resources Canada, R-2000 Standard
oee.nrcan.gc.ca/residential/personal/new-homes/r-2000/standard/standard.cfm?
attr=4

Additional Resources

ACEEE Consumer Guide to Home Energy Savings
aceee.org/consumerguide/chklst.htm
This Home Energy Checklist for Action provides a quick introduction to the ACEEE
Consumer Guide.

ACEEE Most Energy-efficient Appliances
aceee.org/consumerguide/index.htm
Consumers shopping for new appliances can find a complete listing of energy-
efficiency information in *The Most Energy-Efficient Appliances booklet.*

Advanced Energy Corporation
advancedenergy.org/buildings
Great publications, particularly *Building Solutions On-line* and *High Performance
Homes.*

American Solar Energy Society (ASES)
ases.org
ASES is a national organization dedicated to advancing the use of solar energy for the benefit of US citizens and the global environment. ASES promotes the widespread near-term and long-term use of solar energy.

Building Green TV
buildinggreentv.com
Building Green TV's mission is to provide homeowners with a glimpse of just how easy, cost-effective and healthy it is to go green, while dispelling the myth that an environmentally conscious lifestyle means doing without.

Building Science Consortium
buildingscience.com/bsc/
Building America team leader with newly revised website. Lots of practical text and graphic resources on energy-efficient design and construction, particularly under "Houses That Work" and "Case Studies."

Building Science Glossary
buildingscienceconsulting.com/resources/glossary.htm
Here are the ABCs of building science terminology, according to Building Science Consulting. There are a lot of construction glossaries available, on and off the Web. This one is unique in that it is centered on building science and uses the Builder's Guides as a primary reference and source of terms.

BuildingOnline
BuildingOnline.com
BuildingOnline is a comprehensive website for homeowners, do-it-yourselfers and the entire residential building industry.

The Carpet and Rug Institute
carpet-rug.org/commercial-customers/green-building-and-the-environment/green-label-plus/
The Carpet and Rug Institute's Green Label and Green Label Plus Certifications ensure that customers are purchasing among the lowest-emitting carpet, adhesive and cushion products on the market.

Center on Sustainable Communities
icosc.com
The Center on Sustainable Communities educates consumers and professionals about sustainable residential building practices.

Congress for the New Urbanism
CNU.org
The leading organization promoting walkable, neighborhood-based development as an alternative to sprawl.

Consortium for Advanced Residential Buildings (CARB)
carb-swa.com
Building America team leader, Steven Winter Associates. Check out their "Projects" and "CARB-News."

DSIRE: Database of State Incentives for Energy Efficiency and Renewable Energy
dsireusa.org
This database is a comprehensive source of information on state, local, utility and
selected federal incentives that promote renewable energy.

Efficient Windows Collaborative
efficientwindows.com
Unbiased information on the benefits of energy-efficient windows, descriptions of
how they work and recommendations for their selection and use.

Energy Codes, Office of Building Technology, State and Community Programs
energycodes.gov
DOE's Building Energy Codes Program is an information resource on national model
energy codes.

Energy Efficiency and Renewable Energy
eere.energy.gov
The DOE website for the Energy Efficiency and Renewable Energy Clearinghouse
(EREC/EREN) encompasses a wide variety of information including Home Energy
magazine.

Energy Savers
energysavers.gov
A clearinghouse of government online resources dealing with sustainability.

Environmental Protection Agency Global Warming
epa.gov/globalwarming
Learn about global warming and what it means for you. You will find information on:
science of global warming, projected impacts, international and US government policies and programs, latest developments and more.

Environsense
envirosense.org
Solutions and strategies to address indoor air quality and related environmental issues
focused on a "total systems approach."

Florida Solar Energy Center
fsec.ucf.edu
The largest and most active state-supported renewable energy and energy-efficiency
research, training, testing and certification institute in the United States.

Forest Stewardship Council
fscus.org
The FSC has developed a set of principles and criteria for forest management that are
applicable to all FSC-certified forests throughout the world.

Good to be Green
goodtobegreen.com
Information on green building products, sustainable building materials and green
building services providers.

Green Building Resource Guide
greenguide.com
This site has some good FAQs and a database of over 600 green building materials.
There is also a salvaged building materials board where people may sell or acquire
used building materials.

Green Home Guide
greenhomeguide.com
Unbiased reviews and advice from professionals and homeowners like you.

Green Sage
greensage.com
This online source for green and sustainable building materials and furnishings provides links to sellers of sustainable products, sustainable practitioners and online ref-
erences.

Green2Green
green2green.com
Comprehensive information regarding green building products, materials and practices. Side-by-side comparisons of products using a variety of environmental, technical and economic criteria.

The Healthy Building Network
healthybuilding.net
The Healthy Building Network (HBN) is a national network of green building professionals, environmental and health activists, socially responsible investment advocates
and others who are interested in promoting healthier building materials as a means of
improving public health and preserving the global environment.

Home Footprint Calculator
nature.org/initiatives/climatechange/calculator
Use the Nature Conservancy's online carbon footprint calculator to measure your —
or your household's — climate impact. The calculator will estimate how many tons of
carbon dioxide and other greenhouse gases your choices create each year.

Incentive Insulation Database
simplyinsulate.com
A searchable database for access to local information on incentive programs for making energy-efficient improvements. This website was created and is maintained by
North American Insulation Manufacturers Association (NAIMA).

Inhabitat
inhabitat.com
Inhabitat.com is a weblog devoted to the future of design, tracking the innovations in
technology, practices and materials that are pushing architecture and home design towards a smarter and more sustainable future.

Modern Green Living
moderngreenliving.com
The Modern Green Living Home Directory enables you to find green architects, builders, remodelers, interior designers, realtors and green building consultants near you.

National Energy Affordability and Accessibility Project
neaap.ncat.org/db/
The Residential Energy Efficiency Database helps consumers find out what energy-efficiency programs a utility or state offers to help save energy and money.

National Renewable Energy Laboratory
nrel.gov
The National Renewable Energy Laboratory (NREL) is the primary laboratory in the US for renewable energy and energy-efficiency research and development.

NAHB Research Center
nahbrc.org
The NAHB Research Center is a separately incorporated, wholly owned, not-for-profit subsidiary of the National Association of Home Builders (NAHB). The Research Center's adherence to objective research, combined with an affiliation with NAHB, provides a unique opportunity to access the real world of home building through NAHB's 200,000-plus members who are builders, remodelers, manufacturers and other housing industry professionals from across the US.

Partnership for Advancing Technology in Housing (PATH)
pathnet.org
PATH is dedicated to accelerating the development and use of technologies that radically improve the quality, durability, energy-efficiency, environmental performance and affordability of Americans' housing.

Rate It Green
rateitgreen.com
Visitors can search for products and services, read peer reviews and rate products and services.

Residential Energy Efficiency Database (Canada)
its-canada.com/reed/
The Residential Energy Efficiency Database, designed as an educational tool to promote the benefits of energy efficiency, is maintained as a free, online information service.

Savings Starts @ Home
ftc.gov/energysavings
This site from the Federal Trade Commission provides a basic introduction to various aspects of energy-efficient homes.

SunAngle
susdesign.com/sunangle
Located at the Solstice website, this new release of the SunAngle calculator calculates the position of the sun and other terrestrial/solar angles based on your location and the time of day and year.

Southface Energy Institute
southface.org
Southface Energy Institute, a Building America partner, posts great resources under "Journal" and "Fact Sheets."

Sustainable Buildings Industry Council (SBIC)
sbicouncil.org
National resource clearinghouse for whole building design, product information, professional training, consumer education and analytic tools.

Sustainable Sources
greenbuilder.com
This website has a searchable directory of green building professionals, a calendar of green building events and a link to the Sustainable Building Sourcebook, which has detailed information about different aspects of green building and green building materials.

Sustainable-USA Network
sustainableausa.org
Showing that economic growth, environmental protection and increased opportunity for all Americans go hand-in-hand.

Tree Hugger
treehugger.com
TreeHugger is a leading media outlet dedicated to driving sustainability into the mainstream. It strives to be a one-stop shop for green news, solutions and product information.

WaterSense
epa.gov/watersense
Sponsored by the EPA, WaterSense is committed to protecting our future water supply by promoting and enhancing the market for water-efficient products and services.

ZIP-Code Program for Insulation
ornl.gov/sci/roofs+walls/insulation/ins_05.html
A computer program is available to help you calculate the amount of insulation appropriate for your house. The program is called the ZIP-Code because it includes weather and cost information for local regions defined by the first three digits of each postal service zip code.

Endnotes

Chapter 1

1. US Energy Information Administration [online], eia.doe.gov/emeu/recs/recs 2001/ce_pdf/enduse/ce1-7c_4popstates2001.pdf, accessed October 13, 2007, Table CE1-7c.
2. This is true, even with homebuilding in dramatic recession in 2006 and 2007.
3. Realty Times [online], realtytimes.com/rtcpages/20060323_greenhousegas.htm, accessed October 12, 2007.
4. US Environmental Protection Agency [online], December 2004, *Buildings and the Environment: A Statistical Summary*, epa.gov/opptintr/greenbuilding/pubs/ gbstats.pdf, retrieved October 13, 2007.
5. US Environmental Protection Agency [online], epa.gov/watersense/pubs/supply .htm, accessed October 13, 2007.
6. National Association of Home Builders [online], nahb.org/fileUpload_details.as px?contentTypeID=7&contentID=2028, accessed October 13, 2007.
7. Thegreenguide.com [online], thegreenguide.com/doc/108/wood, accessed December 2007.
8. USEPA [online], epa.gov/water/waternews/2006/060612.html, accessed December 2007.
9. Terrapass.com [online], terrapass.com/blog/posts/2007/02/104-pounds-in-18-seconds.html, accessed December 2007.
10. American Council for an Energy-Efficient Economy [online], aceee.org/pubs/ a981.htm, accessed December 2007.
11. California Energy Commission, Consumer Energy Center [online], consumer energycenter.org/home/windows/todays_windows.html, accessed December 2007.
12. Bob Falk and Brad Guy. *Unbuilding: Salvaging the Architectural Treasures of Unwanted Houses*, Taunton Press, 2007.
13. Paul Scheckel. *The Home Energy Diet*, New Society Publishers, 2005, p. 113.
14. Marla Cone. *US Rules Allow the Sale of Products Others Ban, Los Angeles Times*, October 8, 2006 [online], commondreams.org/headlines06/1008-01.htm.
15. Blanche Evans. *New Homes: Will the Big Home Downsize? Realty Times* [online], realtytimes.com/rtpages/20060619_downsizinghomes.htm, accessed December 2007.
16. Census: September 21, 2006. Heather, Whipps, US Household Size Shrinking [online], msnbc.msn.com/id/14942047, accessed December 2007.

17. Interview, Dina Gundersen, Monte Hewett Homes, Atlanta, Georgia, July 2007.

18. Interview with Nat Hodgson, V-P of Construction, Pulte Homes, Las Vegas Division, July 2007.

19. Interview with Rich Coyle, VP of Building Science, Sacramento Division, DR Horton, July 2007.

20. Interview with Steve Tapio, Quality Control Manager and Building Science Team Leader, New Tradition Homes, July 2007.

21. Interview, Larry Brittain, Carsten Crossings, homeowner, July 2007.

22. Interview, Kenny Trapp, Ideal Homes, homeowner, July 2007.

23. Jeff also works for the Noisette Company, the developer of Oak Terrace Preserve.

Chapter 2

1. Interview with Sam Rashkin, US Environmental Protection Agency, Washington DC, August 2007.

2. Interview with Rich Coyle, VP of Building Science, DR Horton, Sacramento Division, July 2007.

3. Interview with Steve Hayes, Division President, McGuyer Homebuilders, Inc., Dallas, Texas, July 2007.

4. Interview with Richard Barna, Pepper Viner Homes, July 2007.

5. Interview with Jeff Baxter, Oak Terrace Preserve, homeowner, July 2007.

6. Dr. Joe Lstiburek. "Understanding Drainage Planes," accessed December 2007, buildingscienceconsulting.com/resources/walls/drainage_planes.pdf.

7. Building Science Corporation. "Hygro-Thermal Regions," accessed December 23, 2007, buildingscienceconsulting.com/designsthatwork/hygro-thermal.htm.

8. Building Science Consulting [online], accessed December 22, 2007, building scienceconsulting.com/resources/presentations/BuildBoston/2007/Serendipity_ Building_Science=Green.pdf, slide 16 from presentation to the National Association of Home Builders conference, January 2007.

9. Data provided by Tom Hoyt at the Builder to Builder Green Summit, San Francisco, May 29, 2007.

Chapter 3

1. Green Home Guide [online], greenhomeguide.org/news_and_events/news_ item_1.html, accessed December 19, 2007.

2. Interview with Steve Rypka, Las Vegas, Nevada, July 2007.

3. Interview with Paul Kriescher, Denver, Colorado, July 2007.

4. Interview with Amy Macklin, Glenwood Park, homeowner, July 2007.

5. Interview, Kenny Trapp, Ideal Homes, homeowner, July 2007.

6. Interview with J. R. Kramer, August 2007.

7. Interview, Larry Brittain, Carsten Crossings, homeowner, July 2007.

Chapter 4

1. Interview with John Gilvasy, Gentrac Building Corporation, President, Ontario, July 2007.

2. The Energy Policy Act of 2005 provided a tax credit of $2,000 to builders who built a home 50 percent above a 2004 standard.

3. Interview with Nat Hodgson, Pulte Homes, Las Vegas, Nevada, July 2007.

4. This is a Michigan licensee of Colorado GreenBuilt, the original program, and identical to it.

5. Interview with Jeff Wassenaar, Legacy Homes, Grand Rapids, Michigan, August 2007.

6. Interview with Tom Hoyt, McStain Neighborhoods, Denver, Colorado, August 2007.

7. Betsy Pettit. "Toward Zero Impact Homes: Ten Case Studies," Build Boston 2007 presentation, accessed December 24, 2007, and available at buildingsciencecon sulting.com/resources/presentations/BuildBoston/2007/Toward_Zero_Impact_ Homes.pdf.

8. Efficient Windows Collaborative [online], efficientwindows.org/lowe.cfm, accessed January 5, 2008.

9. *Arizona Daily Star*, December 24, 2007, p. C6.

10. Toolbase [online], toolbase.org/Technology-Inventory/Whole-House-Systems/ structural-insulated-panels, accessed January 5, 2008.

11. Structural Insulated Panel Association [online], sips.org/content/news/index .cfm?PageId=191, accessed December 24, 2007.

12. Structural Insulated Panel Association [online], sips.org/content/green-building /#4, accessed December 24, 2007.

13. Toolbase [online], toolbase.org/Technology-Inventory/walls/Insulating-Con crete-Forms, accessed January 5, 2008.

14. Insulating Concrete Form Association [online], forms.org/?act=typesoficf1, accessed December 25, 2007.

15. Amvic Systems [online], amvicsystem.com/Homeowners.aspx, accessed December 25, 2007.

16. US Department of Energy [online], energy.gov/news/3097.htm, accessed December 24, 2007.

17. Air Conditioning Contractors of America [online], acca.org/press/news.php?id =160, accessed December 24, 2007.

18. US Department of Energy [online], www1.eere.energy.gov/femp/procurement/ eep_gas_furnace.html, accessed December 24, 2007.

19. US Department of Energy [online], accessed December 24, 2007, eere.energy .gov/consumer/your_home/insulation_airsealing/index.cfm/mytopic=11900.

20. Fortifiber [online], fortifiber.com/weather_resistive_barriers.htm, accessed December 24, 2007.

21. *Washington Post*, January 21, 2007, "New Toilets Are Going Green to Halt Gallon Guzzling."

22. US EPA [online], epa.gov/watersense/pp/find_het.htm, accessed December 24, 2007.

23. "Atlanta Suffers as Southeast Drought Continues," *ABC News* [online], October 15, 2007, abcnews.go.com/GMA/story?id=3730145&page=1, accessed December 24, 2007.

24. US EPA [online], energystar.gov/index.cfm?c=cfls.pr_cfls, accessed December 24, 2007.

25. Wal-Mart [online], walmartfacts.com/articles/5328.aspx, accessed December 24, 2007.

26. US Senate Committee on Energy and Natural Resources [online], summary of HR 6, energy.senate.gov/public/_files/HR6EnergyBillSummary.pdf, accessed December 24, 2007.

27. Ken Butti and John Perlin. *A Golden Thread: 2500 Years of Solar Architecture and Technology*, Cheshire Books, 1980, out of print.

28. Other state incentives for renewable energy and energy efficiency can be viewed at dsireusa.org.

29. Jerry Yudelson. *Green Building: A to Z* , New Society Publishers, 2007, pp. 180–181.

Chapter 5

1. US EPA [online], energystar.gov/ia/new_homes/features/HERSrater_062906 .pdf, accessed December 25, 2007.

2. RESNET, natresnet.org/, accessed December 25, 2007.

3. US EPA [online], energystar.gov/index.cfm?c=bldrs_lenders_raters.nh_HERS, accessed December 25, 2007.

4. US EPA [online], energystar.gov/ia/new_homes/features/AdvancedLighting_ 062906.pdf, accessed December 25, 2007.

5. US EPA [online], energystar.gov/index.cfm?fuseaction=qhmi.showHomes MarketIndex.

6. US EPA [online], energystar.gov/index.cfm?fuseaction=qhmi.showHomes MarketIndex, footnote 1, accessed December 25, 2007.

7. US EPA [online], energystar.gov/index.cfm?c=bldrs_lenders_raters.nh_per formance, accessed December 25, 2007.

8. National Association of Home Builders [online], nahb.org/news_details.aspx? newsID=4776, accessed December 25, 2007. NAHB says that about 97,000 homes have been certified since 1997, or 10,000 per year, and about 40,000 since sometime in 2004.

9. ENERGY STAR website and KB Home data.

10. Interview with Lisa Kalmbach, KB Home, October 2007.

11. New York Energy Smart [online], getenergysmart.org, accessed December 28, 2007.

12. LOHAS [online], lohas.com/articles/100911.html, accessed December 28, 2007.

13. NAHB [online], nahb.org/publication_details.aspx?publicationID=1994&section ID=155, accessed December 25, 2007.

14. NAHB [online], nahb.org/news_details.aspx?newsID=5791, accessed December 25, 2007.

15. Congressional testimony by Brian Catalde, NAHB President, June 2007, nahb .org.

16. nahb.org/publication_details.aspx?publicationID=1994&sectionID=155, accessed April 1, 2007, at page 7.

17. NAHB Model Green Home Guidelines [online], nahb.org/fileUpload_details .aspx?contentTypeID=7&contentID=1994, p. 41, accessed December 26, 2007.

18. See for example, The Green Building Initiative, [online], thegbi.org/residential, accessed December 25, 2007.

19. Built Green Colorado, builtgreen.org, accessed December 25, 2007.

20. Built Green Colorado, builtgreen.org/about/overview.htm, accessed December 25, 2007.

21. Built Green Washington [online], builtgreenwashington.org, accessed December 25, 2007.

22. Built Green Society of Canada [online], builtgreencanada.ca, accessed December 25, 2007.

23. Hawaii BuiltGreen [online], bia-hawaii.com/subpage.asp?section=70, accessed December 25, 2007.

24. greenbuilder.com/general/BuildingSources.html, accessed December 26, 2007.

25. California Green Builder [online], cagreenbuilder.org, accessed December 25, 2007.

26. Author's estimates, based on industry data.

27. Interview with Emily Mitchell, Assistant Program Manager LEED for Homes, USGBC, August 2007.

28 LEED may move to a sampling program in 2008.

29. US Green Building Council, "LEED Numbers," dated December 5, 2007, furnished to the author.

30. treehugger.com/files/2007/12/al_gore_gets_go.php, accessed December 16, 2007.

31. The Green Home Guide [online], accessed December 26, 2007, greenhomeguide .org/green_home_programs/LEED_for_homes_points.html.

32. greenhomeguide.org/green_home_programs/LEED_for_homes_points.html, accessed December 26, 2007.

33. Interview with Dick Peterson, Austin Energy, July 2007.

34. Interview with Randy Hansell, Earth Advantage, July 2007.

35. Interview with Duane Woik, Earth Advantage, July 2007.

36. Interview with Linda Douglas-Worthy, Tucson Electric Power, July 2007.

37. Interview with Anthony Floyd, Green Building Manager, City of Scottsdale, July 2007.

38. EarthCraft House [online], earthcrafthouse.com, accessed December 26, 2007.

39. Interview with Laura Uhde, July 2007.

40. Interview with Jackie Benson, July 2007.

41. Interview with Dina Gundersen, Monte Hewett Homes, August 2007.

42. Build It Green [online], builditgreen.org, accessed December 26, 2007.

43. Build It Green [online], accessed December 26, 2007, builditgreen.org/system/ files/uploads/GreenPoint%20Rated/Guidelines_checklists/2007-New-Home-Guidelines.pdf.

44. Interview with Brian Gitt, executive director of Build It Green, August 2007.

45. Florida Green Building Coalition [online], floridagreenbuilding.org/db/stan dards/pdf/HomeVer5/Version%205%20APPROVED%20BY%20BOARD.pdf, accessed December 26, 2007.

46. ENERGY STAR for New Homes [online], esnewhomes.ca, accessed December 26, 2007.

47. Taken from eflbuilder.com and eflhome.com, accessed December 25, 2007.

48. Environments for Living [online], eflhome.com/index.jsp?action=fl_builder_ general&st=FL, accessed December 25, 2007.

49. GE ecomagination [online], geconsumerproducts.com/pressroom/press_ releases/appliances/energy_efficient_products/ecomaginationhomebuilder program.htm, accessed December 25, 2007.

50. Interview with Michelle Cote, Account Manager, EnerQuality Corporation, August 2007.

51. "GE makes a push for greener housing developments," Carol Lloyd, *San Francisco Chronicle* [online] sfgate.com/cgi-bin/article.cgi?f=/c/a/2007/10/21/BUULSS CBM.DTL, accessed October 21, 2007.

52. Interview with Robert Moffitt, director of Health House program, American Lung Association. healthhouse.org/build/TopTenQuestionsbooklet.pdf, accessed December 26, 2007.

53. Interview with Al Nichols, President, Al Nichols Engineering, Inc., Tucson, Arizona, July 2007.

Chapter 6

1. US EPA [online], energystar.gov/index.cfm?c=behind_the_walls.btw_landing, accessed December 27, 2007.

2. US Green Building Council [online], usgbc.org/DisplayPage.aspx?CMSPageID =147#projects, accessed December 27, 2007.

3. Interview with Steve Tapio, Building Science Team Leader and Quality Control Manager, New Tradition Homes, September 2007.

4. New Tradition Homes [online], newtraditionhomes.com, accessed December 30, 2007.

5. High Point [online], thehighpoint.com, accessed December 30, 2007.

6. Shamrock Heights, green brochure, camwest.com/community/brochure.pdf, accessed December 29, 2007.

7. Interview with Carolyn L. Gladwell, August 2007.

8. Issaquah Highlands [online], issaquahhighlands.com, accessed December 30, 2007.

9. J.A. Gause, ed. *Developing Sustainable Planned Communities*, Urban Land Institute, 2007, pp. 170–181.

10. Pringle Creek [online], pringlecreek.com, accessed December 30, 2007.

11. NorthWest Crossing [online], northwestcrossing.com, accessed December 30, 2007.

12. Interview with Eric Clifton, VP, Sustainable Business Development, Newland Communities, July 2007.

13. Green Home Guide [online], greenhomeguide.org/documents/pp_carsten_ crossings.pdf, accessed December 28, 2007.

14. US Green Building Council [online], usgbc.org/ShowFile.aspx?DocumentID= 3119, accessed December 28, 2007.

15. Carsten Crossing [online], grupe.com/communities/carsten, accessed December 30, 2007.

16. Lennar SolarPlus Communities [online], lennarsolarplus.com, accessed December 30, 2007.

17. DR Horton [online], drhorton.com, search for Provence/Sacramento.

18. Colony at Alamo Creek, colonydanville.com, accessed December 2007.

19. Information in this section was contributed by James Hackler, Victory Homes, victoryhomesinc.com.

20. Gause, ibid., pp. 212–221.

21. Interview with Dan Byrnes, July 2007.

22. Interview with Richard Barna, Pepper Viner Homes, July 2007.

23. Interview with Melissa Knott, Forest City Stapleton, July 2007.
24. Contributed by James Hackler. New Town Builders, newtownbuilders.com.
25. Interview with Tom Hoyt, McStain Neighborhoods, August 2007.
26. Interview with Steve Hayes, Division President, McGuyer Homebuilders Inc., Dallas, Texas, July 2007.
27. Gause, ibid., pp. 142–151.
28. Interview with Kimberly Miller, September 2007.
29. Interview with Jeff Baxter, Noisette Company, July 2007.
30. Interview with Eric Clifton, June 2007.
31. Contributed by James Hackler. Leyland Alliance, warwick-grove.com.
32. Interview with Jeff Wassenaar, Legacy Homes, August 2007.
33. Gause, ibid., pp. 202–211.
34. EnerQuality Corporation. "Backgrounder: EnerQuality & ENERGY STAR® for New Homes," October 2007.
35. Personal communication, Jennifer Talsma, Natural Resources Canada, December 31, 2007.
36. Ibid.
37. Canadian Architect [online], canadianarchitect.com/issues/ISarticle.asp?id=154300&story_id=30247112855&issue=08012004&PC=&RType=, accessed April 1, 2007.

Chapter 7

1. Gerding Edlen [online], gerdingedlen.com/files/pdf/thecaseygreenestbuilding intheus_12_07.pdf, accessed December 31, 2007.
2. Dockside Green [online], docksidegreen.com, accessed December 31, 2007.
3. Ankrom Moisan Associated Architects [online], amaa.com, accessed December 31, 2007.
4. Lighthouse Sustainable Building Centre [online], sustainablebuildingcentre.com /forum-topic/some_builders_pulling_out_the_stops_to_get_leed_condos, accessed December 31, 2007.
5. *This Magazine* [online], thismagazine.ca/issues/2006/07/greeninside.php, accessed December 31, 2007.
6. urbandb.com/canada/ontario/toronto/minto_gardens_east/, accessed December 31, 2007.
7. Rethinking Building [online], rethinkingbuilding.com/projects/design.php?c=2_1, accessed December 31, 2007.
8. The Qube Exchange [online], thequbeexchange.com/2007/08/25/boston -macallen-building-sets-green-standard-for-condos/, accessed January 2, 2008.
9. Cosentini Associates [online], cosentini.com/portfolio/res_rvrhse.html, accessed December 31, 2007.
10. housemedianetwork.com/archive/article.php?issue=43&dept=80&id=699, accessed December 31, 2007.
11. VE Solutions Group [online], vesolutionsgroup.com/p_lucida.php, accessed December 31, 2007.
12. Sustainable Design Consulting [online], sustaindesign.net/content/projects_ multifamily.php, accessed December 31, 2007.

Chapter 8

1. Internal Revenue Service [online], irs.gov/newsroom/article/0,,id=153397,00 .html, accessed December 26, 2007.
2. Tax Incentives Assistance Project [online], energytaxincentives.org/consumers/ solar.php, accessed December 26, 2007.
3. Tax Incentives Assistance Project [online], energytaxincentives.org/consumers/ heating-cooling.php, accessed December 26, 2007.
4. US EPA [online], energystar.gov/index.cfm?c=products.pr_tax_credits#s6, accessed December 26, 2007.
5. Database of State Incentives for Renewables and Efficiency, dsireusa.org, accessed December 27, 2007.
6. For example, Fannie Mae has a fact sheet available at fanniemae.com/homebuy ers/pdf/findamortgage/mortgages/Energy_Efficient_Mortgage_Fact_Sheet.pdf, accessed December 27, 2007.
7. US EPA [online], energystar.gov/index.cfm?c=bldrs_lenders_raters.energy_effi cient_mortgage, accessed December 27, 2007.
8. CMHC [online], cmhc-schl.gc.ca/en/co/moloin/moloin_008.cfm, accessed December 27, 2007.
9. Rick Nevin, et al. "Evidence of rational market valuations for home energy efficiency," *The Appraisal Journal*, October 1998, 66(4), pp. 401–409; "More evidence of rational market valuations for home energy efficiency," *The Appraisal Journal*, October 1999, 67(4), pp. 454–460.

Chapter 9

1. Interview with Melissa Knott, Forest City Stapleton, July 2007.
2. Interview with J.R. Kramer, August 2007.
3. For one example, see "For 'green,' buyer beware: Homes may not be that environmentally friendly," Chuin-Wei Yap, St. Petersburg, Florida, *Times*, December 30, 2007, sptimes.com/2007/12/30/State/For__green___buyer_be.shtml, accessed December 30, 2007.
4. Interview with Richard Michal, Tucson, Arizona, July 2007.
5. Ibid.

Chapter 10

1. Joe Lstiburek and Terry Brennan. "Healthy and affordable housing: Practical recommendations for building, renovating and maintaining Housing – Read this before you move in," n.d., Asthma Regional Coordinating Council of New England, accessed December 24, 2007, and available at buildingscienceconsulting .com/resources/mold/Read_This_Before_You_Move_In.pdf.
2. The American Rainwater Catchment Systems Association is a good starting place for information. arcsa-usa.org. The *Texas Manual on Rainwater Harvesting*, 3rd edition, 2005, is the classic reference work and is available as a free download from: twdb.state.tx.us/publications/reports/RainwaterHarvestingManual_3rdedi tion.pdf, accessed December 30, 2007.
3. Arizona also exempts PV and solar thermal systems from an 8 percent state sales tax.

4. Assumes $12,000 PV system and $4,500 solar water heating system, $2,000 maximum credit per system.

5. 10 percent state tax credit, capped at $1,000 for all solar systems.

6. $3,000 per kW for a 1.5 kW system.

7. US Department of Energy [online], eere.energy.gov/greenpower/resources/tables/pdfs/0307_topten_pr.pdf, accessed December 30, 2007.

8. Global Footprint Network [online], footprintnetwork.org/gfn_sub.php?content=footprint_overview, accessed December 30, 2007.

9. Global Footprint Network [online], footprintnetwork.org/gfn_sub.php?content=national_footprints, accessed December 30, 2007, calculations by the author.

10. b-e-f.org.

11. "Interface aims to extend efficiency from in-house to at-home," *Portland Daily Journal of Commerce*, February 20, 2007, p. 1.

12. blogs.business2.com/greenwombat/2007/03/bank_america_co.html, accessed March 23, 2007.

13. Mayors Climate Protection Center [online], usmayors.org/climateprotection/news.htm, accessed December 30, 2007. American College and University Presidents Climate Change Commitment, see aashe.org.

Chapter 11

1. Borrego Springs Zero Energy Demonstration Homes [online], clarumzeroenergy.com, accessed January 13, 2008

2. BASF Press Release, January 24, 2007.

3. BioRegional's Response to UK Government's Announcements on Zero Carbon Homes [online]. [Cited January 13, 2007]. December 20, 2006. bioregional.com/news%20page/news_stories/ZED/zerocarbon%20201206.htm.

4. Top Global Companies Join with WBCSD to Make Energy Self-Sufficient Buildings a Reality [online]. [Cited January 13, 2007]. wbcsd.org/plugins/DocSearch/details.asp?type=DocDet&ObjectId=MTg2MTU.

5. Interview with Tom Hoyt, McStain Neighborhoods, Denver, August 2007.

Glossary

1. For example, the *Inconvenient Truth* website: climatecrisis.net/takeaction/carbon calculator.

2. American Council for an Energy-Efficient Economy [online], aceee.org/press/op-eds/op-ed1.htm, accessed December 24, 2007.

3. A Sourcebook for Green and Sustainable Building [online], greenbuilder.com/sourcebook/ConstructionWaste.html, accessed December 24, 2007.

Index